SARMATIA EUROPEA
GNA
MARE CASPIUM
ARMENIA
PONTUS EUXINUS
Nicopolis
Satala
Byzantium
Philippi
Nicomedia
Melitene
arissa
MARE AEGAEUM
Ancyra
Sardis
PERSIA
Athenae
Tarsus
Antioch
daemon
Rhodos
Palmyra
Cnossus
Jerusalem
yrene
Alexandria
ARABIA MAGNA

Written by Richard Bodley Scott,
Simon Hall and Terry Shaw

FIELD of GLORY

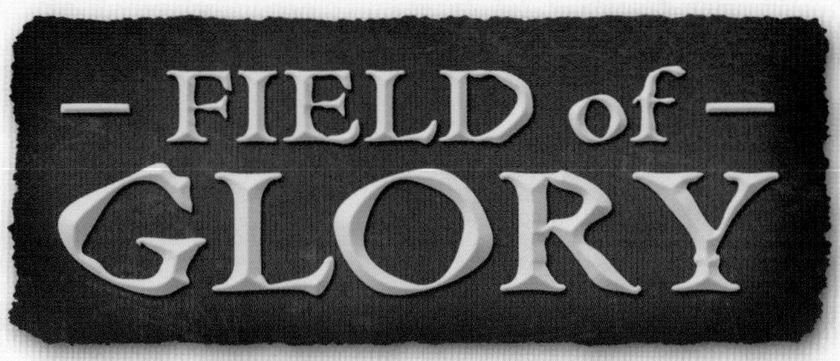

WARGAMING RULES FOR ANCIENT AND MEDIEVAL TABLETOP GAMING

Written by Richard Bodley Scott,
Simon Hall and Terry Shaw

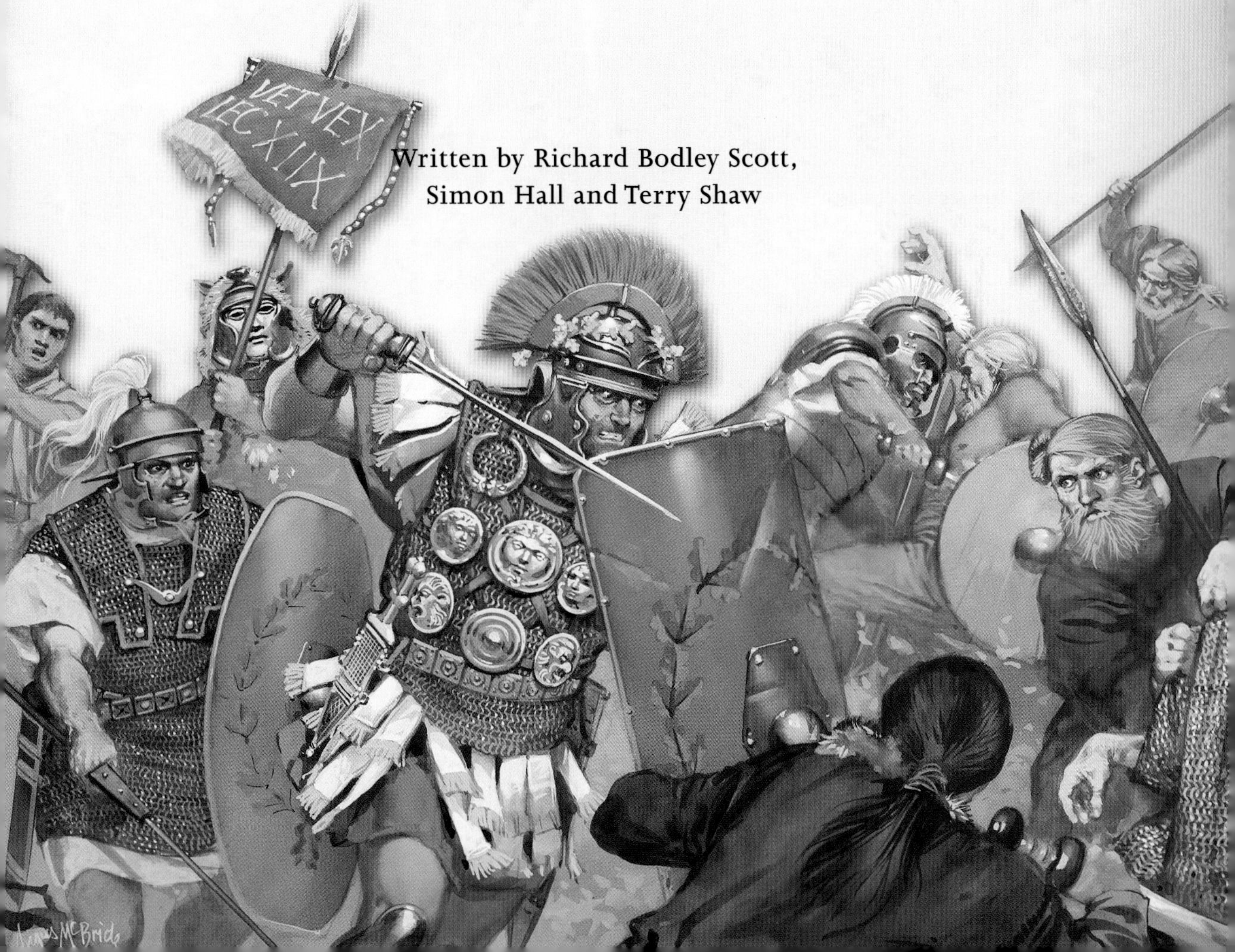

First published in Great Britain in 2008 by Osprey Publishing Ltd.

Osprey Publishing
Midland House, West Way, Botley, Oxford OX2 0PH, UK
443 Park Avenue South, New York, NY 10016, USA
E-mail: info@ospreypublishing.com

Slitherine Software UK Ltd
The White Cottage, 8 West Hill Avenue, Epsom, KT19 8LE, UK
E-mail: info@slitherine.co.uk

A CIP catalogue record for this book is available from the British Library

ISBN: 978 1 84603 313 1

Page layout by Myriam Bell
Index by Alan Thatcher
Typeset in Joanna Pro and Sleepy Hollow
Cover artwork by Peter Dennis
Photography supplied by Duncan MacFarlane – Wargames Illustrated
Diagrams by Claudio Berni – Baueda Wargames Ltd

Text editing by Roger Greenwood
Project management by JD McNeil & Simone Drinkwater
Technical management by Iain McNeil
Originated by PDQ Media, UK
Printed in China through Worldprint Ltd

08 09 10 11 12 13 12 11 10 9 8 7 6 5 4 3

EDITOR DEDICATION

Special thanks to Paul Robinson, James Hamilton, Nik Gaukroger, Russell Henley and Laurence Greaves.

FOR A CATALOGUE OF ALL BOOKS PUBLISHED BY OSPREY MILITARY AND AVIATION PLEASE CONTACT:

NORTH AMERICA
Osprey Direct, c/o Random House Distribution Center,
400 Hahn Road, Westminster, MD 21157
E-mail: info@ospreydirect.com

ALL OTHER REGIONS
Osprey Direct UK, P.O. Box 140 Wellingborough,
Northants, NN8 2FA, UK
E-mail: info@ospreydirect.co.uk

FOR DETAILS OF ALL GAMES PUBLISHED BY SLITHERINE SOFTWARE UK LTD
email: info@slitherine.co.uk

Osprey Publishing is supporting the Woodland Trust, the UK's leading woodland conservation charity, by funding the dedication of trees.

www.ospreypublishing.com
www.slitherine.com

CONTENTS

- INTRODUCTION 7
  - Introduction to *Field of Glory*
  - Design Philosophy
- THE BASICS 11
  - What You Need to Play *Field Of Glory*
  - Measurement
  - Bases
- TROOPS 13
  - Troop type
  - Troop Function Categories
  - Camps
- BATTLE GROUPS 21
  - Battle Group Formations
  - Battle Group Quality (Quality Re-Rolls)
  - Battle Group Cohesion Levels
  - Battle Group Disorder
- COMMAND AND CONTROL 27
  - Commanders
  - Battle Lines
- STARTER ARMIES 31
- PLAYING THE GAME 35
  - Setting up a game
  - Playing the game
  - Turns and Phases
- GENERAL MOVEMENT RULES 39
  - Movement Rules
  - Move Distances and Disorder
  - Simple and Complex Moves
  - Difficult Forward Moves
  - Advances
  - The Complex Move Test (CMT)
  - Wheeling
  - Turning 90 Degrees
  - Turning 180 Degrees
  - Shifting
  - Expansions
  - Contraction
  - Variable Moves
  - Moving Through Friendly Troops
  - Movement of Commanders
  - Moving From an Overlap Position
  - Troops Leaving the Table
- IMPACT PHASE 51
  - Declaration of Charges
  - Legal Charge Contact
  - Charging With Your Battle Groups
  - Formation Changes When Charging
  - Charging to Contact and Stepping Forwards
  - Charging a Flank or Rear
  - Troops Who Cannot Charge
  - Troops Who May Charge Without Orders
  - Attempts to Charge or Receive a Charge With Skirmishers
  - Charging With Missile-Armed Foot Troops
  - Attempts to Charge When Disrupted or Fragmented
  - Being Charged While Fragmented
  - Possible Responses to Charges
  - Sequence of Charges and Responses
  - Resolving Impact Phase Combat
- MANOEUVRE PHASE 69
  - Reforming
  - Conforming to The Enemy in Close Combat
  - Feeding More Bases Into an Existing Melee
  - Restricted Area
  - Second Moves
  - Moving Into Contact With Enemy Battle Groups

Battle Groups Already in Contact But Not Yet Committed to Close Combat
Moving Into Contact With the Enemy Camp

■ SHOOTING PHASE 79
Ranges
Movement and Shooting
Target Priority
Arc of Fire
Line of Sight and Visibility
Overhead Shooting
Shooting and Close Combat
Resolving Shooting

■ MELEE PHASE 85
Overlaps
Melees That Cannot Line Up
Fighting The Enemy in Two Directions
Resolving Melees
Sacking Camps

■ THE COMBAT MECHANISM 89
Deciding How Many Dice to Roll
Allocating Combat Dice
Scoring Hits – Points of Advantage
Accumulating Hits and Taking Cohesion Tests
Support Shooting in the Impact Phase
Commanders in Close Combat
Fighting Broken Troops
Movement of Broken Troops and Pursuers
An Example of Close Combat

■ JOINT ACTION PHASE 105
Outcome Moves in The Joint Action Phase
Commanders in The Joint Action Phase

■ BATTLE GROUP DETERIORATION 111
Cohesion Tests
The Test
The Effect of Cohesion Levels
Death Rolls
Base Removal
Autobreak

■ VICTORY AND DEFEAT 117

■ SPECIAL FEATURES 119
Elephants and Camels
Scythed Chariots
Field Fortifications
Portable Defences
Orb Formation

■ REFERENCE SECTION 123
Appendix 1: Scales, Base Sizes and Detailed Troop Types
Appendix 2: Battlefield Terrain, Visibility and Disorder Effects
Appendix 3: Glossary Of Terms
Appendix 4: Set Up Rules
Appendix 5: Army Composition and the Points System
Appendix 6: Choosing, Painting and Using Your Army
Appendix 7: Examples of Unusual Situations
Appendix 8: Full Turn Sequence

FURTHER INFORMATION 169

INDEX 171

PLAYSHEETS 173

INTRODUCTION

The battle of Nicosia, Cyprus, *AD* 1229, by Christa Hook © Osprey Publishing Ltd. Taken from *Warrior* 18: Knight of Outremer AD 1187–1344.

INTRODUCTION TO FIELD OF GLORY

Field of Glory has been designed in an approachable and easy to learn manner that allows players to concentrate on realistic deployments and battlefield tactics, eliminating much of the extraneous minutiae of past rules and allowing us to capture the atmosphere of battles ranging from the dawn of history to medieval times. This series is intended to give both beginner and expert wargamers everything they need to play the battles of the ancient and medieval worlds on their tabletops.

This book is designed to both explain the game and be a reference guide when playing. To make the rules easier to follow, we have included numerous diagrams and photographs, together with a number of useful **TIPS** to assist your game-play.

We have also included detailed systems, examples and explanations, such as the precise definition of troop types, along with some guides to choosing and painting an army and battlefield tactics to get you going, but these have been put in appendices at the end so as to make the reading of the core rules easier.

WHAT IS MINIATURE WARGAMING?

Historical miniature wargaming as a popular hobby can be traced back to 1913 when the famous author H.G. Wells conceived and wrote the first commercial set of wargames rules "Little Wars." In fact it goes back further still with Kriegsspiel in the early 19th century, and the ancient pharaohs were rumoured to have used model figures to plan their military campaigns.

We've come a long way since then. Today wargaming is an absorbing and fascinating pastime involving elements of tactical skill and chance, where armies of accurately researched and painted figurines march across realistically modelled battlefields to re-fight bygone wars. Have you got it in you to become an Alexander the Great?

Games can range from re-fights of actual historical battles to speculative "what ifs" matching armies against foes that never met. They can be stand-alone games in which a points system is used to ensure that both armies have a fair chance, scenario games with unequal forces such as an attack on a marching army or the defence of a river line, or even complex campaigns in which logistics and strategy are as important as tactical skill.

Ancient/Medieval wargaming covers the widest period of all, from the first organised armies circa 3,000 BC until the rising dominance of gunpowder weapons at the end of the 15th Century AD. The armies are colourful and varied and come equipped with all sorts of weaponry ranging from simple slings to the dreaded war elephants and scythed chariots.

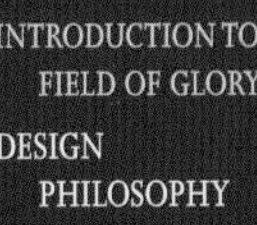

Greek Commander plans his campaign

DESIGN PHILOSOPHY

This section explains the rationale behind the different terms used, and outlines the design concepts and approaches that we have adopted.

Each member of the *Field of Glory* design team has a keen interest in ancient and medieval history, and between us we have amassed over 100 years of wargaming experience.

In this *Field of Glory* rulebook, you take the role of the army commander and his senior generals, giving the rules a top down style and feel. Historical accounts describe battles as a series of events and phases, rather than solely an account of constant action. With *Field of Glory*, we have also tried to reflect this ebb and flow of events on the battlefield.

Armies of this era had a common theme, whatever their organisation at the micro level. Each had a commander-in-chief and a few senior commanders who would take control of a wing, or the centre, or a sweeping charge. Subordinate to these was another layer of commanders who controlled the various tactical formations which generally consisted of a number of units grouped together. In *Field of Glory* we call these formations ***battle groups***.

In *Field of Glory* you will take command of an army which consists of approximately 10-15

War elephants attack!

battle groups led by the C-in-C and his senior commanders. The game has been designed to ensure that, just as in reality, the commanders (you) are fully occupied with decision making from the outset. Your key objective is to outmanoeuvre the enemy army and concentrate your forces at critical points in the battle. This will then destroy the enemy's will to fight, deal a devastating blow to the morale of their commanders (your opponent) and allow you to win.

Our companion army list books will contain historical overviews and the organisation of hundreds of accurately researched armies, ensuring that your battles will be able to have a realistic and historical feel.

Also, in reality, some armies would be relatively small, consisting of as few as 5,000 men, whilst others would be enormous. *Field of Glory* will allow you to see what might have been had these forces been equally matched, using a points system, as each army can then be scaled up or down whilst retaining an individual mix and balance of troops to create "what if" encounters.

We started with a blank sheet of paper and looked at a wide range of possible mechanisms. Some concepts are entirely new. Others may look familiar at first glance, but interact with the rest of the rules in a completely new way, giving *Field of Glory* a style all its own.

In *Field of Glory* our most important objective is to make the game fun to play whilst retaining a strong historical feel. So whether you fancy being Alexander the Great or Ghengis Khan, it's up to you, happy gaming and may your dice roll high!

A Chinese Army prepares for battle

THE BASICS

The battle of Bruranburh, by Gerry Embleton © Osprey Publishing Ltd. Taken from *Warrior 3: Viking Hersir 793–1066 AD.*

WHAT YOU NEED TO PLAY FIELD OF GLORY

- An opponent: games can be played with one player on each side, solo, or with multiple players on each side.
- A tabletop/board – the game is ideally designed to be played on an area of 180cm (or 72") x 120cm (or 48"), but smaller or larger spaces can be used.
- Two opposing armies of miniature figurines, painted and mounted on bases of the same width. These figurines can be of any scale. However, those which work best with the rules are 15mm or 25/28mm tall. These can be easily obtained, either painted or unpainted from a wide range of suppliers.
- Terrain for your battlefield, such as hills, rivers, marshes and so on. These are all commercially available and described in more detail later.
- Dice: Normal cubes numbered 1 to 6 (d6). Ideally, each player should have about 10 of one colour and 5 each of two other colours.
- A means of measuring distances: a tape measure or a set of measuring sticks marked off in inches or mm.

TIP!

Which figure scale you choose is unimportant in Field of Glory as the rules are designed to suit any scale.

MEASUREMENT

Measuring distances in *Field of Glory* is by **movement units**. One movement unit, or MU for short, is either 25mm or 1 inch, as agreed by the players or decided by tournament organisers.

BASES

A base is a rectangle on which model figurines are mounted. The number and type of figurines gives a visual indication of the troops involved. Each base represents a certain number of actual men, and this is explained in further detail in Appendix 1. In *Field of Glory*, the number of bases needed to form a battle group is specified in our companion army list books. These are the playing pieces in *Field of Glory*.

All the figurines used in *Field of Glory* are mounted on bases of the same width. When using 15mm or smaller scale figures, the base needs to be 40mm wide. For 25/28mm figures, it is 60mm wide. The depth of bases and the number of figures which can be mounted on each base are listed in Appendix 1.

Field of Glory features a wide range of different ***troop types***. These reflect the huge variety that existed in armies of the period. Bases of different troop types are represented in a number of ways. Fast moving, lightly equipped troops will usually have fewer figurines on a base than slower moving, heavily armed warriors.

TROOPS

Sir John Cheyney and man-at-arms, 1485, by Gerry Embleton © Osprey Publishing Ltd. Taken from *Men-at-Arms 145: The Wars of the Roses.*

Gauls and Numidians clash with Roman Cavalry and Hastati

The photograph above shows several different types of troops. These are defined by five parameters: **troop type**, **armour**, **quality** (skill), **manoeuvre training** and **combat capabilities**. It is this mix of parameters that allows *Field of Glory* to accurately portray the wide variety of troop types which existed in the ancient and medieval world.

TROOP TYPE

Troop types are divided into two basic categories, and then several sub-categories, according to how they moved and fought on the battlefield. Different troop types are based in different ways. The two main categories are foot and mounted, and they are sub-divided as follows (see *Appendix 1* for further information).

FOOT

They can be: ***heavy foot***, ***medium foot***, ***light foot***, ***mob***, ***battle wagons***, ***light artillery*** or ***heavy artillery***.

MOUNTED

They can be: ***knights***, ***cataphracts***, ***light horse***, ***cavalry***, ***camelry***, ***elephants***, ***heavy chariots***, ***light chariots*** or ***scythed chariots***.

ARMOUR

Some troops benefit from wearing armour or carrying shields. For others, factors such as their mounts or vehicles make armour and shields less relevant. There are four levels of **armour** used in *Field of Glory*. These are, in order of decreasing protection: ***heavily armoured***, ***armoured***, ***protected*** and ***unprotected***.

All troop types have one of these armour qualifiers, except for the following: ***battle wagons***, ***elephants***, ***artillery*** of all types and ***chariots*** of all types.

In the photograph below, the Roman cavalry are described as "cavalry, armoured". The Carthaginian elephants are simply "elephants".

QUALITY

Some troops were better fighters because of their morale, training and/or weapon skills. *Field of Glory* has four categories of troop quality: **elite**, **superior**, **average** and **poor**.

Only exceptional troops with the highest morale are classified as **elite**. Some of history's most famous armies have contained a high proportion of superior combatants, whilst others have consisted of average or even poorer quality troops. Generally, an army of poorer quality troops will be weaker than a superior force. To compensate for this, in *Field of Glory* it costs fewer points per base, (see our companion army list books for more information on troop point values) so the poorer army can be much larger.

TRAINING

Troops used to obeying orders and who practiced moving together in formation are classified as **drilled**. All others are **undrilled**.

The close formation Roman foot in the photograph overleaf are legionaries. These are described as "heavy foot, armoured, superior,

TIP!

A small force of high quality troops applied at the right time and place can often shatter larger poorer quality forces, which would lead to a breakthrough that should be exploited.

Roman cavalry face an impossible task.

Lakedaimonian battle drill, by Adam Hook © Osprey Publishing Ltd. Taken from Warrior 27: Greek Hoplite 480–323 BC.

drilled". The Gallic Warriors in the Carthaginian army are classified as "medium foot, protected, average, undrilled". They are each treated differently in the rules.

CAPABILITIES

The weapons and tactical abilities that influence combat effectiveness are called **capabilities**. The names of some capabilities are well-known terms, others less so and have been created for *Field of Glory* to give memorable names to particular behaviour or weapons training. In *Field of Glory* it is not enough to simply possess a weapon to be regarded as "capable" - troops are only classified as having a capability if use of such a weapon and fighting technique was a major part of their tactical methods or doctrine. E.g. Ghilman cavalry sometimes carried a lance but their main fighting method was as mounted bowmen with a sword or mace, and it is therefore only these latter capabilities that we recognise.

The list of capabilities are: *longbow*, *crossbow*, *bow*, *bow**, *firearm*, *javelins*, *sling*, *swordsmen*, *skilled swordsmen*, *offensive spearmen*, *defensive spearmen*, *pikemen*, *impact foot*, *heavy weapon*, *lancers*, *light spear*, *light artillery* and *heavy artillery*.

IN SUMMARY

The five qualifiers: **type**, **armour**, **quality**, **training** and **capabilities** are used together to describe a base of figurines. Although initially this may appear a little complicated, it can be picked up very quickly, and will only aid gameplay. Our companion army list books describe the troop types in detail. A little knowledge of history can help with tactical decisions e.g. the motivation of a group of charging elephants is not a big issue (**average**). Also, they are unlikely to be trying to keep in step (**undrilled**). Contrast this with well-disciplined ranks of armoured Roman infantry (**heavy foot, armoured, superior, drilled**). They are equipped with the pilum, which is thrown at short range (**impact foot**), before closing to fight with shield and gladius (**skilled swordsmen**). The relevant strengths and weaknesses of each troop type will become easier to understand and master as you play.

TIP!

Pick an army from a period of history that interests and enthuses you. You will find this much easier to paint and as there are no "super armies" in *Field of Glory*, each has its strengths and weaknesses. E.g a Spartan army consists mainly of hoplites (heavy foot, armoured, superior, drilled, offensive spearmen). They are easy to control, very solid and extremely tough. They fear little frontally but are slow to react. Compare this with a Skythian army with lots of horse archers (light horse, unprotected, average, undrilled, bow, swordsmen). They are extremely manoeuvrable, skirmishing with bow to weaken their opponent before charging home. Both quite different armies with completely contrasting fighting doctrines. Both have the potential to win if used well. The choice is yours.

The drilled Legionaries clash with Hannibal's Gauls

Spartan hoplites stand firm against Persian horse archers

TROOP FUNCTION CATEGORIES

The troop types noted above are easily grouped into the following categories to describe the function they performed on the battlefield. These terms are used throughout the rules to avoid the need for repetition:

SKIRMISHERS:

- battle groups entirely of light foot
- light horse

> **TIP!**
>
> Knowing how to utilise your troops the way a commander of this era would do is a great benefit when playing e.g. use your skirmishers to chase off enemy skirmishers or soften up enemy battle troops. They are not close combat troops.

BATTLE TROOPS (NON-SKIRMISHERS):

- any troops other than light foot or light horse
- mixed battle groups of heavy or medium foot with supporting light foot

SHOCK TROOPS:

- any mounted with lancers capability, except light horse
- heavy chariots
- scythed chariots
- foot with impact foot capability
- foot with offensive spearmen capability
- foot with pikemen capability

The field headquarters of the Duke of Burgundy

CAMPS

Each army has a **supply camp**. If an enemy battle group ends a move in contact with an unfortified supply camp, the camp is immediately sacked and lost.

A fortified supply camp is assumed to be defended by camp guards, who must be defeated before the camp can be sacked.

TIP!

Place your camp somewhere relatively safe and protect it. Armies who lost their supply camp were generally in serious trouble. In *Field of Glory* this will weaken your army, possibly contributing to your defeat.

BATTLE GROUPS

Roman Legionaries, by Angus McBride © Osprey Publishing Ltd. Taken from *Warrior* 72: Imperial Roman Legionary AD 161–284.

Now that you understand bases and troop types, we will explain how these are grouped together into battle groups.

A typical army has ten to fifteen battle groups. Each battle group consists of between two and twelve bases of figurines, usually of the same troop type. The arrangement of the bases in a battle group can change, but they always move together as a group. The bases cannot be separated, except where this is specifically allowed by the rules. Even in these cases, the separation is temporary. Bases cannot switch from one battle group to another during the game.

Each battle group is assumed to comprise several individual units/warbands/tribal contingents under the command of a junior commander, who is not represented in the game.

All of the bases of a battle group must be of the same quality and training. Except where the list specifies mixed battle groups, they must also be of the same armour class. Where an army list permits a choice of quality, training or armour class, this allows individual battle groups to differ from each other. It does not permit variety within a battle group.

Each battle group must initially have an **even number of bases**. The only exception to this rule is where an army list book specifies battle groups consisting of ⅔ of one type and ⅓ of another. In this circumstance it can have 9 bases, but only if this falls within the battle group size range specified by the list. The army's **supply camp** is not a battle group.

Training day for the Knights of Outremer, by Christa Hook © Osprey Publishing Ltd. Taken from *Warrior 18*: Knight of Outremer AD 1187–1344.

African veterans lead the attack

BATTLE GROUP FORMATIONS

In general, troops must be in a **rectangular formation** with all bases facing in the same direction, in edge and corner contact with each other. Only the rear rank of a battle group is allowed to have fewer bases. So, for example, a battle group of 8 bases could be deployed 1 wide and 8 deep, 2 wide and 4 deep, 3 wide with only 2 bases in the third rank, 4 wide and 2 deep and so on.

There are four exceptions to this general case:

1. **Columns** – a battle group that is one base wide is a column of march and must be "kinked" at points where it has wheeled (e.g. to follow a road) until the whole column has passed that point.
2. A battle group that is, or has been, **fighting the enemy in two directions** will have bases facing in different directions until it reforms.
3. A **compulsory move** specified by the rules can temporarily force a battle group out of formation until it reforms.
4. Some battle groups can form **orb formation**, which results in bases facing outwards.

SOME EXAMPLES OF PERMITTED FORMATIONS

Carthaginian battle groups

BATTLE GROUP QUALITY (QUALITY RE-ROLLS)

The effect of the quality difference of troop types is determined by re-rolling dice. Where a section of the rules states "**quality re-rolls apply**" the following rules are used:

- Elite troops can re-roll 1's and 2's.
- Superior troops can re-roll 1's.
- Poor troops must re-roll 6's.
- A dice is only re-rolled once.
- If a *battle line* of mixed quality troops re-rolls, it re-rolls as the worst quality battle group in the line.

TIP!

Make good use of your quality troops. You will not win battles by relying on your weaker troops. Choose carefully whether to put a commander into combat for extra benefit. Once committed to the fight, he is there to the finish and risks being lost. The loss of command and control could be catastrophic.

A commander fighting in the front rank of a battle group in close combat temporarily upgrades the quality of the battle group he is with. This allows the close combat "to hit" dice (but not any other type of dice rolls) of that battle group to be one re-roll level higher. Elite troops re-roll 1's, 2's and 3's; superior 1's and 2's; average 1's and poor troops need not re-roll their 6's.

For any re-roll of 1's, 2's and 3's, the re-rolled dice is never taken as less than the original roll. This is rare but possible, e.g. an elite battle group rolling two 2's for a score of four gets two re-rolls. If these come up say 6 and 1, the score is counted as eight, 6 and 2. The re-rolled 2 cannot go down to a 1.

BATTLE GROUP COHESION LEVELS

All battle groups begin the game in good order, and we refer to this as **steady**. As they suffer battle damage, their willingness and effectiveness in battle is reduced, resulting in changes to their **cohesion level**. These changes can occur gradually or suddenly and represent a mixture of morale effects and loss of formation. There are four levels of **cohesion**:

- **Steady**: the battle group is in good order and ready to fight
- **Disrupted**: reduced in effectiveness, but still in the fight (DISR)

Carthaginian battle group

BASE METHOD AND COUNTERS

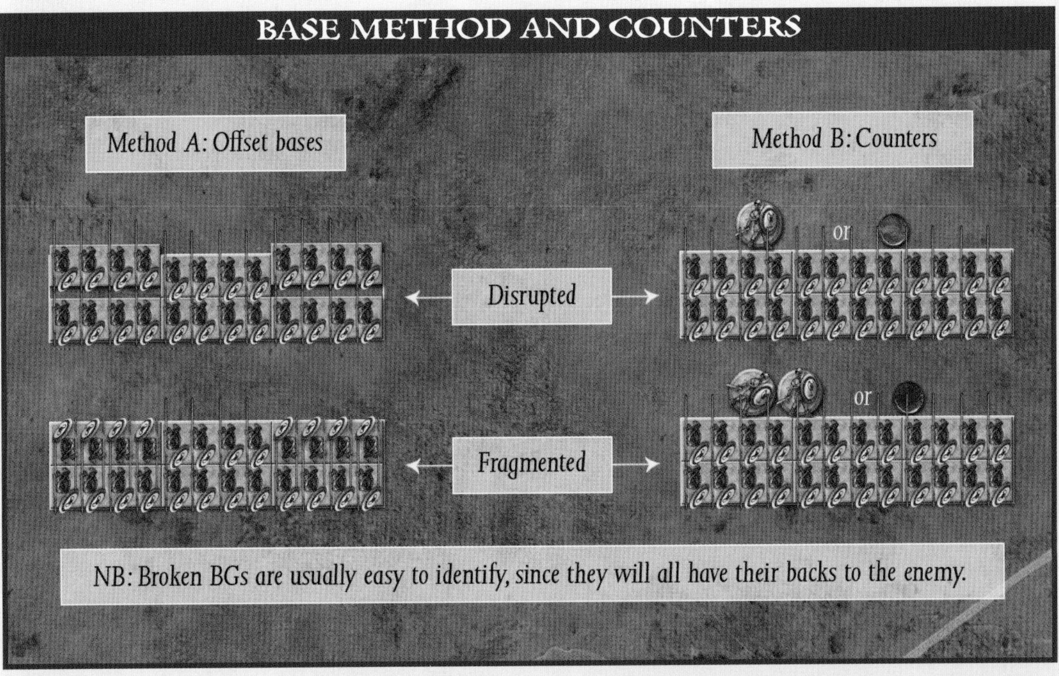

TIP!

Battle group cohesion is an accurate indicator of how the battle is going. To be victorious in *Field of Glory*, it is necessary to break the opposing army's will to fight on, by forcing their battle groups down the cohesion "ladder" until they break. When enough of them become fragmented or broken, the enemy army will collapse and rout.

- **Fragmented**: in a critical state, unable to fight effectively (FRAG)
- **Broken**: no longer able to fight, fleeing, or about to flee

Cohesion states can be indicated by positioning the bases of a battle group as a visual reminder, or you may prefer to use counters. These alternative methods are shown above. In all cases, when a battle group is broken, its bases are turned around and it will then flee at the time specified in the turn sequence.

Skirmishers battle through the rough terrain

BATTLE GROUP FORMATIONS
BATTLE GROUP QUALITY (QUALITY RE-ROLLS)
BATTLE COHESION LEVELS
BATTLE GROUP DISORDER

BATTLE GROUP DISORDER

Bases of a battle group positioned in certain types of **terrain** can be disordered, making them function less effectively, especially if they are of a type that depends on keeping formation to be fully effective. E.g. a phalanx of pikemen relies on keeping close order and is therefore badly affected by anything other than good terrain, whilst foot skirmishers never suffer such problems as their loose formation permits them to operate effectively in almost any type of terrain.

A HASTATI BATTLE GROUP STRADDLING DISORDERING TERRAIN

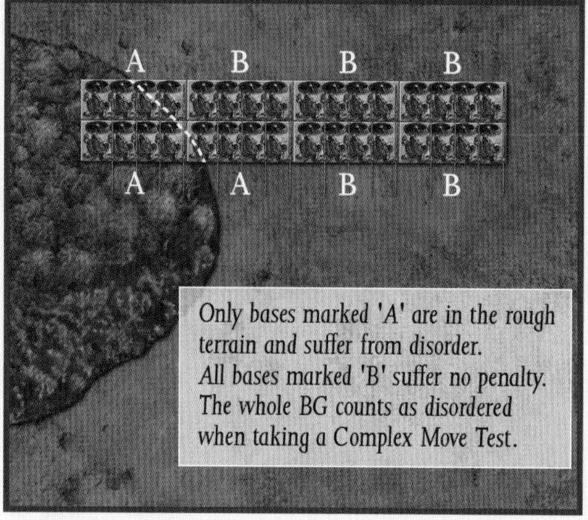

A B B B

A A B B

Only bases marked 'A' are in the rough terrain and suffer from disorder. All bases marked 'B' suffer no penalty. The whole BG counts as disordered when taking a Complex Move Test.

Terrain can also affect the movement distances of battle groups. The **General Movement Rules** section fully details how and where battle groups are affected in this way.

Individual bases that are in more than one type of terrain are affected by the terrain that reduces their movement most or causes them the most disorder. Only bases that are at least partially in the terrain are affected, e.g. if a battle group has 8 bases of Macedonian pikemen, 4 fully in "good going" and 4 in a wood, only the 4 in the wood are affected by terrain. This will cause disorder and reduce movement, consequently reducing the movement of the entire battle group.

Good order recovers automatically when a base leaves the terrain that caused the disorder.

In the diagram to the left, the Roman *hastati* battle group is partly in "rough going". The left hand file has both bases disordered. The next file has one base in good order and one disordered. The rest of the bases of the battle group are in good order. For movement purposes the entire battle group is disordered and movement is reduced. If it has to take any tests the battle group is considered to be disordered.

TIP!

Before playing a game, it is useful to study the troop types available to the enemy (see the companion army list books). Try to place or arrange terrain that will create a tactical advantage for your army. E.g. if you have a lot of medieval knights you need open spaces; if you have lots of foot skirmishers you might select steep hills. Once the battle field is laid out, deploy your troops to take best advantage of the available terrain and try to dominate areas where you have an advantage. It is seldom wise to contest areas where you are at a disadvantage or disperse your "bad terrain" troops too thinly to contest a tactically important terrain piece.

COMMAND AND CONTROL

The Black Prince, by Christopher Rothero. Taken from MAA 111: The Armies of Crecy and Poitiers.

COMMANDERS

In this chapter you will learn how to control and manage your battle groups on the battlefield.

With the exception of **commanders**, all bases must be part of a battle group. Commanders are represented by individual bases and can move independently or with a battle group they have temporarily joined. Each army must have a ***commander-in-chief*** and 1 to 3 ***subordinate*** or ***allied commanders***.

A commander is an individual of high rank, responsible for influencing one or more battle groups. A base representing a commander must be easily distinguishable from other bases in the army. All commanders have a ***command range***: i.e. the distance within which they can influence battle groups. There are three levels of commander and those available are set out in the companion army list books:

- **Inspired commander (IC)**, command range 12 MU: Julius Caesar, Ghengis Khan, Timur, Hannibal, Pyrrhus and Alexander all fit this category.
- **Field Commander (FC)**, command range 8 MU: A competent commander, able to command an army, or a reliable subordinate.
- **Troop commander (TC)**, command range 4 MU: A junior officer able to command a small part of the army or a very weak commander of a large army, such as Darius.

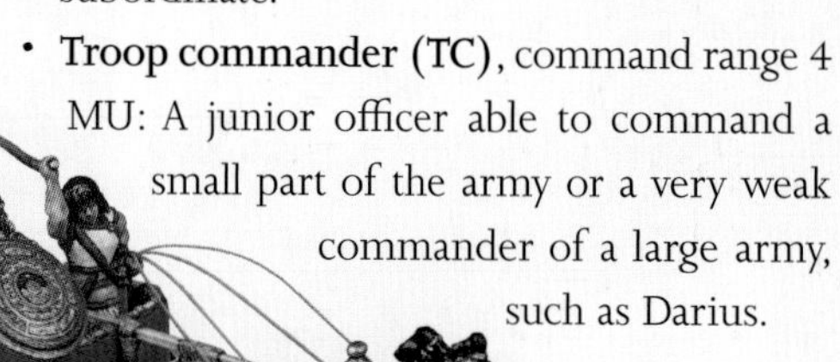

ACHILLES

Hannibal

A commander can only be with one battle group at a time. When that battle group is in close combat, he can elect either to fight in the front rank or to encourage the battle group from the rear. Unless he is fighting in the front rank in close combat, he can influence other battle groups that are in his command range and not in close combat.

If with a battle group, a commander's base must always be placed in edge to edge and corner to corner contact with a base of this one battle group. If operating independently, his base must not be touching any battle group.

HECTOR

Praetorians attempt to capture the eagle of legio ii Parthica, Immae, AD 218, by Angus McBride © Osprey Publishing Ltd. Taken from Warrior 72: Imperial Roman Legionary AD 161–284.

LINE OF COMMAND

Commanders can only affect battle groups for which they are **in line of command**. The C-in-C and subordinate commanders are in line of command for all battle groups in the main army, but not for any in ***allied contingents***.

Some armies can have one or more allied contingents. Allied commanders are only in line of command for battle groups of their own contingent.

TIP!

Deciding which commanders to select and how to use them is a key consideration. Do you commit them to lead the attack at a crucial moment, by fighting in the front rank to inspire the troops, or do you keep them behind your lines for command and control? Making this decision wisely can often be the key to success in *Field of Glory*.

BATTLE LINES

A **battle line** is a collection of battle groups with each in at least partial edge to edge contact with another and all facing in the same direction. It can be formed at deployment or during the game by moving battle groups into such a position. In order to operate as a battle line it must have a commander in line of command with it. He must be with one of its battle groups, and his **command range** must reach every battle group in the battle line.

The following restrictions apply:

- Severely disordered, fragmented or broken troops cannot be part of a battle line.
- Scythed chariots can never be part of a battle line.
- Foot and mounted troops cannot be mixed in the same battle line except:
  - Light foot can be in a battle line with mounted troops.
  - Elephants can be in battle line with foot troops.
- Battle groups that are part of an allied contingent can only form a battle line with other battle groups of the same allied contingent.

The principal advantage of a battle line is that it allows multiple battle groups to perform certain actions together as if each had a commander with it.

TIP!

Deploying and operating in battle lines is a sound historical tactic that will gain you significant advantages when manoeuvring, often allowing you to gain the initiative.

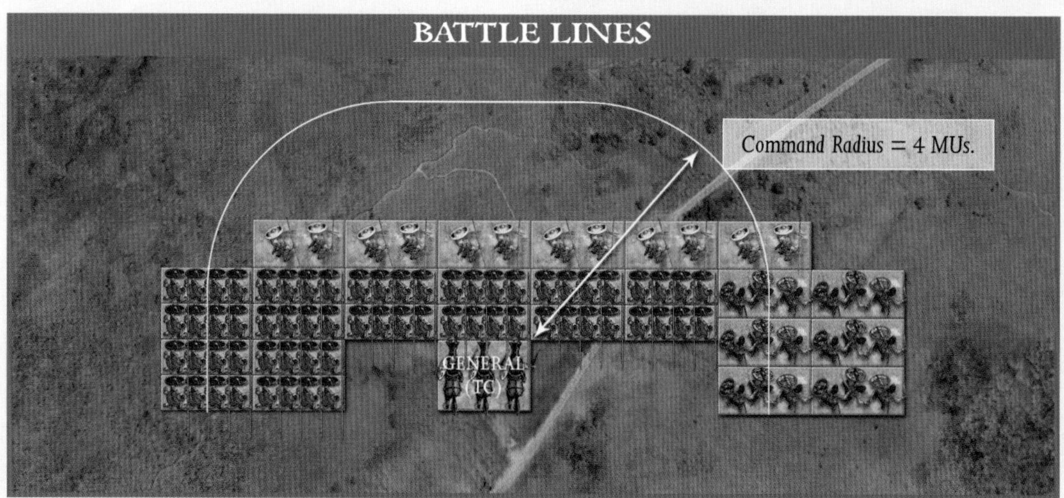

The Third Praetorian Cohort, by Richard Hook © Osprey Publishing Ltd. Taken from Elite 50: The Praetorian Guard.

Now that you understand how an army operates it, is time to look at some typical armies. The following are "starter" armies loosely based on the opposing forces at the Battle of Trebia (218 BC). We will use these armies and troop types to guide you through the remainder of the rules. At Trebia a Carthaginian army under Hannibal defeated a Roman army led by Sempronius Longus.

ROMAN ARMY UNDER SEMPRONIUS	
C-in-C: Sempronius Longus	Field Commander
Sub-Commander: Gaius Fulvius	Troop Commander
Sub-Commander: Lucius Lucretius	Troop Commander
4 x Cavalry	Cavalry, Light Spear, Swordsmen, Armoured, Undrilled, Average
4 x Cavalry	Cavalry, Light Spear, Swordsmen, Armoured, Undrilled, Average
4 x Hastati & Principes	Heavy Foot, Impact Foot, Skilled Swordsmen, Armoured, Drilled, Superior
4 x Hastati & Principes	Heavy Foot, Impact Foot, Skilled Swordsmen, Armoured, Drilled, Superior
2 x Triarii	Heavy Foot, Offensive Spearmen, Armoured, Drilled, Elite
4 x Velites	Light foot, Javelin, Light Spear, Protected, Drilled, Average
4 x Hastati & Principes	Heavy Foot, Impact Foot, Skilled Swordsmen, Armoured, Drilled, Superior
4 x Hastati & Principes	Heavy Foot, Impact Foot, Skilled Swordsmen, Armoured, Drilled, Superior
2 x Triarii	Heavy Foot, Offensive Spearmen, Armoured, Drilled, Elite
4 x Velites	Light foot, Javelin, Light Spear, Protected, Drilled, Average
8 x Italian foot	Medium Foot, Light Spear, Swordsmen, Protected, Drilled, Average
Fortified Camp	

Roman army stands ready

ROMAN ARMY UNDER SEMPRONIUS
CARTHAGIAN ARMY UNDER HANNIBAL
FRENCH ARMY UNDER KING PHILIPPE
ENGLISH ARMY UNDER KING EDWARD

The Carthaginian army advances

CARTHAGINIAN ARMY UNDER HANNIBAL	
C-in-C: Hannibal	Inspired Commander
Sub-Commander: Hasdrubal	Troop Commander
Sub-Commander: Mago	Troop Commander
4 x Gallic Cavalry	Cavalry, Light Spear, Swordsmen, Armoured, Undrilled, Superior
4 x Spanish Cavalry	Cavalry, Light Spear, Swordsmen, Protected, Undrilled, Superior
4 x Numidian Cavalry	Light horse, Javelin, Light Spear, Unprotected, Undrilled, Average
4 x Numidian Cavalry	Light horse, Javelin, Light Spear, Unprotected, Undrilled, Average
6 x African Spearmen	Heavy Foot, Offensive Spearmen, Protected, Drilled, Average
6 x African Spearmen	Heavy Foot, Offensive Spearmen, Protected, Drilled, Average
8 x Gallic Foot	Medium Foot, Impact Foot, Swordsmen, Protected, Undrilled, Average
6 x Spanish Foot	Medium Foot, Impact Foot, Swordsmen, Protected, Undrilled, Average
2 x Elephants	Elephants, Undrilled, Average
6 x Numidian Foot	Light foot, Javelins, Light Spear, Unprotected, Undrilled, Average
4 x Balearic Slingers	Light foot, Sling, Unprotected, Undrilled, Superior
Fortified Camp	

Here is another pair of "starter" armies, based loosely on the opposing forces at the battle of Crécy (1346 AD). At this battle, an English army under King Edward III defeated a French army under King Philippe VI.

FRENCH ARMY UNDER KING PHILIPPE

C-in-C: King Philippe VI	Troop Commander
Sub-Commander: Charles, Comte d'Alençon	Troop Commander
Sub-Commander: Rudolph, Duc de Lorraine	Troop Commander
4 x Men-at-arms	Knights, Lancers, Swordsmen, Heavily Armoured, Undrilled, Superior
4 x Men-at-arms	Knights, Lancers, Swordsmen, Heavily Armoured, Undrilled, Superior
4 x Men-at-arms	Knights, Lancers, Swordsmen, Heavily Armoured, Undrilled, Superior
4 x Men-at-arms	Knights, Lancers, Swordsmen, Heavily Armoured, Undrilled, Superior
8 x Genoese Crossbowmen	Medium Foot, Crossbow, Protected, Drilled, Average
6 x French Crossbowmen	Medium Foot, Crossbow, Protected, Undrilled, Average
6 x French Crossbowmen	Medium Foot, Crossbow, Protected, Undrilled, Average
12 x Peasants	Mob, Unprotected, Undrilled, Poor
Unfortified Camp	

ENGLISH ARMY UNDER KING EDWARD

C-in-C: King Edward III	Field Commander
Sub-Commander: Edward, The Black Prince	Troop Commander
Sub-Commander: William de Bohun, Earl of Northampton	Troop Commander
4 x Dismounted men-at-arms	Heavy Foot, Heavy Weapon, Heavily Armoured, Drilled, Superior
4 x Dismounted men-at-arms	Heavy Foot, Heavy Weapon, Heavily Armoured, Drilled, Superior
4 x Dismounted men-at-arms	Heavy Foot, Heavy Weapon, Heavily Armoured, Drilled, Superior
8 x Longbowmen	Medium Foot, Longbow, Swordsmen, Protected, Drilled, Average
8 x Longbowmen	Medium Foot, Longbow, Swordsmen, Protected, Drilled, Average
6 x Longbowmen	Medium Foot, Longbow, Swordsmen, Protected, Drilled, Average
8 x Welsh spearmen	Medium Foot, Offensive Spearmen, Unprotected, Undrilled, Average
2 x Guns	Light Artillery, Undrilled, Average
12 x Prepared ditches and pits	Field Fortifications
Unfortified Camp	

PLAYING THE GAME

The battle of Andraedsweald, by Gerry Embleton © Osprey Publishing Ltd. Taken from *Warrior 5: Anglo-Saxon Thegn AD 449–1066.*

SETTING UP A GAME

The first task is to position the terrain on the battlefield and then deploy the armies. You can do this in a number of ways, depending on the type of game to be played. If you are re-fighting an historical battle or campaign, it is likely that you will have researched the terrain and battlefield deployments. This will therefore dictate your layout. However, if this information is not available or you simply want an "equal points" battle you can follow the system described in the appendices at the back of this book.

A game in progress: **Trojans defend Troy**

PLAYING THE GAME

The game is played over a number of turns with players alternating who is "active" in each successive turn, until the scenario is complete, one army routs or time runs out. We consider that three hours should be sufficient time for two players of average experience to complete a game. During his turn, the active player can declare charges and manoeuvre his troops. His

ATTRITION POINTS	
Each battle group currently BROKEN, routed off table or destroyed	2
Each battle group straggling or evaded off table	1
Each battle group currently FRAGMENTED	1
Camp sacked by enemy	2

opponent can make only those response moves permitted by the rules. Both players' troops can shoot and fight, and both players can move their commanders in the final phase of the turn. The following turn, the active player is changed and the process is repeated till the game ends.

The game ends either when time runs out or at the end of the current phase if one army (or both) has suffered an **army rout**. An **army rout** occurs when an army's attrition points, calculated as per the table above, is equal or greater to the number of battle groups in the army at the start of the game. It is possible for both armies to break at the same time.

Note that scythed chariot battle groups do not count for attrition, neither in the original count of battle groups nor when calculating attrition points. Their loss is expected.

TURNS AND PHASES

A turn is divided into five phases. These are played strictly in the following order:

1. **The Impact Phase**: The impact phase covers charges and any combats resulting from these. The active player can initiate charges intended to result in close combat. The opposing player can respond with ***evades*** or ***interception charges*** where permitted. Impact combat is then resolved. Historically, a ferocious charge by certain troop types could break the enemy on contact or cause serious disruption or worse. Troops with the **lancers** or **impact foot** capability should do well here.
2. **The Manoeuvre Phase**: The active player moves any of his troops that did not move in the impact phase. Troops who are **undrilled** will often find it harder to change direction or formation than **drilled** troops.
3. **The Shooting Phase**: Both sides must shoot with any troops able to shoot at enemy bases in this phase.
4. **The Melee Phase**: All troops still in close combat now fight again. Melee combat is

TIP!

You will often have crucial decisions to take in the Joint Action Phase. Do you use your commanders to bolster the morale of your main attack or attempt to rally the battle group that's got into trouble? Just be careful not to chase a lost cause. The choices you make here will often decide the battle.

separate and distinctly different from impact combat. This allows us to accurately model historical differences in troop behaviour. Some troops depended on sweeping all before them in a ferocious charge whilst others were more steadfast in the push and grind of hand to hand combat that we model in melee. Armour and capabilities such as **swordsmen** are now important.

5. **The Joint Action Phase**: Occurs at the end of each player's turn, but does not 'belong' to either player. In this phase, both players can move their commanders. This is an important feature of *Field of Glory*. Players need to make effective use of their commanders, by positioning them carefully to influence troops in the coming turn or by joining any battle group needing assistance e.g. to bolster its cohesion or rally it from rout.

The sequence must be played in strict order. The full and detailed sequence of play is shown in the appendices at the back of the book.

GENERAL MOVEMENT RULES

The Ancient Greeks, 349 BC, by Angus McBride © Osprey Publishing Ltd. Taken from Elite 7: The Ancient Greeks.

This chapter covers all of the movement rules that are not phase specific. Note that some move types are unavailable to certain troop types and others are not available in all the phases. The restrictions are detailed in the relevant sections.

MOVEMENT RULES

- A permitted move of any battle group or commander can be taken back and redone, but only if its initial position was marked or can be unambiguously referenced. Otherwise the move is over.
- A battle group or commander's move is over if the player moves another battle group or commander, or makes a dice roll for another battle group.
- Movement is made by an individual battle group, by multiple battle groups moving together as a battle line, or by commander's bases moving independently.

MOVE DISTANCES AND DISORDER

The following table cross references troop type with terrain to show the effect on order and maximum move distances in MUs. For movement purposes, a terrain type is assigned one of four difficulty levels: **open**, **uneven**, **rough** or **difficult**. The effect of terrain types is covered in Appendix 2.

- The lower move distance applies **to the whole move** if any part of any base of the battle group is in distance-reducing terrain at any stage of its move. As a result, sometimes battle groups can reach the edge of a piece of terrain but not enter it. e.g. if cavalry have moved at least 3 MU in the open and meet rough terrain, they have already moved their maximum rough terrain distance, so cannot enter it.

TROOP TYPE	OPEN	UNEVEN	ROUGH	DIFFICULT
Light foot	5	5	5	4
Medium Foot	4	4	4	3
Heavy Foot	3	2	2	1
Light horse and Commanders	7	7	5	3
Cavalry	5	4	3	1
Knights and Cataphracts	4	3	2	1
Elephants	4	4	3	1
Light Chariots	5	3	2	1
Heavy and Scythed Chariots	4	2	1	N/A
Battle Wagons	3	2	1	N/A
Light Artillery	2	1	1	N/A

□ No effect
□ Disorder
■ Severe disorder

MOVEMENT RULES
MOVE DISTANCES AND DISORDER
SIMPLE AND COMPLEX MOVES
DIFFICULT FORWARD MOVES
ADVANCES
THE COMPLEX MOVE TEST (CMT)
WHEELING
TURNING 90 DEGREES
TURNING 180 DEGREES
SHIFTING
EXPANSIONS
CONTRACTION
VARIABLE MOVES
MOVING THROUGH FRIENDLY TROOPS
MOVEMENT OF COMMANDERS
MOVING FROM AN OVERLAP POSITION
TROOPS LEAVING THE TABLE

- Troops in column move at +1 MU along roads or through any terrain if the indicated move distance is less than their move distance in **open terrain**.
- Battle groups with mixed troop-types have the move distance of the slower type.
- Battle lines have the move distance of their slowest battle group.
- Battle groups moving through more than one type of terrain are limited to the shortest move distance shown for any of those terrain types. Battle groups with mixed troop types use the shortest move distance that would apply to any base in the battle group, even if that base is clear of the terrain. e.g. heavy foot backed by a rank of light foot move at 2 MU in rough terrain, even if only the rear rank of light foot is in the rough terrain.

SIMPLE AND COMPLEX MOVES

Moves fall into three categories: simple, complex or impossible. The table below cross references move types against troop types and shows the category of move. A move must be from a single section of the table (e.g. charges, advances or expansions). Moves by lone commanders are always simple.

A complex move requires a test to be passed before it can be made. All types of moves can be constrained by other restrictions, described later in this chapter, or by limitations imposed in specific phases.

- Battle lines are limited to the 'Advances' section of the table.
- Scythed chariots are limited to the 'Charges' and 'Advances' section of the table.
- Heavy artillery cannot move at all.
- Light artillery and battle wagons (or a battle line including either of these) must pass a Complex Move Test or CMT (see below) to carry out any move, whether simple or complex.

DIFFICULT FORWARD MOVES

A **difficult forward move** is one that includes a single **wheel** and/or is less than the troops' full available move distance - unless either:

a) All of the movement is more than 6 MU from any enemy (including the enemy camp but not an enemy commander's base), or
b) A commander is with the battle group or battle line. He must start the phase with a battle group and remain with it for the whole phase.

ADVANCES

An **advance** is a move from the 'Advances' section of the table. Some moves from other sections are permitted to include an **advance**.

SIMPLE & COMPLEX MOVES (Simple, Complex, Impossible)		Troop type			
			Battle troops		
Type of move	Move to be made	Skirmishers	Drilled	Undrilled Cavalry or Light Chariots	Other Undrilled
Charges	Charge directly forwards	Simple	Simple	Simple	Simple
	Wheel and charge enemy in range	Simple	Simple	Simple	Simple
Advances	*Difficult forward moves* (see above) with no more than a single wheel	Simple	Simple	Simple	Complex
	Any other forward move with no more than a single wheel	Simple	Simple	Simple	Simple
Double Wheels	A forward move including 2 wheels	Simple	Simple	Simple	Complex
Expansions	Expand frontage by 1 or 2 bases while stationary	Simple	Simple	Complex	Complex
	Expand frontage by 1 or 2 bases followed by a SIMPLE *advance*	Simple	Complex	Impossible	Impossible
Contractions	Contract frontage by 1 or 2 bases with a SIMPLE *advance* of at least 3 MUs before or after	Simple	Simple	Simple	Complex
	Contract frontage by 1 or 2 bases while stationary or with *advance* of less than 3 MUs before or after	Simple	Complex	Complex	Impossible
Turns	Turn 90 or 180 deg while stationary	Simple	Simple	Simple	Complex
	Turn 90 deg with a SIMPLE *advance* before or after	Simple	Complex	Complex	Impossible
	Turn 180 deg with a SIMPLE *advance* before or after	Simple	Impossible	Impossible	Impossible
	Turn 180 deg, move <=3 MUs in a SIMPLE *advance* and turn back again	Complex	Impossible	Impossible	Impossible

THE COMPLEX MOVE TEST (CMT)

The following procedure must be followed if a complex move test is required:

COMPLEX MOVE TEST	
Roll two dice, apply quality re-rolls, and add the scores. Apply the following modifiers.	
+1 if a commander in *line of command* is in *command range*	
+1 if this same commander is with the battle group or battle line which is taking the test	
+1 if this same commander is an inspired commander	
-1 if any of the bases are DISRUPTED or DISORDERED	Count the worst of these two, but never both
-2 if any of the bases are FRAGMENTED or SEVERELY DISORDERED	
Score to pass	7 if drilled or skirmishers
	8 if other undrilled

POINTS TO NOTE ON THE CMT:

- If a battle group or battle line fails its CMT, it can make a simple move.
- Once the dice have been rolled, that battle group or battle line must make its move, if any, before others are moved or tested. It is **not** permitted to arrange to conditionally make or change a move depending on the result of a subsequent battle group's test.
- Only one commander can influence the test.
- To be able to influence a CMT, a commander must be with the testers from the start of the phase to count as with them, and in command range from the start of the phase to count as in command range.
- If a commander is with a battle group or battle line when it takes a CMT, he must remain with the same battle group for the rest of the phase.
- A mixed battle group or battle line tests using the worst applicable column in the Simple and Complex Move table.
- Quality re-rolls apply to the CMT. When testing a battle line, its quality is that of its lowest quality battle group.

TIP!

Think ahead. Wherever possible, avoid complex moves, or make them early so you get time for a second chance. Wheel your troops while more than 6 MUs from the enemy to avoid taking CMTs that might stall your advance.

WHEELING

Wheeling is a change of direction by rotating around one front corner of the battle group or battle line. One corner of the front edge remains in the same position. For ease of measuring, the distance moved during the wheel is taken as the straight line from the starting position to the ending position of the moving front corner.

TIP!

When wheeling, be careful not to slide the corner on which the battle group is pivoting as this is not permitted by the rules.

MOVEMENT RULES
MOVE DISTANCES AND DISORDER
SIMPLE AND COMPLEX MOVES
DIFFICULT FORWARD MOVES
ADVANCES
THE COMPLEX MOVE TEST (CMT)
WHEELING
TURNING 90 DEGREES
TURNING 180 DEGREES
SHIFTING
EXPANSIONS
CONTRACTION
VARIABLE MOVES
MOVING THROUGH FRIENDLY TROOPS
MOVEMENT OF COMMANDERS
MOVING FROM AN OVERLAP POSITION
TROOPS LEAVING THE TABLE

A move cannot include more than two wheels, except by a column moving along a road. A move by a column entirely along a road is always simple, no matter how many wheels are involved. If wheeling a battle line, no battle group can exceed the full move distance of the slowest battle group in the battle line.

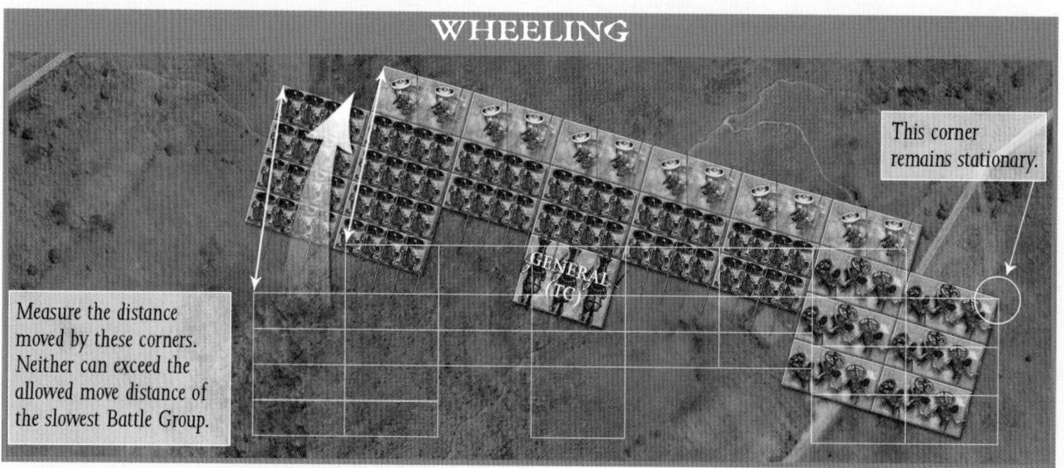

TURNING 90 DEGREES

See the diagram below. The old side edge of the battle group becomes the new front edge. The old front edge becomes the new side edge. The corner in between does not move. The new front edge must consist of the minimum number of bases so that the width of the turned group is at least as wide as it was deep before turning. (For example, in 15mm scale, if the old formation was 45mm deep, the new formation will be two bases – 80mm – wide). Other bases are repositioned behind to make the new formation legal. If the above is not possible due to obstructing troops or impassable terrain, the turn cannot be made.

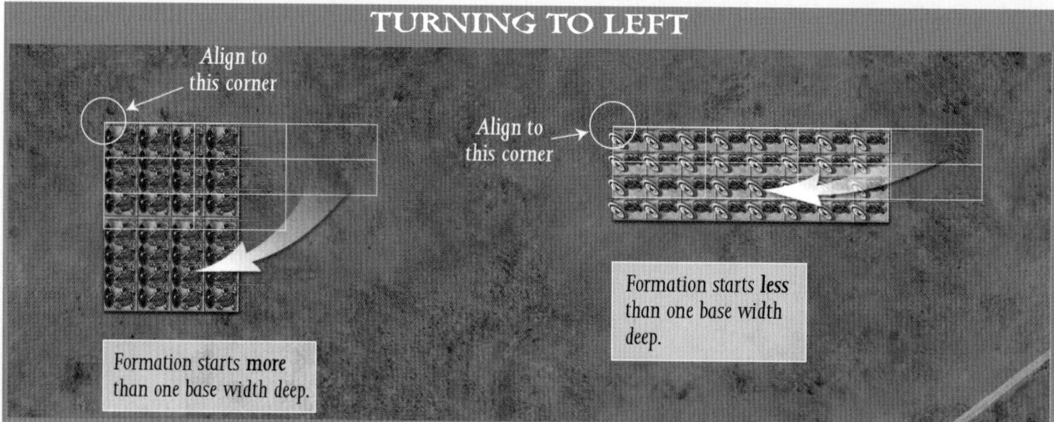

When a mixed battle group turns, its new front edge must, if possible, consist of the same base types as the old front edge. Bases are simply relocated to achieve this.

TURNING 180 DEGREES

The battle group ends in a block of the same width and depth as before, facing in the opposite direction, with its new front edge on the line of its old rear edge. The bases comprising the old front rank become the new front rank, and so forth.

SHIFTING

An **advance** can include a "free" sideways shift in the following circumstances only. The extra distance is not measured:

- Up to one base width sideways if all bases move the full distance straight forward (excluding the shift) and there are no enemy within 6 MUs at any point in the move. This includes the enemy camp but not an enemy commander's base.
- Up to half a base width sideways:
  - If this is necessary to avoid "clipping" terrain or friendly troops, and at least one front corner of the battle group moves at least 1 MU (excluding the shift). The shift cannot be greater than is necessary to avoid the obstacle.
  - To move into an ***overlap position*** against an enemy battle group that is already in close combat to its front.

Shifts are not permitted when ***charging***, nor in ***second moves***, nor with ***double wheels***, ***expansions***, ***contractions*** or ***turns***.

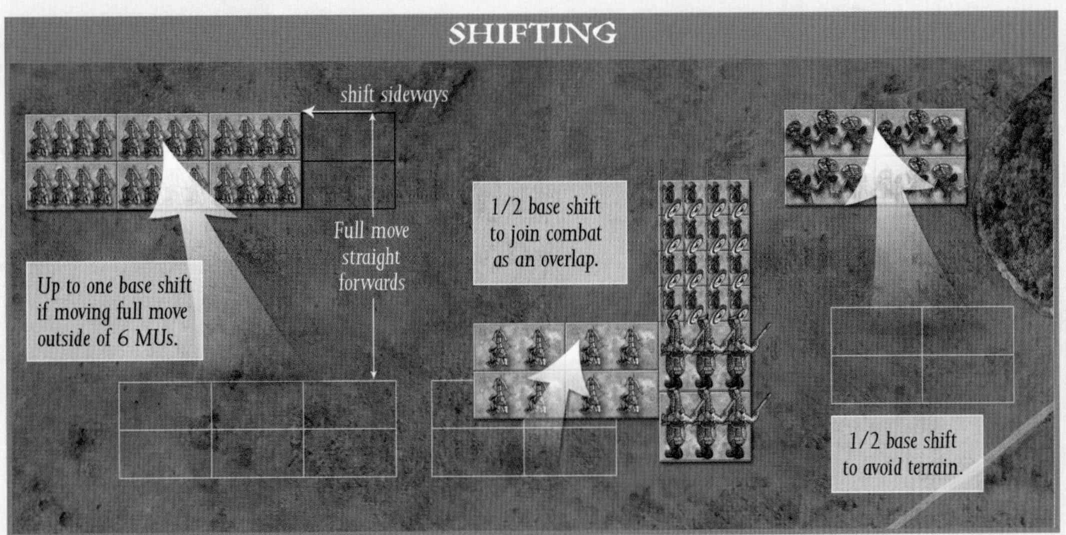

MOVEMENT RULES
MOVE DISTANCES AND DISORDER
SIMPLE AND COMPLEX MOVES
DIFFICULT FORWARD MOVES
ADVANCES
THE COMPLEX MOVE TEST (CMT)
WHEELING
TURNING 90 DEGREES
TURNING 180 DEGREES
SHIFTING
EXPANSIONS
CONTRACTION
VARIABLE MOVES
MOVING THROUGH FRIENDLY TROOPS
MOVEMENT OF COMMANDERS
MOVING FROM AN OVERLAP POSITION
TROOPS LEAVING THE TABLE

EXPANSIONS

Expansion by a battle group that is not in close combat is carried out as follows: Increase the width of the front rank by adding one or two bases taken from other ranks. If two bases are expanded, they can either be added to the same side, or one to each side. Then move bases not in the front rank to make the formation legal.

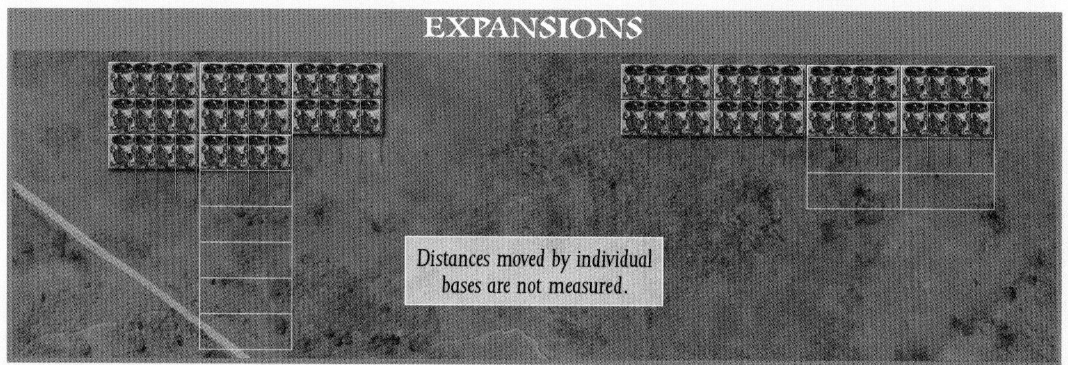

CONTRACTIONS

Contraction by a battle group that is not in close combat is carried out as follows: Remove one or two bases from the same or opposite ends of the front rank and place them in any other rank. Move bases not in the front rank to make the formation legal. To qualify as having advanced at least 3 MUs when contracting, both front corners of the final formation must have moved at least 3 MUs.

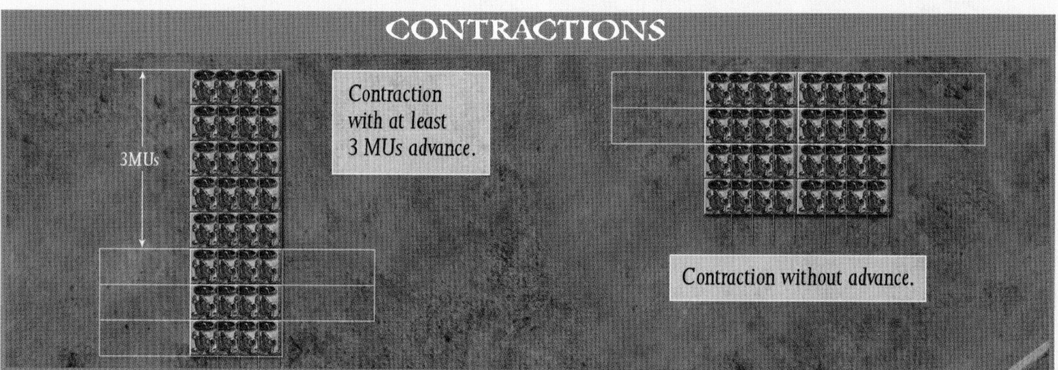

VARIABLE MOVES

In some situations, move distances are not fixed. If the rules state that a variable move must be made, roll one dice and consult the table below to determine any change to the distance to be moved.

This is generally the case when making **evades/charges** or **routs/pursuits**, and will sometimes result in the troops being caught or outdistancing the enemy.

TIP!

Keep variable move distances in mind when approaching enemy troops with skirmishers, as troops that normally move less may still catch you due to the VMD.

VARIABLE MOVEMENT DISTANCE (VMD)	
Roll 1d6	
1	-2 MUs
2	-1 MU
3 or 4	Normal distance
5	+1 MU
6	+2 MUs
Quality re-rolls do not apply	

MOVING THROUGH FRIENDLY TROOPS

In certain circumstances your battle groups can move voluntarily through other friendly troops, but at other times this may happen involuntarily and may cause deterioration in the cohesion of the battle group being passed through.

INTERPENETRATIONS

Interpenetrations are situations where you can choose to move through friendly troops and where there is no penalty for doing so. No interpenetrations are permitted when charging.

INTERPENETRATIONS

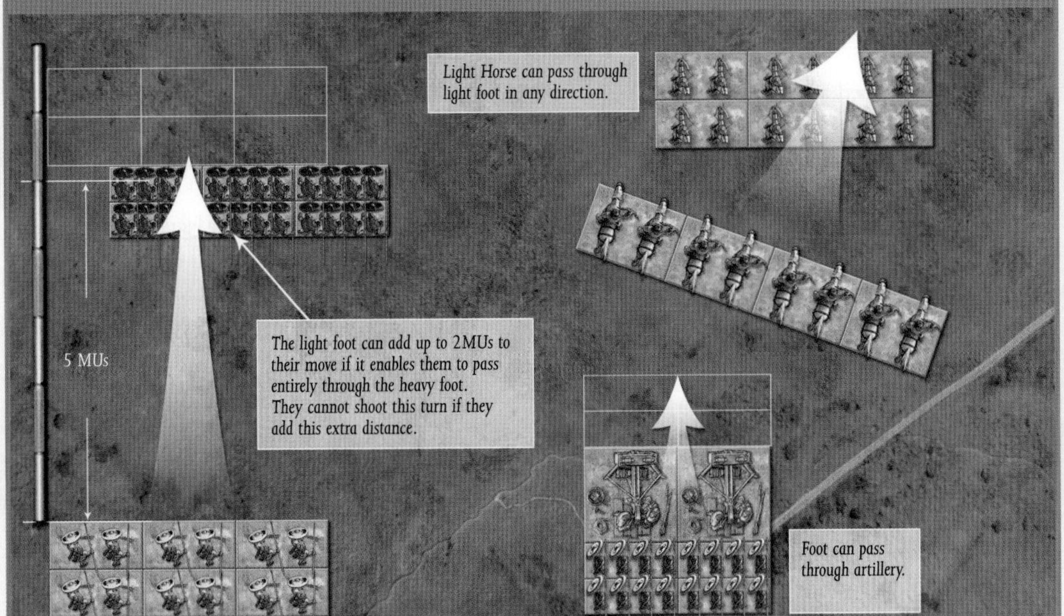

MOVEMENT RULES
MOVE DISTANCES AND DISORDER
SIMPLE AND COMPLEX MOVES
DIFFICULT FORWARD MOVES
ADVANCES
THE COMPLEX MOVE TEST (CMT)
WHEELING
TURNING 90 DEGREES
TURNING 180 DEGREES
SHIFTING
EXPANSIONS
CONTRACTIONS
VARIABLE MOVES
MOVING THROUGH FRIENDLY TROOPS
MOVEMENT OF COMMANDERS
MOVING FROM AN OVERLAP POSITION
TROOPS LEAVING THE TABLE

The following interpenetrations of friendly troops are permitted:

- Commanders can pass through and be passed through by any troops in any direction.
- Light foot can pass through any troops in any direction.
- Cavalry, light horse, light chariots and elephants can pass through light foot in any direction.
- Foot can pass through artillery perpendicularly from back to front or front to back only.
- Some armies are allowed special interpenetrations for troops who were historically capable of this. Where this is permitted, it is shown in the companion army list books. Such interpenetrations must be perpendicular from back to front or front to back only.
- If a battle group does not have sufficient move distance to pass fully through another battle group:
  - Light foot pass completely through if there is room beyond and they do not exceed their normal move distance by more than 2 MUs. They cannot then shoot this turn.
  - In all other cases, bases of the moving battle group that reach the battle group being interpenetrated are moved all the way through and are placed on the far side. Those that did not reach are placed with the front base in contact with the near side. If any do not pass through, the battle group making the interpenetration is DISORDERED until the interpenetration is completed in a subsequent turn. Other battle groups blocking placement of the moving battle group's bases are shifted as far as necessary in the direction of interpenetration to make room. If this is not possible (due to enemy troops, impassable terrain or the table edge) the move is not allowed. When a partial interpenetration has occurred, no wheel or turn by either battle group is permitted (except a 180 degree turn by skirmishers) until either battle group moves clear of the other using a permitted interpenetration.

TIP!

Be careful not to let battle groups become trapped in front of your main battle line with no escape route. Foot skirmishers can interpenetrate in most circumstances, but not always. If you delay too long you might get trapped. Mounted skirmishers always need gaps to pass through.

BURSTING THROUGH FRIENDS

In various circumstances, battle groups may be forced to burst through other battle groups that they cannot normally interpenetrate. This is not voluntary and causes difficulties.

A battle group burst through by friendly shock troops drops one cohesion level:

- Move the shock troops their full move. Then, if necessary, shift back the entire battle group being passed through so that they are behind the shock troops.
- Any other friends behind are shifted back to make room.
- If it is impossible (due to enemy troops, impassable terrain or the table edge) to shift friends back sufficiently to make room, the shock troops do not move at all and (if they were STEADY) drop to DISRUPTED.

A battle group burst through by friendly evaders or routers drops one cohesion level:

MOVEMENT RULES
MOVE DISTANCES AND DISORDER
SIMPLE AND COMPLEX MOVES
DIFFICULT FORWARD MOVES
ADVANCES
THE COMPLEX MOVE TEST (CMT)
WHEELING
TURNING 90 DEGREES
TURNING 180 DEGREES
SHIFTING
EXPANSIONS
CONTRACTION
VARIABLE MOVES
MOVING THROUGH FRIENDLY TROOPS
MOVEMENT OF COMMANDERS
MOVING FROM AN OVERLAP POSITION
TROOPS LEAVING THE TABLE

- Move the evading or routing battle group to the full extent of its move. If its move does not completely clear all friends, it is placed beyond any battle groups(s) it is currently bursting through if there is room for it beyond, otherwise it is destroyed and removed from the table. No cohesion test is taken for friends seeing this.

A battle group that is burst through by more than one friendly battle group in the same phase only drops one cohesion level.

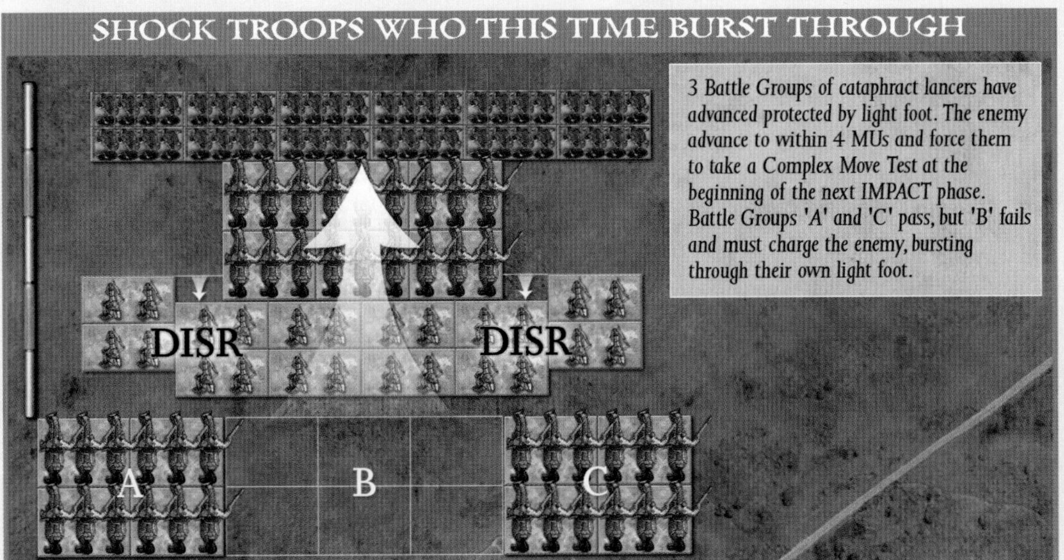

MOVEMENT OF COMMANDERS

- A commander who is with a battle group at the start of a phase can move with the battle group as it moves. A commander not with a battle group, or who wishes to leave a battle group (and is not fighting in the front rank in close combat), can move in the manoeuvre phase of his own side's turn and **again** in every joint action phase.
- Commanders, however depicted, have the move distance of light horse when not with a battle group.
- Commanders can move in any direction without any CMTs and without having to wheel or turn the base to face the direction of movement.
- Commanders' bases represent only the commander and a few aides. Therefore they do not obstruct the movement of other troops. Commanders can interpenetrate any friendly troops in any direction and vice versa.
- When a commander joins a battle-group:
  - His base must be placed in edge to edge and corner to corner contact with a base of the battle group.
  - His base can be moved at any time the minimum necessary to a new such position **if this is necessary** to avoid obstructions or make way for friendly or

enemy troops. (This is not permitted if he is fighting in the front rank - see below). If there is no room left for him to be so placed, a marker must be placed on top of one of the bases of the battle group to represent his position.

- He can only be with one battle group at a time. If possible, he must be placed in a position that makes it clear which battle group he is with. If not, the player must declare which battle group he is with.
- He can only leave the battle group, or voluntarily move to a different position in contact with it, during the manoeuvre or joint action phases. If he moves with the battle group, he must remain in exactly the same position relative to it, unless its formation changes. In that case he moves the minimum necessary to a new permitted position.

- If a commander is declared to be fighting in the front rank, his base is placed anywhere in the front rank (player's choice) to show that he is fighting. The base(s) he displaces is (are) placed behind him, but still count as fighting as if in their original position. Once declared as fighting in the front rank, the commander cannot leave the front rank of that battle group until it is no longer in close combat and no longer in contact with enemy routers.
- If a battle group's move would take it into contact or within shooting range of an enemy commander who is not with a battle group, he must immediately move (in any phase or turn) to join a friendly battle group, if there is one within his normal move distance. If not, he does not move and is immediately lost. It is not necessary for the enemy to declare a charge on him, nor to halt their move at the point of contact.

MOVING FROM AN OVERLAP POSITION

A battle group which fought in melee in a previous turn as an overlap only, can choose to charge a different enemy or evade in the impact phase, move normally in the manoeuvre phase, or continue to fight against its existing opponents in the next melee phase.

TROOPS LEAVING THE TABLE

- If any part of any base of a battle group leaves the table, that battle group is removed from play and cannot return during the game. If it routed off the table, it counts as 2 attrition points towards its side's defeat. If it evaded off the table, it counts as 1 attrition point.
- Except by evading, battle groups cannot voluntarily leave the table except in campaign games or in scenario games where this is allowed by the scenario.
- A charging or pursuing battle group whose move would take any part of it off the table edge instead halts its move at the table edge.
- In situations where battle groups are shifted to make room for others, they cannot be shifted if this would take any part of any base off the table.
- If a commander is routing or evading with a battle group that leaves the table, he is removed from play for the remainder of the game. It is not necessary to take a cohesion test for battle groups seeing this.

IMPACT PHASE

Early Mycenaean infantry, by Angus McBride © Osprey Publishing Ltd. Taken from Elite 130: The Mycenaeans c. 1650–1100 BC.

The **impact phase** is divided into four stages:

- Declaring charges. (In addition, some troops may charge without orders.)
- Troops responding to charges by intercepting or evading the chargers.
- Moving the chargers into contact.
- Resolving combats for battle groups that have come into contact.

All activity in the impact phase is resolved by battle groups. Battle lines are not used in the impact phase at all. We start by showing a straightforward sequence of events detailing what happens in a charge when there is no special reaction possible by the opponent. We then consider battle groups that are unable or unwilling to charge or that make an involuntary charge. Finally, we consider what happens when troops intercept or evade the chargers.

DECLARATION OF CHARGES

The active player declares which of his battle groups are to charge and by convention places a dice behind each to note this. To be allowed to declare a charge, there must be a visible enemy base that can be "legally" contacted by the charging battle group within its normal move distance through the terrain to be crossed. A battle group can declare charges on as many enemy battle groups as can be "legally" contacted within this move distance. When the charge declaration stage is over, no charge declarations can be rescinded, nor additional voluntary charges declared.

Any enemy battle group in the path of a charge counts as being charged if it can be "legally" contacted, even if it was not one of the originally declared targets of the charge. This applies even if it can only be contacted by bases stepping forward (see below). It does not apply if, due to intervening friends, it could not be contacted even by stepping forward bases – unless the situation changes, as follows: If a battle group is revealed and can now be contacted due to friends evading or breaking and routing, it becomes a target of the charge and will therefore take any required tests once the evade or rout move has occurred.

If a CMT is required to make a charge against certain troops, it must be taken if required for any of the battle groups that can be "legally" contacted in the chosen direction of charge, including by stepping forward bases. It need not and cannot be taken for those that can only be contacted if another battle group evades or routs.

LEGAL CHARGE CONTACT

A battle group makes a "legal" charge contact if at least one of its bases contacts an enemy base either:

a) with its front edge, or
b) with its front corner only against the enemy base's edge.

Other bases of the charging battle group may contact the enemy in other ways (e.g. only corner to corner), but will not be eligible to fight in the impact phase combat.

The King of France and his nobles thunder towards the enemy.

CHARGING WITH YOUR BATTLE GROUPS

A charging battle group must make a charge move in one of two ways:

1. Advance directly ahead, up to the full extent of its charge move (plus any variable move distance to contact evaders) to "legally" contact any part of the target battle group(s).
2. Combine such an advance with a single wheel, made at any stage during the charge move. Any troops can wheel during a charge without taking a CMT. Unless required to avoid friends, a wheel cannot be made if this would result in less bases being eligible to fight in the impact phase combat than would occur if the battle group charged straight ahead. A wheel while charging cannot be more than 90 degrees.

A charge cannot be declared if it would contact only the flank or rear edge of an enemy base which is already in melee to its front, except by a "legal" flank or rear charge. (See overleaf) A battle group unable to charge in such a case may be able to move into an overlap position in the manoeuvre phase.

> **TIP!**
>
> If your troops are best at impact, make sure your charges arrive with as many bases in contact as possible. Don't waste valuable shock troops such as knights in small scale contacts where only a few will fight at impact.

DECLARATION OF CHARGES
LEGAL CHARGE CONTACT
CHARGING WITH YOUR BATTLE GROUPS
FORMATION CHANGES WHEN CHARGING
CHARGING TO CONTACT AND STEPPING FORWARDS
CHARGING A FLANK OR REAR
TROOPS WHO CANNOT CHARGE
TROOPS WHO MAY CHARGE WITHOUT ORDERS
ATTEMPTS TO CHARGE OT RECEIVE A CHARGE WITH SKIRMISHERS
CHARGING WITH MISSILE-ARMED FOOT TROOPS
ATTEMPTS TO CHARGE WHEN DISRUPTED OR FRAGMENTED
BEING CHARGED WHILE FRAGMENTED
POSSIBLE RESPONSES TO CHARGES
SEQUENCE OF CHARGES AND RESPONSES
RESOLVING IMPACT PHASE COMBAT

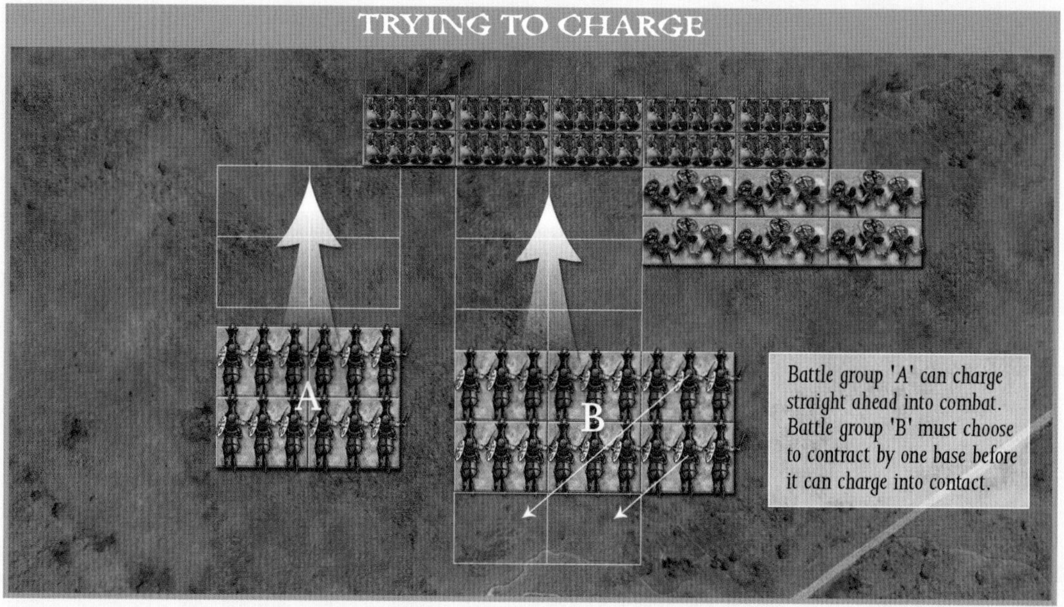

FORMATION CHANGES WHEN CHARGING

The only change in formation that is allowed during a charge move is to contract the battle group's frontage by one base **if necessary** to pass friendly troops. The frontage is reduced and bases fall back behind those in front. A battle group cannot be contracted to avoid hitting enemy who would otherwise be in the path of its charge. No turns or expansions are permitted. If, owing to this, contact is not possible, the charge cannot be made and is cancelled.

CHARGING TO CONTACT AND STEPPING FORWARDS

To charge, move your battle group forward, making any wheels or formation changes allowed, until a "legal" contact is made. If it is now possible to get more bases into contact with the same or different enemy battle groups, you MUST step them forward to make further contacts, unless exempted by the following rules:

To step forward after initial contact, slide any files of your battle group not yet in contact straight forward until the front base makes contact with enemy bases, subject to the following conditions:

- No bases can be stepped forward more than 2MUs from the original line of contact.

DECLARATION OF CHARGES
LEGAL CHARGE CONTACT
CHARGING WITH YOUR BATTLE GROUPS
FORMATION CHANGES WHEN CHARGING
CHARGING TO CONTACT AND STEPPING FORWARDS
CHARGING A FLANK OR REAR
TROOPS WHO CANNOT CHARGE
TROOPS WHO MAY CHARGE WITHOUT ORDERS
ATTEMPTS TO CHARGE OT RECEIVE A CHARGE WITH SKIRMISHERS
CHARGING WITH MISSILE-ARMED FOOT TROOPS
ATTEMPTS TO CHARGE WHEN DISRUPTED OR FRAGMENTED
BEING CHARGED WHILE FRAGMENTED
POSSIBLE RESPONSES TO CHARGES
SEQUENCE OF CHARGES AND RESPONSES
RESOLVING IMPACT PHASE COMBAT

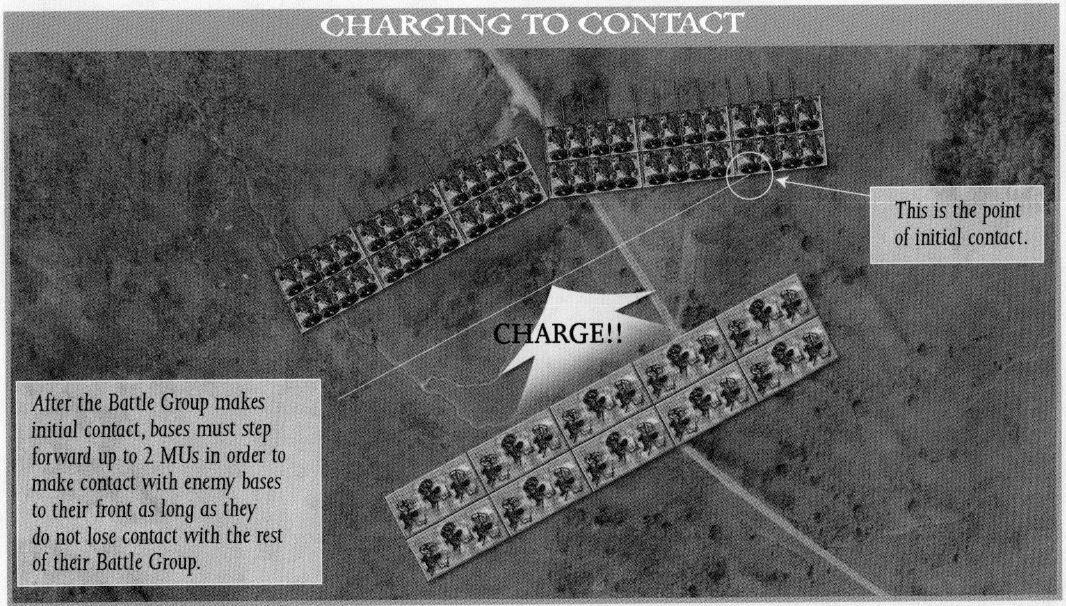

- Every stepped forward front rank base must end in contact with an enemy.
- Every base in a file must step forward the same distance as the front rank base.
- A battle group cannot separate to form multiple groups of bases. There must be at least corner to corner contact throughout.
- The stepped forward distance is additional to the normal move distance plus any variable move distance already added.
- Skirmishers need not step forward into contact with an enemy battle group of non-skirmishers that they otherwise would not contact.

Stepping forward therefore results in a battle group having an uneven line.

CHARGING A FLANK OR REAR

Flank and rear charges can be devastating in effect but arc more difficult to engineer. A battle group charged in the flank or rear may suffer an immediate drop in cohesion and always fights at a major disadvantage in the impact phase. The following rules apply to flank and rear charges:

- A battle group can only charge an enemy battle group in the flank or rear if it starts its charge in a position where both of the following apply (see diagram):
  - The charging battle group starts with no part of any of its bases directly in front of any part of any base of the target battle group.
  - The charging battle group starts with at least one base entirely behind a straight line extending the front edge of the enemy battle group. If the enemy battle

STEPPING FORWARDS INTO COMBAT

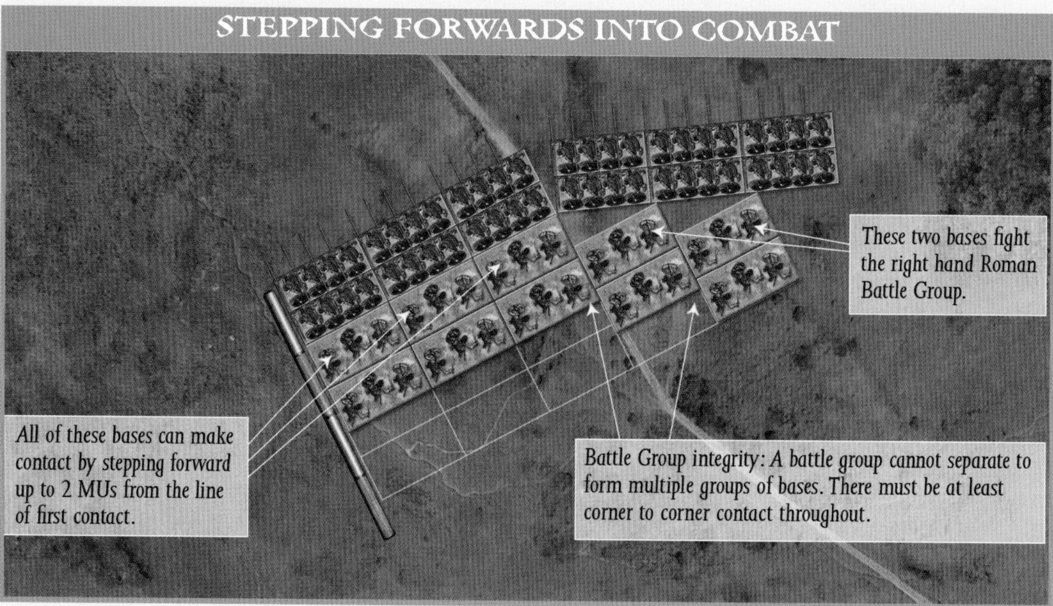

group has some files stepped forward, its front edge is taken as the front edge of the file on the flank charged. If the enemy battle group is facing in more than one direction, it has more than one front edge for this purpose – the above requirement must be satisfied for all of them.

- For a charge to qualify as a flank or rear charge, the first part of the enemy battle group contacted must be the side or rear edge or rear corner of one of its bases.
- For a charge to qualify as a flank charge, it cannot include a wheel unless the charging battle group starts its move with its nearest point at least 1 MU away from the battle group being charged.
- Battle wagons, troops in **orb formation** and troops attacked across fortifications they are defending (see the **Special Features** section) never count as being charged in flank or rear. Battle wagons and troops in orb formation do not turn if contacted on their side or rear base edge.
- Battle groups which are contacted by a flank or rear charge immediately drop one cohesion level unless they are non-skirmishers contacted by skirmishers. (If contacted in flank or rear by more than one enemy battle group in the same turn, they only drop one level.)
- Bases contacted on a side or rear edge, or a rear corner, by an enemy flank or rear charge are immediately turned 90 or 180 degrees to face the chargers, using the normal rules for turning, provided that they are not already in contact with enemy to their front. If all the contacted bases are already in contact with enemy to their front, one of

TIP!

Be careful to protect your flanks. It can be disastrous to get hit in the flank or rear by the enemy.

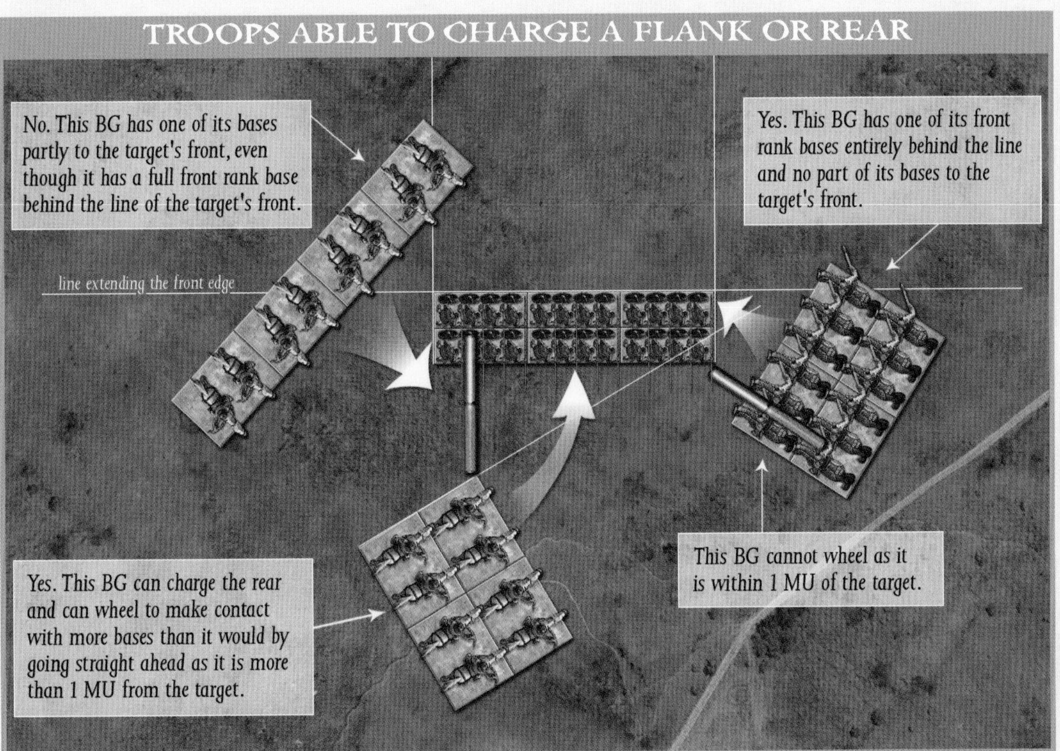

them is turned. If turning creates a gap between the bases that have been turned and the other bases of the battle group, the turned bases are shifted back so as to remain in contact. The flank charging battle group then moves forward to maintain contact even if normal movement distance is exceeded.

- Flank/rear chargers are always on a net ++ **Points of Advantage (POA)** in the impact phase. Bases fighting against a flank or rear charge in the impact phase always fight on a net -- POA. No other POAs apply. (This means that flank/rear chargers always need 3s to hit whilst those being charged need 5s.)
- A charge which does not qualify as a flank or rear charge can still contact the flank edge of an enemy base, provided that it was not already in melee to its front. Such a charge does not count as a flank or rear charge, and is treated as a normal charge on the enemy front. In the manoeuvre phase the chargers must, if possible, align with the enemy front. Even if it is not possible to align, troops charged in this way do not suffer a negative POA in the subsequent melee phase(s) for "fighting enemy in two directions".

TROOPS WHO CANNOT CHARGE

Battle wagons and artillery cannot move in the impact phase. They cannot charge and they cannot intercept.

DECLARATION OF CHARGES
LEGAL CHARGE CONTACT
CHARGING WITH YOUR BATTLE GROUPS
FORMATION CHANGES WHEN CHARGING
CHARGING TO CONTACT AND STEPPING FORWARDS
CHARGING A FLANK OR REAR
TROOPS WHO CANNOT CHARGE
TROOPS WHO MAY CHARGE WITHOUT ORDERS
ATTEMPTS TO CHARGE OT RECEIVE A CHARGE WITH SKIRMISHERS
CHARGING WITH MISSILE-ARMED FOOT TROOPS
ATTEMPTS TO CHARGE WHEN DISRUPTED OR FRAGMENTED
BEING CHARGED WHILE FRAGMENTED
POSSIBLE RESPONSES TO CHARGES
SEQUENCE OF CHARGES AND RESPONSES
RESOLVING IMPACT PHASE COMBAT

TROOPS WHO MAY CHARGE WITHOUT ORDERS

Shock troops are eager to get stuck in and may charge enemy within reach even if the commander (player) does not wish them to. In certain circumstances, shock troops who have **not** declared a charge need to pass a complex move test (see the ***General Movement Rules*** section) to avoid charging without orders. More specifically:

- Mounted shock troops must pass a CMT to prevent them from charging any enemy battle group(s) within charge range.
- Foot shock troops must pass a CMT to prevent them from charging any enemy foot battle group(s) within charge range.

However, shock troops will not charge without orders (and are therefore not required to take a CMT to prevent charging) in the following circumstances:

- If their move could end even partly in terrain that would disorder or severely disorder them.
- If they are medium foot starting wholly in uneven, rough or difficult terrain and the move could end even partly in ***open terrain***.
- If they are foot defending fortifications or a riverbank.
- If they are foot whose move could contact or be intercepted by mounted.
- If their move could end in contact with a fortification, elephants or a riverbank.
- If they are fragmented (they cannot charge).

(If the enemy who would be charged are capable of evading - see later - assume a charge move distance of 2 MUs more than the shock troops' normal move distance. This is the maximum variable move distance that could be added.)

Otherwise, if shock troops would normally be required to test to prevent them from charging without orders, the following rules apply if they could not contact the enemy without passing through friends, even by wheeling and/or dropping back bases:

- They do not test (and will not charge) if the friends are shock troops or already in melee.
- They do not test (and will not charge) if all the enemy in reach are skirmishers.
- Otherwise the battle group must take a CMT as normal. If it fails, it must burst through the friends. (Note that a player cannot choose to allow his shock troops to burst

TIP!

Manoeuvre your shock troops into positions where you would want them to charge. If they are taking tests not to charge without orders, they are usually in the wrong place, your timing has gone awry, or you have failed to screen them from enemy skirmishers.

through in this way, they can only do so if they fail their CMT and charge without orders).

The following additional rules apply to CMTs to avoid charging without orders:

- The CMT is taken by each individual battle group separately, even if it is part of a battle line. A commander cannot therefore be counted as "with" the battle group for the test unless he is actually with the battle group that is testing.
- Mixed battle groups including any shock troops must test as if entirely shock troops.
- **Quality re-rolls do not apply.**

Shock troops charging without orders who cannot contact all potential target battle groups within charge range, charge the one(s) nearest to straight ahead.

Shock troops that successfully test to prevent charging without orders can move normally in the manoeuvre phase. They must take another CMT then if they want to make a complex move.

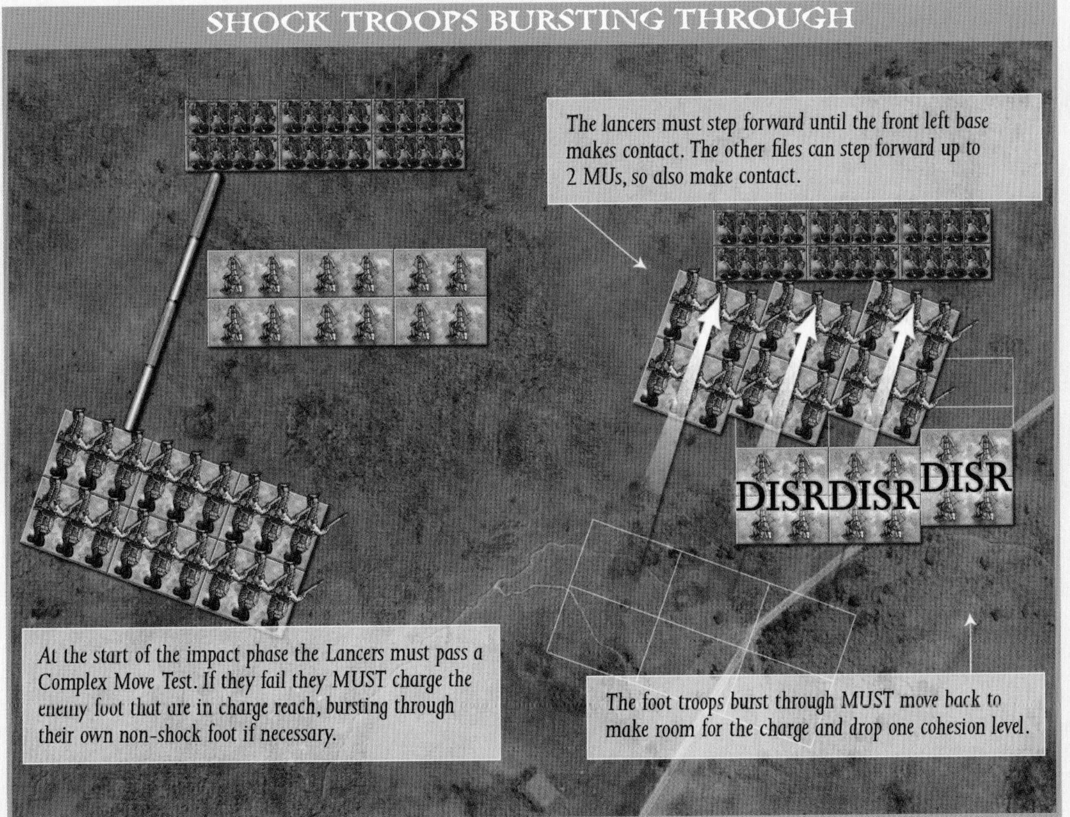

ATTEMPTS TO CHARGE OR RECEIVE A CHARGE WITH SKIRMISHERS

Skirmishers are understandably reluctant to engage in close combat with more heavily equipped troops. As a result:

- A battle group entirely of light foot cannot charge or intercept unbroken non-skirmishers in **open terrain** (even in the flank or rear).
- Light horse must pass a CMT to charge unbroken non-skirmishers (unless charging their flank or rear). They cannot intercept non-skirmishers in any circumstances.
- If any of their charge targets evade, skirmishers must halt their charge 1 MU away from enemy to their front whom they would not normally be allowed to charge without a CMT (unless they passed a CMT to charge them prior to charging).
- A battle-group entirely of light foot or light horse must pass a CMT to receive a charge by enemy non-skirmishers unless it is entirely in uneven, rough or difficult terrain or defending fortifications or a riverbank. If it fails the CMT it must evade.

CHARGING WITH MISSILE-ARMED FOOT TROOPS

Foot armed with long range missile weapons are reluctant to charge, preferring to shoot till the last possible moment. Consequently:

- Non-shock medium foot whose front rank has bow, longbow, crossbow or firearm must pass a CMT to charge or intercept unbroken non-skirmishers (unless charging their flank or rear).

ATTEMPTS TO CHARGE WHEN DISRUPTED OR FRAGMENTED

Troops who are disrupted or fragmented are less keen to charge. As a result:

- DISRUPTED non-shock battle groups must pass a CMT to charge.
- FRAGMENTED battle groups cannot charge.

BEING CHARGED WHILE FRAGMENTED

A fragmented battle group is very vulnerable and is quite likely to turn and flee if charged. As a result:

- FRAGMENTED battle groups must take a cohesion test if being charged by any troops other than light foot.
- If they BREAK as a result of the test, they cause immediate cohesion tests on friendly battle groups in range, and then make an initial rout move before the chargers are moved.

Where a friendly battle group initially blocks them from being contacted by an enemy charge, they need not take a cohesion test unless the friendly battle group moves to clear the path by evading or routing.

POSSIBLE RESPONSES TO CHARGES

Prior to moving chargers, there are three possible responses by the enemy: receiving the charge, interception charges and evade moves. We cover each in turn.

Romans prepare to receive a Carthaginian charge

RECEIVING THE CHARGE

Troops receiving a charge are not moved, and **never** count as "charging" when determining combat factors. However, the combat factors are designed to take account of any appropriate

DECLARATION OF CHARGES
LEGAL CHARGE CONTACT
CHARGING WITH YOUR BATTLE GROUPS
FORMATION CHANGES WHEN CHARGING
CHARGING TO CONTACT AND STEPPING FORWARDS
CHARGING A FLANK OR REAR
TROOPS WHO CANNOT CHARGE
TROOPS WHO MAY CHARGE WITHOUT ORDERS
ATTEMPTS TO CHARGE OT RECEIVE A CHARGE WITH SKIRMISHERS
CHARGING WITH MISSILE-ARMED FOOT TROOPS
ATTEMPTS TO CHARGE WHEN DISRUPTED OR FRAGMENTED
BEING CHARGED WHILE FRAGMENTED
POSSIBLE RESPONSES TO CHARGES
SEQUENCE OF CHARGES AND RESPONSES
RESOLVING IMPACT PHASE COMBAT

response, e.g. legionaries being charged by Gallic warriors respond by hurling their pila and surging forward to meet the Gauls over the last few metres. We do not depict this minor movement on the tabletop, but the combat factors take account of the full interaction.

INTERCEPTION CHARGES

Each battle group has a zone to its front where it can interfere with the charge of an opposing battle group. This mechanism allows you to cover flanks and protect nearby friendly troops. We call this the **Zone of Interception (ZOI)**:

- The ZOI is 2 MUs for foot and 4 MUs for mounted troops. It extends only directly to the intercepting battle group's front and only through terrain that does not disorder or severely disorder it. A battle group cannot intercept an enemy battle group if, due to intervening terrain, no part of the enemy battle group is visible to it before either battle group moves.
- If an enemy battle group attempts to charge through the ZOI of a battle group that is not itself a target of any charge this turn, that battle group has the option of making an interception charge on the chargers.
- DISRUPTED non-shock troops must pass a CMT to intercept.

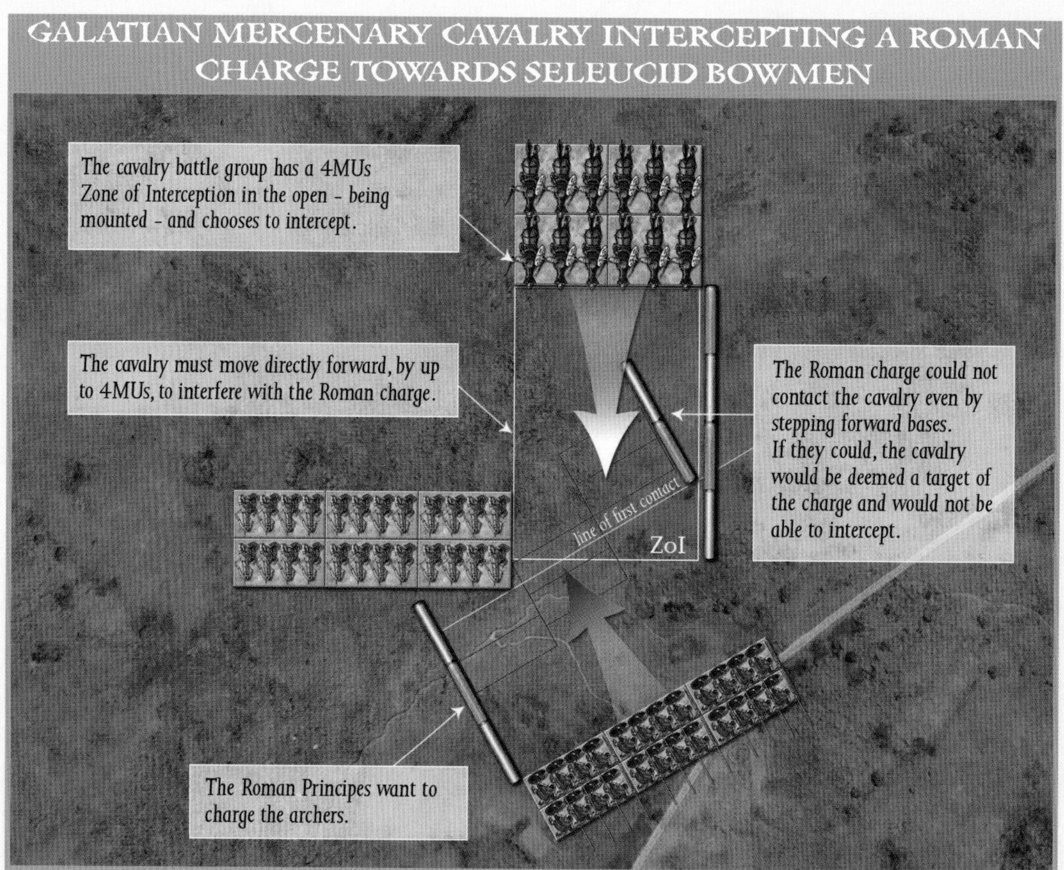

- FRAGMENTED troops cannot intercept.
- Skirmishers cannot intercept non-skirmishers.
- Non-shock missile-armed medium foot (see above) must pass a CMT to intercept non-skirmishers other than by a flank or rear charge.
- A battle group that is itself charged cannot intercept. This applies even if a charge was not declared on it, if it is in the path of a charge and would be contacted (including by bases stepping forward) if no friendly battle group evaded.
- An interception charge must be directly forward (except as below) and can be up to the limit of the battle group's ZOI. It cannot include any shifts, changes of formation or interpenetrations. It must either:
  - Cross the path of the charging enemy battle group. Interceptors move before chargers. If this would result in the enemy chargers contacting its flank, the intercepting battle group can and must wheel towards them to avoid this, its total move distance including the wheel not exceeding 4 MUs if mounted, 2 MUs if foot. If it cannot avoid being contacted in the flank, the interception is cancelled.
  - Contact the flank or rear of the enemy battle group. This is only permitted if the intercepting battle group started in a position to charge the flank or rear of the enemy battle group as previously described. It cancels the enemy battle group's charge completely and despite the fact that it happens in the enemy's turn, is treated as a normal flank/rear charge.

TIP!

Position some of your battle groups so that they can cover your flanks by intercepting enemy chargers.

BLOCKING MOVE BY INTERCEPTING CAVALRY

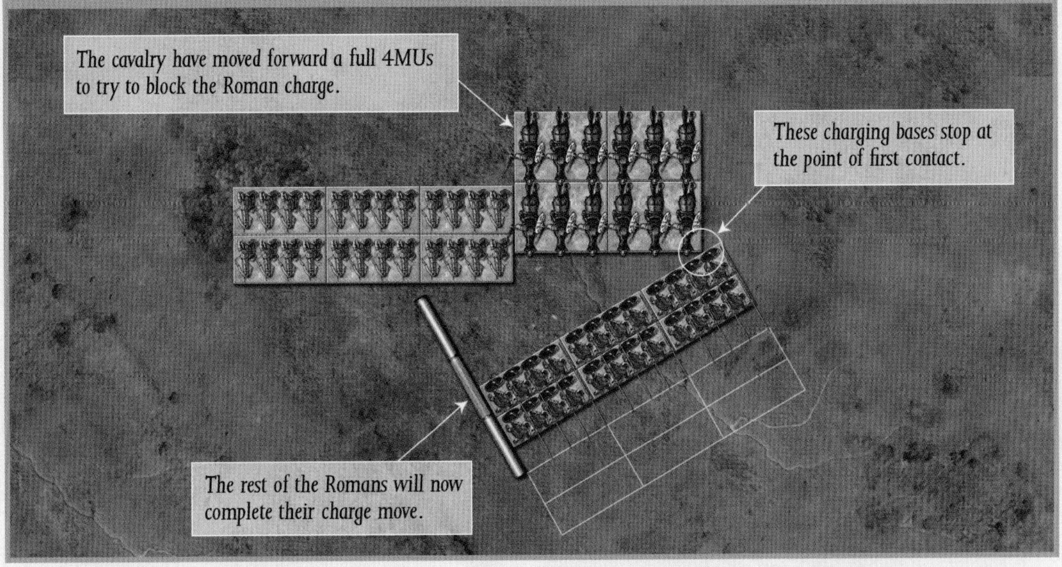

DECLARATION OF CHARGES
LEGAL CHARGE CONTACT
CHARGING WITH YOUR BATTLE GROUPS
FORMATION CHANGES WHEN CHARGING
CHARGING TO CONTACT AND STEPPING FORWARDS
CHARGING A FLANK OR REAR
TROOPS WHO CANNOT CHARGE
TROOPS WHO MAY CHARGE WITHOUT ORDERS
ATTEMPTS TO CHARGE OT RECEIVE A CHARGE WITH SKIRMISHERS
CHARGING WITH MISSILE-ARMED FOOT TROOPS
ATTEMPTS TO CHARGE WHEN DISRUPTED OR FRAGMENTED
BEING CHARGED WHILE FRAGMENTED
POSSIBLE RESPONSES TO CHARGES
SEQUENCE OF CHARGES AND RESPONSES
RESOLVING IMPACT PHASE COMBAT

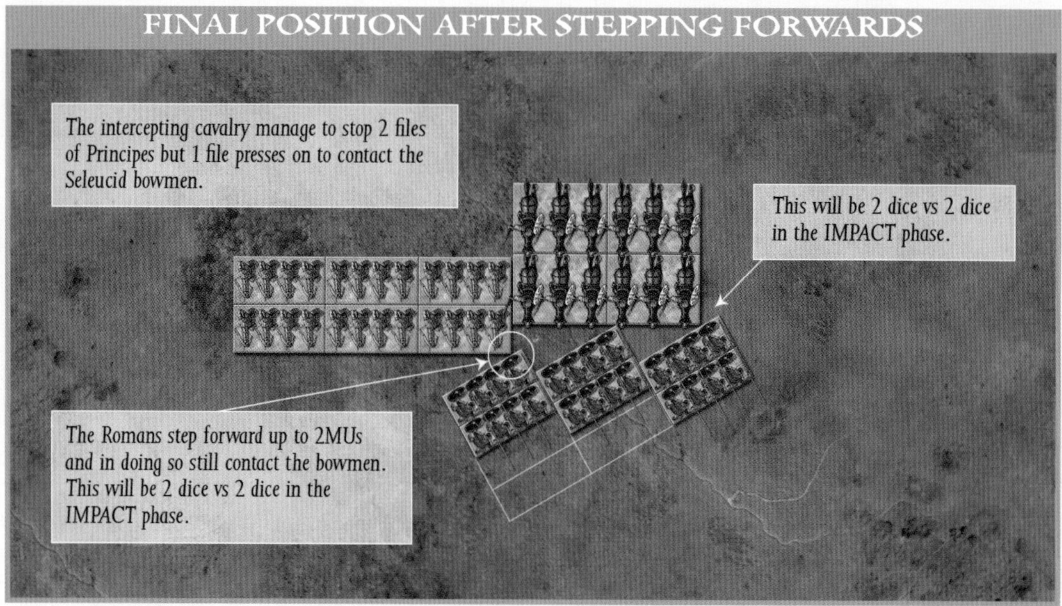

- Unless its charge is cancelled as above, the original charging battle group now completes its charge move. This may partly or wholly contact the intercepting battle group, and may or may not contact the original target of the charge at all.
- An intercepting battle group cannot itself be intercepted.

EVADE MOVES

Some troops are able to harass the enemy then retreat rapidly out of the way if charged. We call this evading. The distance moved by both evaders and chargers is variable so there is a risk that evaders may get caught.

Skirmishers can evade whatever their formation. Non-shock cavalry, camelry and light chariots can evade if they are formed up entirely *1 base deep*. This represents a looser, more flexible formation than when they are deployed 2 or more bases deep, often in reality consisting of small clumps of men separated by gaps. The procedure is as follows:

- Non-shock cavalry, camelry or light chariots entirely 1 base deep or skirmishers can choose to evade an enemy battle group's charge unless they are already in close combat other than only as an overlap. A commander with a battle group that evades must evade with it.
- Skirmishers must pass a CMT not to evade from charging enemy non-skirmishers unless the skirmishers are entirely in uneven, rough or difficult terrain or defending fortifications or a riverbank.

Gallic cavalry ready to charge

SEQUENCE SHOWING A SIMPLE EVADE MOVE OF LIGHT HORSE AWAY FROM ELEPHANTS WITH A SMALL SHIFT

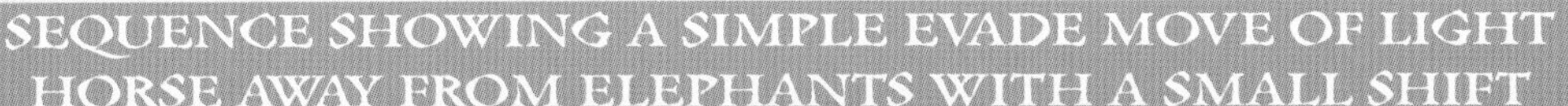

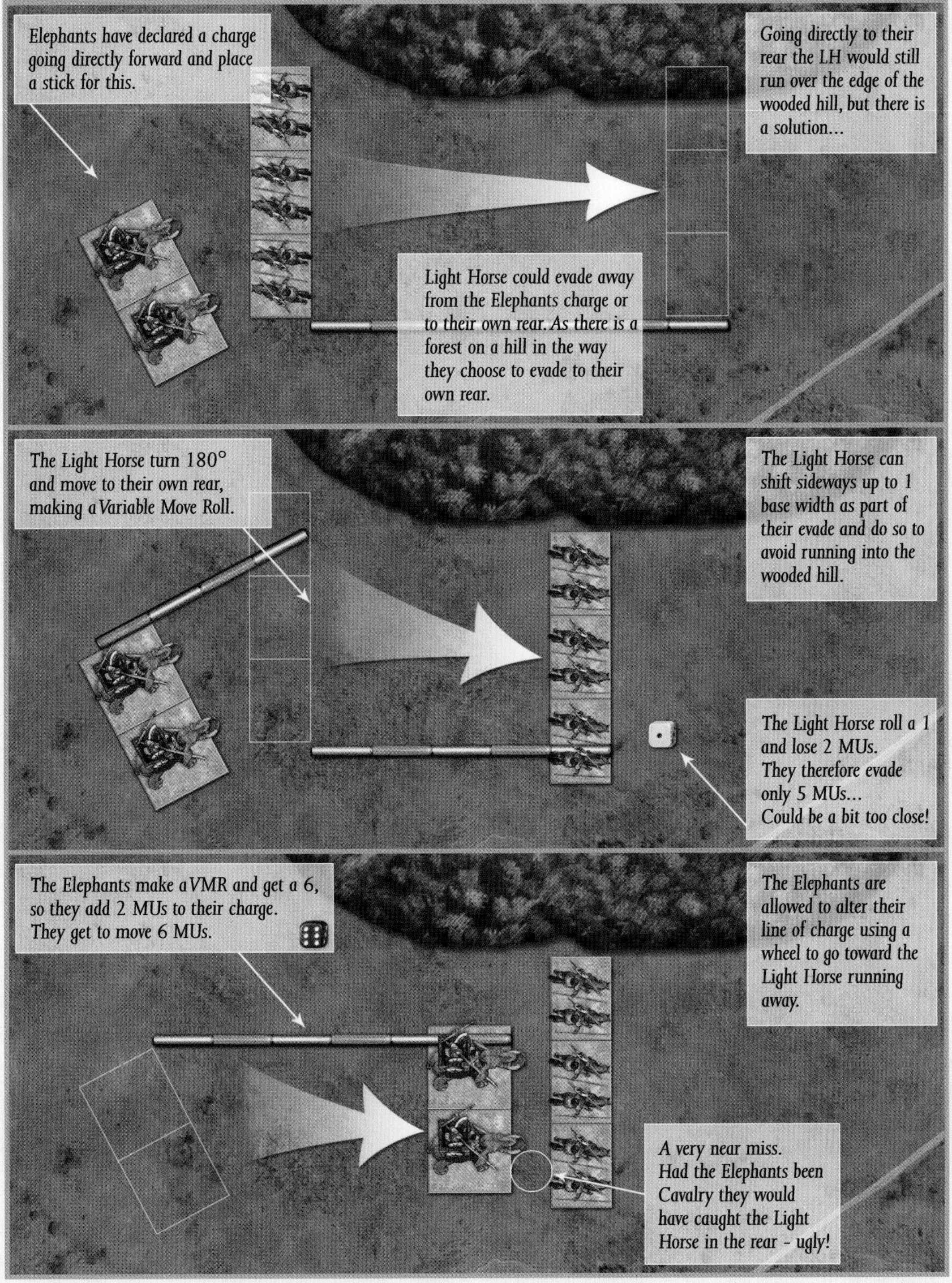
Elephants have declared a charge going directly forward and place a stick for this.
Going directly to their rear the LH would still run over the edge of the wooded hill, but there is a solution…
Light Horse could evade away from the Elephants charge or to their own rear. As there is a forest on a hill in the way they choose to evade to their own rear.
The Light Horse turn 180° and move to their own rear, making a Variable Move Roll.
The Light Horse can shift sideways up to 1 base width as part of their evade and do so to avoid running into the wooded hill.
The Light Horse roll a 1 and lose 2 MUs.
They therefore evade only 5 MUs…
Could be a bit too close!
The Elephants make a VMR and get a 6, so they add 2 MUs to their charge.
They get to move 6 MUs.
The Elephants are allowed to alter their line of charge using a wheel to go toward the Light Horse running away.
A very near miss.
Had the Elephants been Cavalry they would have caught the Light Horse in the rear - ugly!

DECLARATION OF CHARGES
LEGAL CHARGE CONTACT
CHARGING WITH YOUR BATTLE GROUPS
FORMATION CHANGES WHEN CHARGING
CHARGING TO CONTACT AND STEPPING FORWARDS
CHARGING A FLANK OR REAR
TROOPS WHO CANNOT CHARGE
TROOPS WHO MAY CHARGE WITHOUT ORDERS
ATTEMPTS TO CHARGE OT RECEIVE A CHARGE WITH SKIRMISHERS
CHARGING WITH MISSILE-ARMED FOOT TROOPS
ATTEMPTS TO CHARGE WHEN DISRUPTED OR FRAGMENTED
BEING CHARGED WHILE FRAGMENTED
POSSIBLE RESPONSES TO CHARGES
SEQUENCE OF CHARGES AND RESPONSES
RESOLVING IMPACT PHASE COMBAT

- When troops who can evade are charged, their player must decide whether or not they will evade. If they are to evade, the charger then uses a measuring stick or tape to indicate the direction of the charge, which must be achievable by wheeling and which would "legally" contact the evaders had they remained stationary.
- The evading troops then have two choices:
  - They can evade in the direction of the charge. If charged by two or more enemy battle groups, bisect the angle between the enemy charge directions.
  - Unless charged in flank or rear they can evade directly to their own rear.
- After choosing which of the above two options to adopt, the evader makes a variable move distance roll.
- If evading to its own rear, the battle group turns 180 degrees, and moves its full distance directly forwards (which is to its original rear) adjusting for the variable move distance.
- If evading in the direction of the charge, the battle group must first turn 180 or 90 degrees (player's choice) unless its existing facing is closer to the direction of the charge. It must then wheel until it is facing a direction parallel to the chargers' indicated direction of charge. It then completes its full move directly forwards, adjusting for the variable move distance.
- When making a 90 degree turn whilst evading the normal rules for 90 degree turns are followed, except that the positioning of

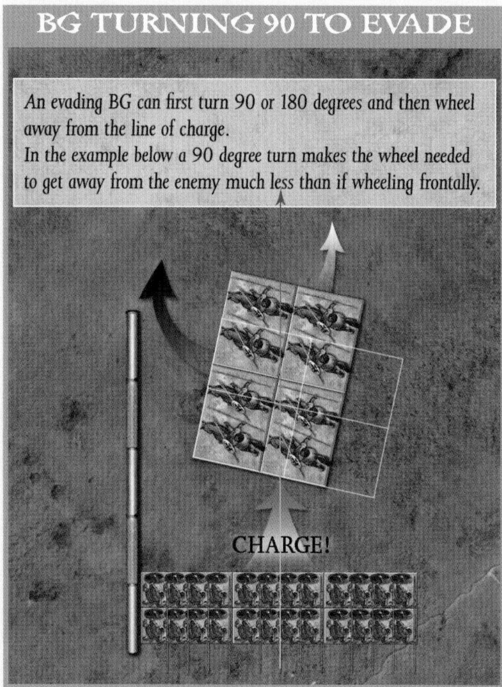

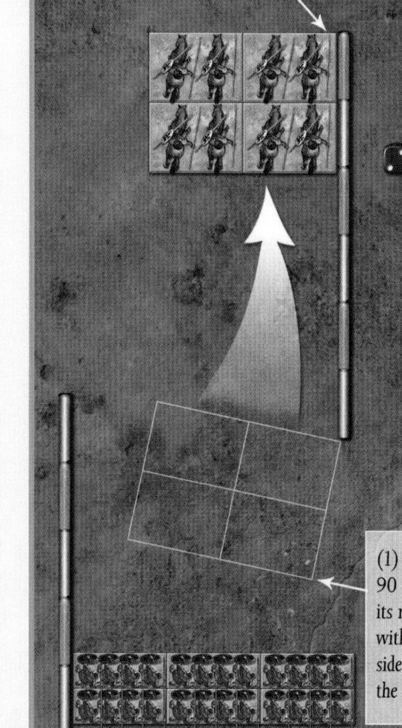

the turned battle group is different: The old side edge nearest the chargers becomes the new rear edge. The old front edge of the battle group becomes the new side edge.

- If an evading battle group encounters any obstructions, the following rules apply:
  - It interpenetrates friends if allowed to do so. (See **interpenetration**).
  - It can shift sideways up to one base width to get past friendly troops it cannot interpenetrate, enemy troops, a camp or terrain, or to avoid leaving the table. All bases must end in edge to edge and corner to corner contact with another base of the battle group. The battle group cannot split.
  - Provided that they do not shift more than one base width sideways, bases that cannot get past an obstruction can be moved to the rear of those bases that have been able to complete their evade move. In this situation the battle group is more likely to get caught, as its rear will not move as far as its front.
  - If the above would not allow all front rank bases to complete their evade move the battle group.
    * must instead burst through any friendly battle group in its normal evade path, with no shifting or contraction being allowed at all. The battle group is moved to the full extent of its evade move and any battle groups even partially burst through drop 1 level of cohesion immediately. (Note that battle groups passed through by evaders who can normally interpenetrate them do not count as burst through.)
    * must instead halt 1 MU away from any enemy battle group in its path, with no shifting or contraction being allowed at all, and if it starts closer to them than 1 MU, does not move at all.
  - If the evading battle group meets terrain it cannot enter, or has too little move to enter, or a camp, it turns 90 degrees and wheels to move parallel to the edge of the terrain or camp in whichever direction is closest to its original evade direction.
  - Battle groups that cannot complete an evade move by any of the above means move as far as they can, and are likely to be caught.
  - If the evading battle group meets a side table edge or the opponent's rear table edge, it can choose to turn 90 degrees and wheel to move parallel to the table edge in whichever direction is closest to directly away from the chargers; otherwise it leaves the table if any base even partly crosses the

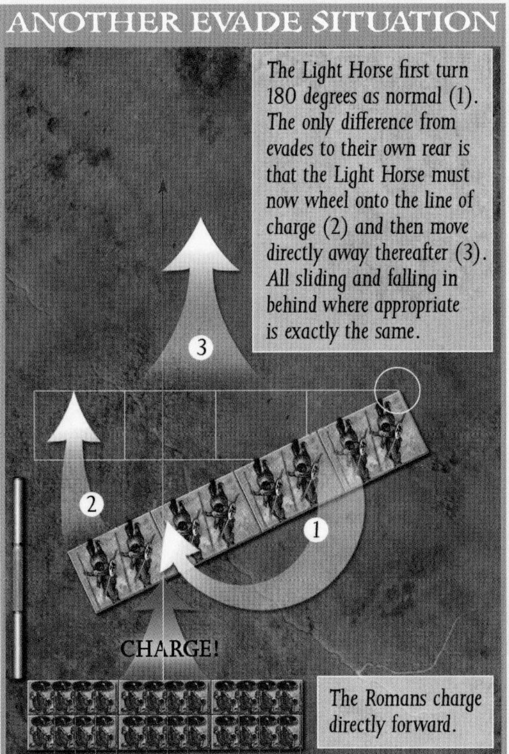

DECLARATION OF CHARGES
LEGAL CHARGE CONTACT
CHARGING WITH YOUR BATTLE GROUPS
FORMATION CHANGES WHEN CHARGING
CHARGING TO CONTACT AND STEPPING FORWARDS
CHARGING A FLANK OR REAR
TROOPS WHO CANNOT CHARGE
TROOPS WHO MAY CHARGE WITHOUT ORDERS
ATTEMPTS TO CHARGE OT RECEIVE A CHARGE WITH SKIRMISHERS
CHARGING WITH MISSILE-ARMED FOOT TROOPS
ATTEMPTS TO CHARGE WHEN DISRUPTED OR FRAGMENTED
BEING CHARGED WHILE FRAGMENTED
POSSIBLE RESPONSES TO CHARGES
SEQUENCE OF CHARGES AND RESPONSES
RESOLVING IMPACT PHASE COMBAT

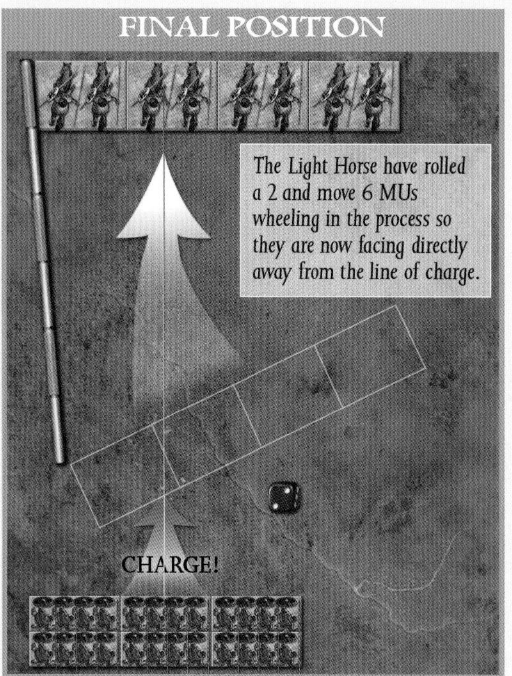

table edge. It cannot turn to avoid leaving its own rear table edge. Troops that evade off the table take no further part in the game and count as 1 attrition point towards army rout.

TIP!

Try to leave gaps for your troops to evade through. If you don't, you may find your main battle line has been burst through, disrupting your forces.

- The chargers now move their charge move, adjusting the move distance by a VMD roll if all their charge targets evaded. If all target battle groups evade out of the original path of the charge, the chargers can wheel in an attempt to catch them. A charging battle group whose move would take any part of it off the table edge instead halts its move at the table edge.
- Evaders who are contacted by chargers always count as having been charged in flank/rear.

Although the rules above cover all complex situations, we have included several further examples in **Appendix** 7.

SEQUENCE OF CHARGES AND RESPONSES

Each charge and any responses to it must be actioned in the order listed in the full turn sequence at the end of the book, but if there is more than one charge the active player chooses the order in which they are actioned. Once all responses and all charge moves have been completed, impact combat is resolved.

RESOLVING IMPACT PHASE COMBAT

The combat for all bases that have made contact during this impact phase is now resolved. Note that where battle groups already had some bases in contact which fought in a previous turn, they do not fight now. Only new impact combats are resolved now. See the **Combat Mechanism** section.

The Ottoman Turks, c. 1400, by *Angus McBride* © Osprey Publishing Ltd. Taken from *Men-at-Arms 140: Armies of the Ottoman Turks 1300–1774.*

In the manoeuvre phase, the active player can move any available battle groups or commanders as permitted by the movement rules. Battle groups cannot be moved in the manoeuvre phase if they are broken, already in close combat or charged in the impact phase. Commanders cannot be moved in the manoeuvre phase if they are fighting in the front rank of a battle group in close combat or are with a battle group that charged in the impact phase. Below are specific movement rules that apply in this phase.

REFORMING

If, as a consequence of previous events, (other than forming **orb** or depicting adverse cohesion states), a battle group is no longer in normal formation, it can reform in **either side's** manoeuvre phase.

- It reforms into normal formation facing the direction previously faced by any of its bases (player's choice) and level with the furthest forward base in that direction. The final position and formation of the reformed battle group must be as close as possible to its position and formation prior to reforming. Bases in contact with the front edge of enemy bases must remain in contact with the same enemy bases.
- A battle group must reform if it is to make any voluntary move. (Other than to feed more bases into an existing melee).
- A battle group completing a previous partial interpenetration reforms at the end of its move. Otherwise, reforming occurs at the start of the manoeuvre phase and does not affect any of the other manoeuvre phase rules.
- A battle group currently fighting in two or more directions against enemy battle groups in close combat cannot reform.
- A battle group that has some of its bases facing the enemy currently in contact with its flank or rear (and no enemy in contact to its front) is not forced to reform. If it does so, however, it must reform to face the enemy in contact.

CONFORMING TO THE ENEMY IN CLOSE COMBAT

At the start of the manoeuvre phase, the active player's battle groups already in close combat with the enemy **must** (unless otherwise stated below or physically impossible) pivot and/or slide bases by the minimum necessary to conform to the enemy bases in contact:

- Conforming usually means lining up each base in full front edge to front edge contact with an enemy base, or conforming to an **overlap position** (see below). If fighting against the flank of bases which were unable to turn to face, it means lining up in front edge contact with the enemy flank edge, with at least one base in front corner contact with an enemy front corner.
- The battle group must end its conform

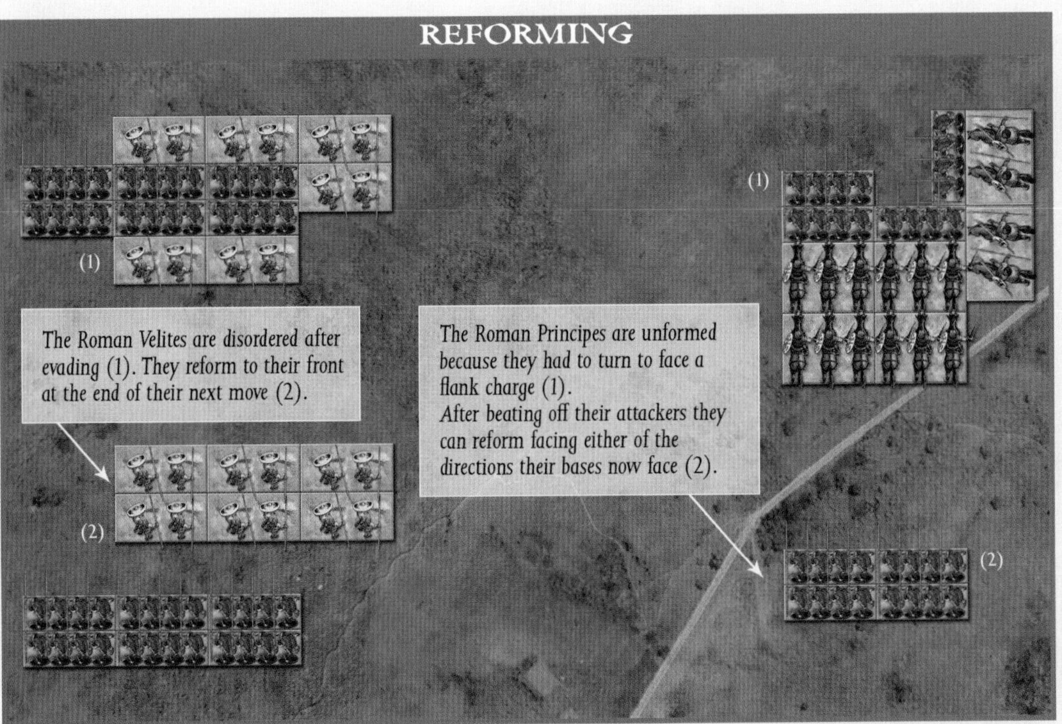

REFORMING
CONFORMING TO TEH ENEMY IN CLOSE COMBAT
FEEDING MORE BASES INTO AN EXISTING MELEE
RESTRICTED AREA
SECOND MOVES
MOVING INTO CONTACT WITH ENEMY BATTLE GROUPS
BATTLE GROUPS ALREADY IN CONTACT BUT NOT YET COMMITTED TO CLOSE COMBAT
MOVING INTO CONTACT WITH THE ENEMY CAMP

move in a normal formation (see **The Basics** section), except that each file steps forward to line up with the nearest file already in contact with the enemy. This may result in additional enemy bases being contacted.

- If bases are in contact with the flank of enemy bases as a result of a charge that did not qualify as a flank or rear charge, the battle group must pivot to conform with the front edge of the enemy battle group, sliding the minimum necessary to contact the front edge of at least one enemy base, or to an overlap position if this is not possible. This may sometimes look odd, but is a game mechanism to provide on-table clarification that the enemy battle group is not **fighting the enemy in 2 directions in the melee phase**. This still applies even if conforming is not possible.
- Friendly battle groups not in contact with the enemy must be shifted sideways sufficiently to make room for the above, provided that this is not blocked by enemy or impassable terrain and no bases would cross the table edge.
- Troops that cannot conform by any of the above methods do not move but continue to fight in an offset formation. They may however be able to conform at a later stage.
- A battle group that has some bases facing at 90 or 180 degrees to the rest (due to enemy contacting its former flank or rear) does not conform to the enemy.
- Battle wagons, artillery, troops in orb formation and troops defending field fortifications or a riverbank, or in a river, do not conform to the enemy.

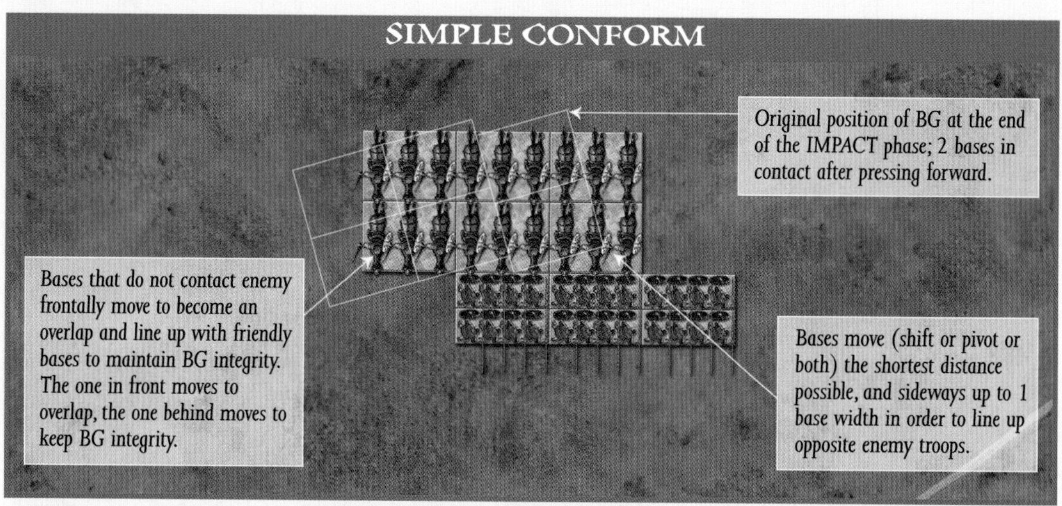

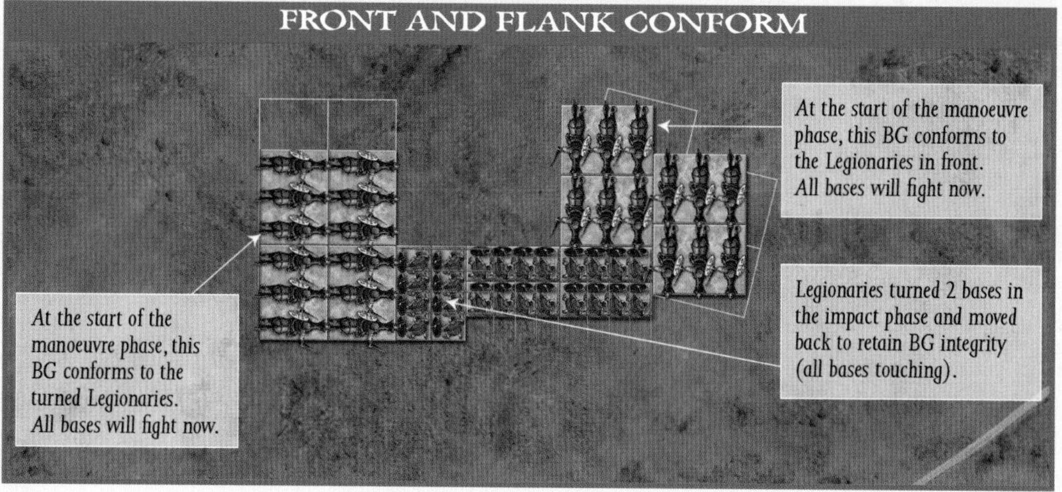

FEEDING MORE BASES INTO AN EXISTING MELEE

A battle group involved in close combat can gradually feed more and more of its troops into a protracted melee until they are all fighting. The following mechanisms are used to represent this (the contraction and expansions mentioned are merely rule mechanisms to achieve this). They do not require a CMT and are not compulsory:

- A battle group that is already in contact with enemy can expand its frontage by one file (a base frontage) on one side only.
- The active player expands first. The non-active player can match this expansion, or expand by one file to match an existing overlap, if there is room to do so. The non-

active player cannot expand unless the active player expanded on the same side or already had troops on that side in position to fight as an overlap in the next melee phase.

- Only bases that fulfil the following criteria can be moved:
  - They must not be in a position to contribute to combat prior to being moved (with dice or by creating a **Point of Advantage (POA)**).
  - They must not have any enemy bases in front edge contact with them, nor able to fight them as an overlap.
  - Moving them must not result in contraction by more than one file on any side of the battle group.
- Troops can thus be moved out from rear ranks that are not fighting, or from an unengaged end of a line to the other end. This represents a gradual spreading of the melee.
- Alternatively, instead of expanding, either player can contract his battle group by one file to move bases fulfilling the above criteria into a rear rank provided that they could then contribute to the melee – (with dice or by creating a POA).
- Bases cannot be "lapped round" the end of an enemy formation to get extra bases in front edge contact.
- Battle wagons and artillery never expand or contract in melee.

TIP!

Make use of your numbers by feeding extra troops into combats to try and overwhelm the enemy.

FEEDING MORE BASES INTO MELEE 1

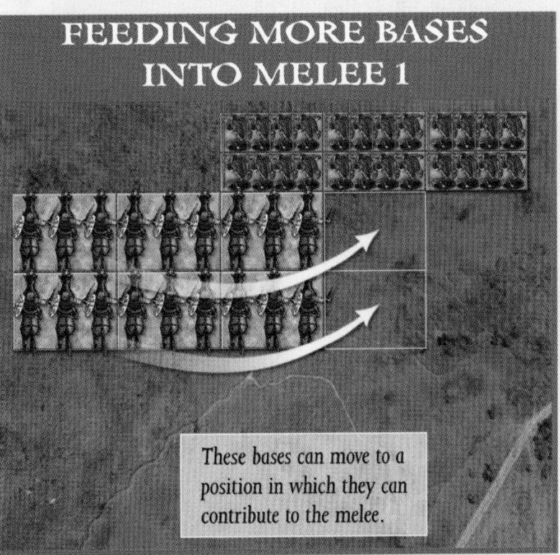

These bases can move to a position in which they can contribute to the melee.

FEEDING MORE BASES INTO MELEE 2

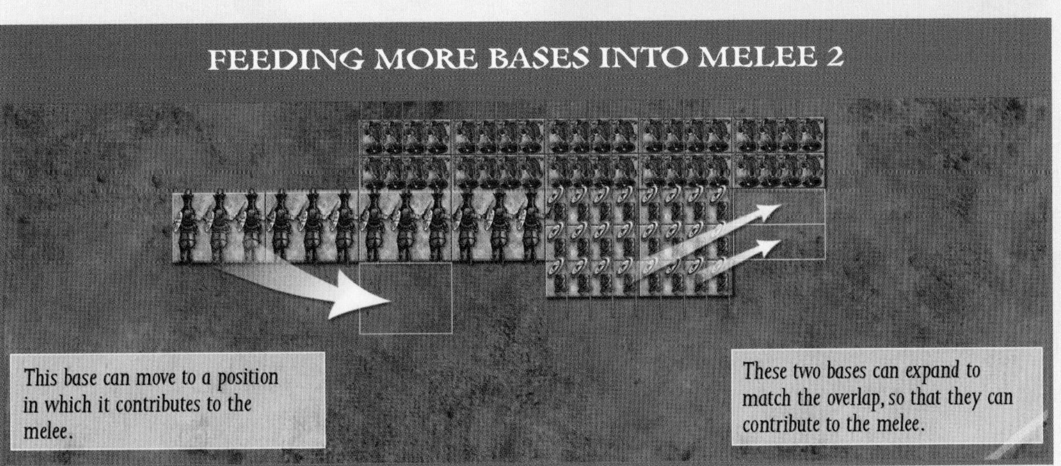

This base can move to a position in which it contributes to the melee.

These two bases can expand to match the overlap, so that they can contribute to the melee.

REFORMING
CONFORMING TO TEH ENEMY IN CLOSE COMBAT
FEEDING MORE BASES INTO AN EXISTING MELEE
RESTRICTED AREA
SECOND MOVES
MOVING INTO CONTACT WITH ENEMY BATTLE GROUPS
BATTLE GROUPS ALREADY IN CONTACT BUT NOT YET COMMITTED TO CLOSE COMBAT
MOVING INTO CONTACT WITH THE ENEMY CAMP

RESTRICTED AREA

- For normal movement only, a battle group within 2 MU directly in front of an enemy battle group is considered to be pinned. It can only perform a limited number of actions:
  - Advance directly towards that enemy battle group.
  - Wheel towards that enemy battle group until its front is parallel to the enemy front, or wheel as far as it can towards such a position; advancing thereafter if it wishes to do so.
  - Remain in place. (It can expand or turn, but not contract).
  - Make a move that ends further away from that enemy battle group. (i.e. at the end of the move, the nearest point of the battle group is further away from the enemy battle group than its nearest point was at the start of the move.)
  - Conform to an **overlap position** against another enemy battle group.
- In each of the above cases, the battle group must end its move at least partly in front of the enemy battle group, or the move is not permitted.
- If pinned by more than one enemy battle group it can choose which of these it responds to, and any restrictions apply relative to that battle group only.
- Non-skirmishers ignore the restricted area of enemy skirmishers.
- Battle wagons, artillery and troops in **orb formation** exert no restricted area.
- The restricted area only applies in the manoeuvre phase. It does not affect moves (such as charges) that take place in other phases.

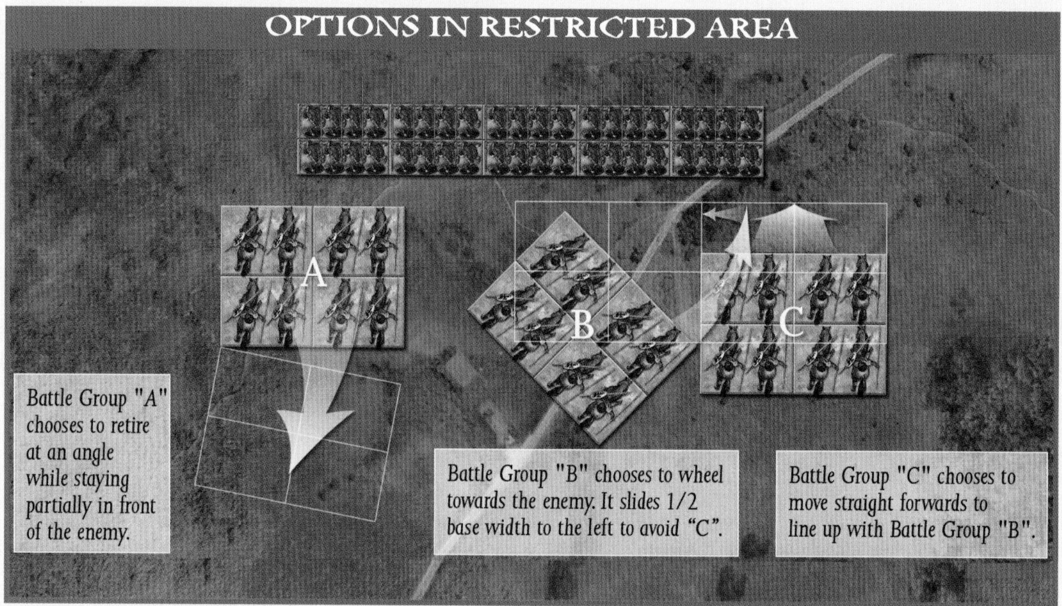

REFORMING
CONFORMING TO TEH ENEMY IN CLOSE COMBAT
FEEDING MORE BASES INTO AN EXISTING MELEE
RESTRICTED AREA
SECOND MOVES
MOVING INTO CONTACT WITH ENEMY BATTLE GROUPS
BATTLE GROUPS ALREADY IN CONTACT BUT NOT YET COMMITTED TO CLOSE COMBAT
MOVING INTO CONTACT WITH THE ENEMY CAMP

SECOND MOVES

Battle groups or battle lines with a commander, and commanders on their own, can move **twice** if they fulfil the following conditions:

- Neither the 1st nor the 2nd move can start, end or go within 6 MUs of any enemy (including the enemy camp but not an enemy commander's base).
- There must be a commander in line of command with the battle group or battle line from the start of the manoeuvre phase and throughout both moves.
- A battle line must remain together throughout the 1st and 2nd moves. It cannot be formed as a 1st move, then moved together as a 2nd move. It cannot 'drop off' or 'pick up' battle groups during the moves.
- The second move by a battle group or battle line must be a simple **advance**.
- Light artillery and battle wagons (or a battle line including either of these) must pass a second CMT to make a second move. They can only do so after first passing a CMT for, and making, a first move.
- If during a second move a battle group comes within visibility range of an enemy **ambush marker**, the ambush is immediately revealed. Unless it was a **dummy marker**, the move ends at that point if already within 6 MUs of the ambushers.

The second move must be carried out immediately after the first.

MOVING INTO CONTACT WITH ENEMY BATTLE GROUPS

Battle groups can only move into contact with enemy battle groups in the manoeuvre phase, but only to join an existing melee in an overlap position. This is the only situation in which battle wagons can move into contact with enemy.

Such a move can include a sideways shift of up to half a base width. It is exempt from any requirement to pass a CMT to wheel or move less than full distance. It is not a charge, so is not subject to the restrictions that apply to charges. It is not affected by the restricted area of other enemy battle groups.

Any other contact must wait until the next impact phase and is initiated by charging.

An **overlap position** is one with a base in any of the following situations:

- Full or partial side edge to side edge contact with an enemy base that is in front edge contact with friends.
- Front corner to front corner and side edge to side edge contact with a friendly base facing the same direction that has its full front edge in contact with an enemy base. (The base in overlap will therefore have a corner to corner contact with that enemy base.).
- Front corner to front corner and side edge to side edge contact with a friendly base facing the same direction that has all or part of its front edge in contact with the flank edge of an enemy base. (The base in overlap

may therefore not be in contact with that enemy base.) This situation can occur when a flank contact is made on a base that is wider than it is deep.

- In cases where it was not possible to conform the troops already in melee: Front corner to front corner and side edge to side edge contact with a friendly base counting as fighting as if in front edge contact with enemy. (See the **Melee Phase** section).

TIP!

Try to get as many overlaps as you can. Numbers have a quality all of their own.

BATTLE GROUPS ALREADY IN CONTACT BUT NOT YET COMMITTED TO CLOSE COMBAT

FRONT CORNER TO FRONT CORNER ONLY

This can happen, for example, when a battle group breaks its frontal opponents and does not pursue. It may then be in front corner to front corner contact only with an enemy battle group that was fighting it only as an overlap. Battle groups in front corner to front corner contact only are not committed to close combat, and are free to move away. If they do not move away, no combat occurs unless they are eligible to fight as an overlap. If not, they can engage in melee as follows:

A battle group that is only in front corner to front corner contact with an enemy battle group, and not eligible to fight as an overlap, can shift 1 base width sideways to create a front edge to front edge contact, but only if both of the following apply:

- It is not in frontal contact with, nor eligible to fight as an overlap against, any other enemy battle group.
- It is not in the restricted area of another enemy battle group of a type it does not ignore.

No CMT is required. If the enemy are non-shock cavalry, camelry or light chariots entirely **1 base deep** or skirmishers, and are not already in close combat other than only as an overlap, they can evade directly to their own rear. Otherwise the two battle groups fight normally in the melee phase. (There is no impact combat).

SIDE EDGE TO SIDE EDGE ONLY

This can happen, for example, when a battle group breaks its frontal opponents and pursues, leaving it in side edge to side edge contact with an adjacent enemy battle group. Battle groups in side edge to side edge contact are not committed to close combat, and are free to move away. If they do not move away, no combat occurs unless they are eligible to fight as an overlap. If not, they can engage in melee as follows:

REFORMING
CONFORMING TO TEH ENEMY IN CLOSE COMBAT
FEEDING MORE BASES INTO AN EXISTING MELEE
RESTRICTED AREA
SECOND MOVES
MOVING INTO CONTACT WITH ENEMY BATTLE GROUPS
BATTLE GROUPS ALREADY IN CONTACT BUT NOT YET COMMITTED TO CLOSE COMBAT
MOVING INTO CONTACT WITH THE ENEMY CAMP

A battle group that is in side edge to side edge contact with an enemy battle group can turn 90 degrees to face it, provided that it is not in the restricted area of another enemy battle group of

Greek Hoplites, 413 BC, by *Angus McBride* © Osprey Publishing Ltd. *Taken from Elite 7*: The Ancient Greeks.

a type it does not ignore. A CMT must be taken if this would normally be required for a stationary turn, and if it fails the CMT it cannot turn. If it does turn, it fights the enemy battle group as normal in the melee phase. (There is no impact combat.)

If the enemy are non-shock cavalry, camelry or light chariots entirely ***1 base deep*** or skirmishers, and are not already in close combat other than only as an overlap, they can evade directly to their own rear or directly away from the turned battle group.

If it does not evade, the enemy battle group can choose whether or not to turn bases to face:

- If it does not turn bases to face, it will get no dice in the melee, but will not count as **fighting enemy in 2 directions** if it is also fighting enemy to its front.
- If it does turn bases to face:
  - If it is already in close combat, it turns the contacted bases as if charged in the flank (see the Impact Phase section). It will then count as **fighting enemy in 2 directions**.
  - If it is not already in close combat, it can either turn only the contacted bases as if charged in the flank, or the whole battle group can turn to face, using the normal rules for a 90 degree turn. In either case it will not count as **fighting enemy in 2 directions**.

MOVING INTO CONTACT WITH THE ENEMY CAMP

Troops move into contact with the enemy camp in the manoeuvre phase. This is not a charge.

SHOOTING PHASE

Battle of *Agincourt*, 1415, by Gerry Embleton Taken from *Warrior* 11: English Longbowman 1330–1515.

In the shooting phase the effect of shooting with long-range missile weapons is resolved. Only bases that have a shooting capability listed in their troop description in our companion army list books can shoot.

Both players normally shoot with all bases that are eligible to shoot in the shooting phase. Shooting is carried out in the order chosen by the active player. However, both sides shoot before any outcomes are resolved, so no advantage can be gained from choosing the order.

The primary objective of shooting (in the game) is to cause deterioration of the enemy by forcing **cohesion tests**. Causing base losses is very much secondary.

Shooting is only adjudicated if there is the potential to force a **cohesion test** or **death roll** on the target. If the number of dice to be rolled is less than the number of hits required to force either test, no dice are rolled. This speeds up play and reflects the historical reality that minor harassment would not materially affect the cohesion of large bodies of troops.

The Burgundian army of Charles the Bold deploy their guns

RANGES
MOVEMENT AND SHOOTING
TARGET PRIORITY
ARC OF FIRE
LINE OF SIGHT AND VISIBILITY
OVERHEAD SHOOTING
SHOOTING AND CLOSE COMBAT
RESOLVING SHOOTING

RANGES

A front rank base is in range if a front corner or any part of its front edge is within range of the target. Rear rank bases shoot as if at the same range as the front rank, even if the front rank cannot shoot. The table opposite shows the range of different weapons in MUs.

SHOOTING RANGES (MUS)	EFFECTIVE	MAXIMUM
Foot bows, longbows or crossbows	4	6
Sling, mounted bows or crossbows	4	-
Javelins or firearms	2	-
Heavy artillery	6	12
Light artillery	6	-

MOVEMENT AND SHOOTING

- Light artillery whose battle group moved in any way during the preceding manoeuvre phase cannot shoot in the shooting phase. This includes light artillery mounted on battle wagons. The shooting of other troop types is not affected by having moved during the manoeuvre phase.
- No troops can shoot if they moved in the impact phase.
- Some troops receiving a charge take shooting into account in the combat resolution of the impact phase. This is dealt with in the combat section of the rules. It is the **only** shooting that is permitted in the impact phase. Chargers and evaders cannot shoot. (We judge that any such shooting would be too ineffective to have a significant effect.)

TARGET PRIORITY

A front rank base that shoots can only shoot at its priority target. A base eligible to shoot from another rank has target priority as if in the front rank. A target must be legitimate in terms of line of sight, visibility and arc of fire (see below). Targets are selected in the following order of priority:

- A targetable enemy base in effective range and at least partly straight ahead. If there are two such targets, shoot at the nearest. If both are at exactly the same distance, shoot at the one most directly to the front.
- The nearest targetable enemy base in the arc of fire. If two are at exactly the same distance, shoot at the one most directly to the front.
- If two targets are of equal priority, the shooting player chooses whether to target the one on the left or the one on the right. He cannot choose to target some of his bases to the left and some to the right in order to get extra bases shooting at the same battle group.

ARC OF FIRE

Subject to target priority:

- A base can shoot at an enemy base that is not directly ahead, provided that some part of the enemy base is inside a straight line projecting forward parallel to, and at the following distance from, the shooting base's side edge:
  - 2 base widths if no base of the shooting battle group is in effective range of that enemy battle group.
  - 1 base width otherwise.
- A base can only shoot at an enemy base if at least part of the enemy base is forward of a straight line extending the shooting base's front edge.
- Light horse and light chariots can also shoot backwards (with a negative modifier), treating their rear edge as their front edge.
- Battle wagons can shoot from either long side of their base, as chosen by the shooting player. They shoot as if 2 bases side by side. The long edge that is shooting is treated as their front edge. They cannot shoot from a short edge.

LINE OF SIGHT AND VISIBILITY

Line of sight is always drawn from the front rank of the shooting battle group, even if the front rank is not shooting. A file can shoot at a target base if it is possible to draw straight lines from both front corners of its front rank base to a single point on the target base without passing through:

- Terrain that would block line of sight.
- Friendly troops, except as specified in the overhead shooting section below.

If any target is thus disqualified, the shooter moves on to its next target priority until a permitted target (if any) is found.

OVERHEAD SHOOTING

- Chariots and artillery only shoot with their front rank. Light chariots shooting to their rear treat their rear rank as their front rank. Battle wagons only shoot with one file.
- Other troops shoot only with bases in the 1st and 2nd ranks. (The effect of shooting by 3rd rank supporting light foot archers is dealt with in impact phase combat). Light horse shooting to their rear treat their rear rank as their front rank.
- Battle groups on higher ground can shoot over friends if either of the following apply:
  - The intervening friends are over 1 MU from the shooters and over 1 MU from the target base, measured along the line of the shortest distance between shooter and target.
  - The shooters are artillery and the intervening friends are light foot.

RANGES
MOVEMENT AND SHOOTING
TARGET PRIORITY
ARC OF FIRE
LINE OF SIGHT AND VISIBILITY
OVERHEAD SHOOTING
SHOOTING AND CLOSE COMBAT
RESOLVING SHOOTING

ARC OF FIRE AND LINE OF SIGHT

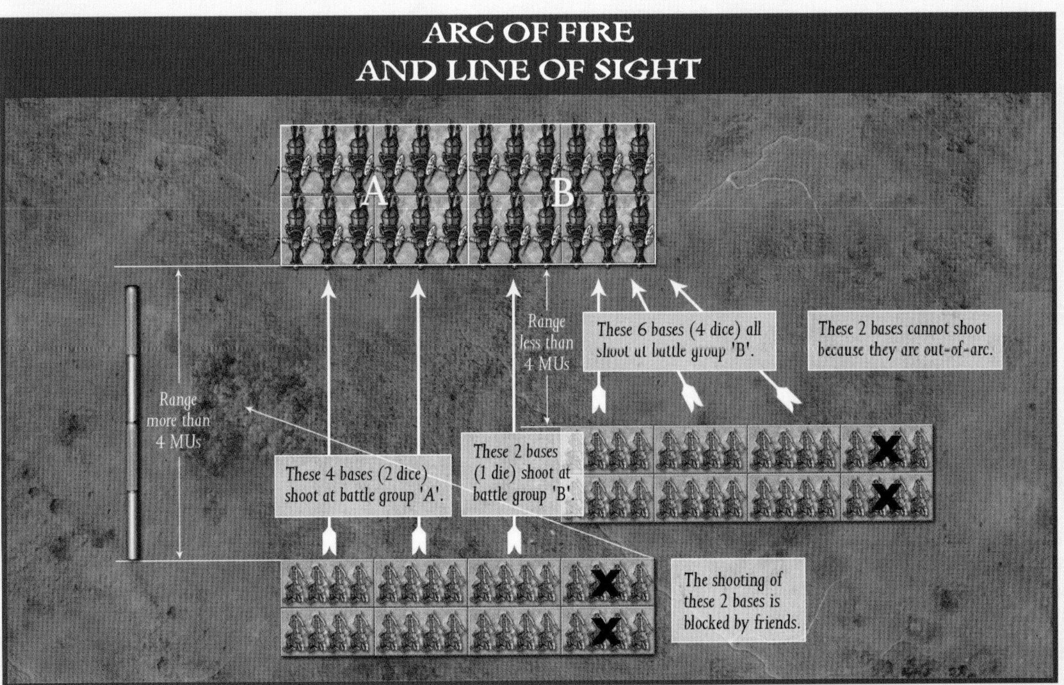

ARC OF FIRE AND TARGET PRIORITY AT EFFECTIVE AND MAXIMUM RANGES

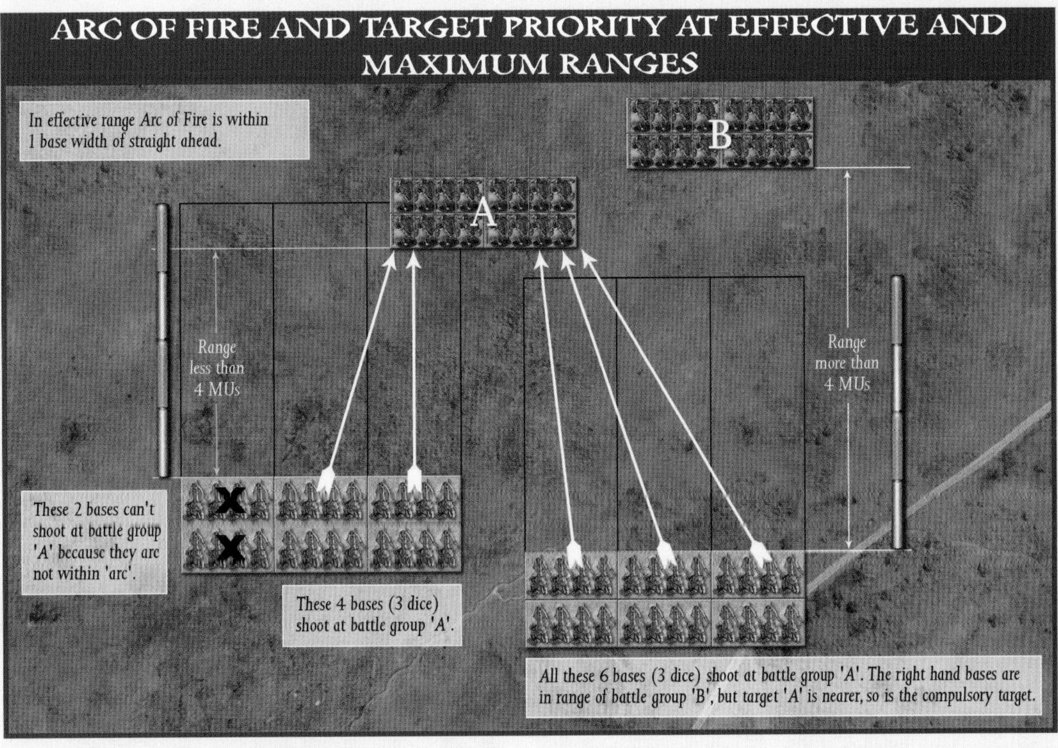

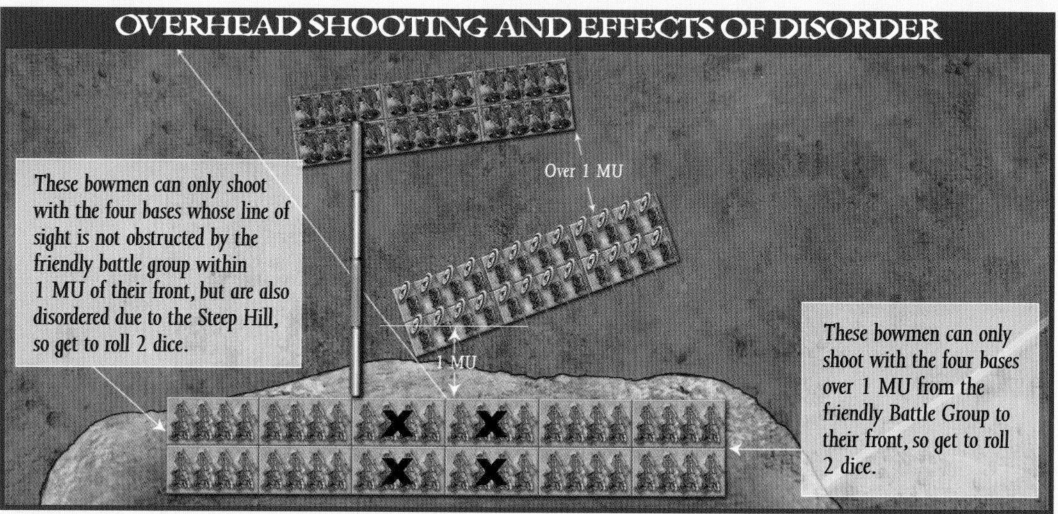

SHOOTING AND CLOSE COMBAT

Bases that are engaged in close combat cannot shoot or be shot at. As a result:

- A base cannot shoot if it is in a position to fight as a 1st or 2nd rank or overlap in melee this turn.
- A base cannot be shot at if it is in a position to fight as a 1st or 2nd rank or overlap in melee this turn.
- A battle group cannot be shot at if it is pursuing routers and still in contact with them.
- A battle group can be shot at if attacking a camp but not if looting it.
- 2nd or 3rd rank bases of foot who were charged this turn can sometimes shoot as part of impact phase combat. This is dealt with in the combat section of the rules.

See the Combat Mechanism section for Resolving Shooting.

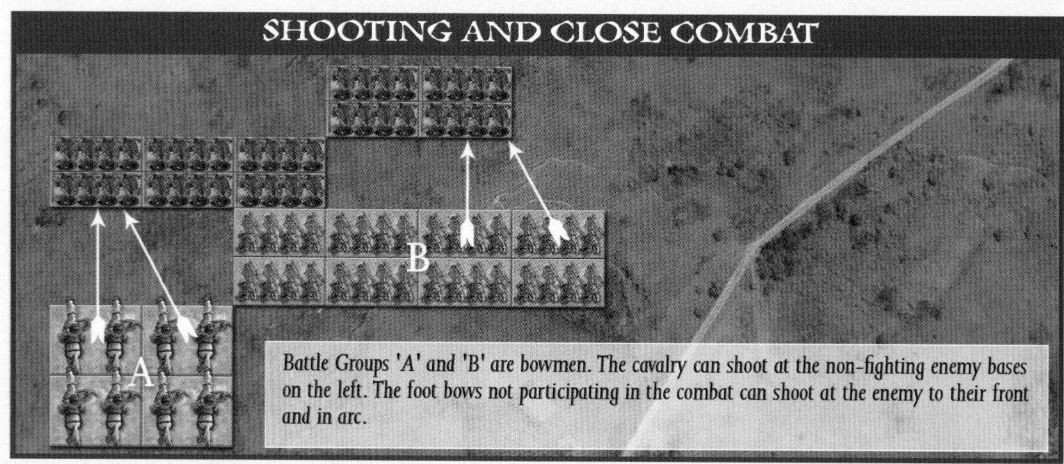

MELEE PHASE

The battle of The Sambre, 57 BC, by *Wayne* Reynolds © Osprey Publishing Ltd. Taken from *Warrior* 30: Celtic *Warrior* 300 BC–AD 100.

In the melee phase, all bases in front edge contact with unbroken enemy, or in an overlap position, and who are not themselves broken, are eligible to fight in close combat. Other ranks can also be eligible to fight if so specified in the combat section.

Battle groups which survived combat in the impact phase, and remain in contact with an unbroken enemy, will fight for a second time in the turn, often with more bases engaged as they are fed into the melee (see the **Manoeuvre Phase** section).

OVERLAPS

Overlap positions are defined in the manoeuvre phase section. Each overlapping file fights with the same net *Points of Advantage (POA)* and same number of ranks as if it was in front edge contact with the overlapped enemy base. Restrictions:

- A battle group can only be overlapped by one file at each end of any of its four edges, even if it is stepped forward.
- A base that is in contact with the front edge of enemy bases on more than one of its edges cannot be overlapped on the corner between two contacted edges.
- Bases overlapping two enemy battle groups can only contribute melee dice against one of them. (As chosen by the player whose battle group they belong to).
- A base that can contribute to close combat to its front (with dice or by creating a **Point of Advantage (POA)**) cannot fight as an overlap.

BASES ELIGIBLE TO FIGHT IN MELEE

All 'blue' bases are elegible to fight in the melee phase, either with the enemy bases in contact to their front or as an overlap, with the exception of those marked 'A'. These cannot fight because of the rule which states:

"A base that is in contact with the front edge of enemy bases on more than one of its edges ('B') cannot be overlapped on the corner between two contacted edges."

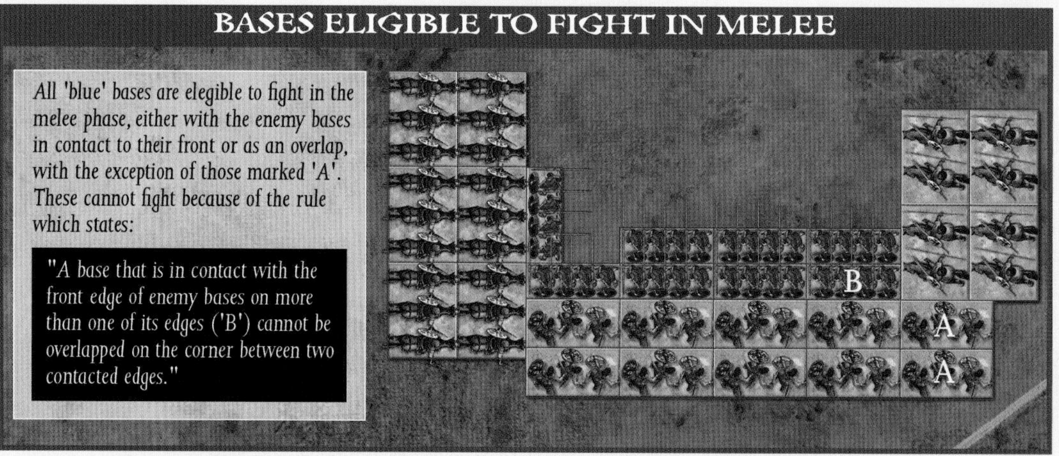

MELEES THAT CANNOT LINE UP

If it is not possible for battle groups in contact to line up, they continue to fight in an offset position with the same number of bases counting as 'in front edge contact' or 'overlapping' as if they had conformed. If two bases would conform to the same enemy base then the one which has the

OVERLAPS
MELEES THAT CANNOT LINE UP
FIGHTING THE ENEMY IN TWO DIRECTIONS
RESOLVING MELEES
SACKING CAMPS

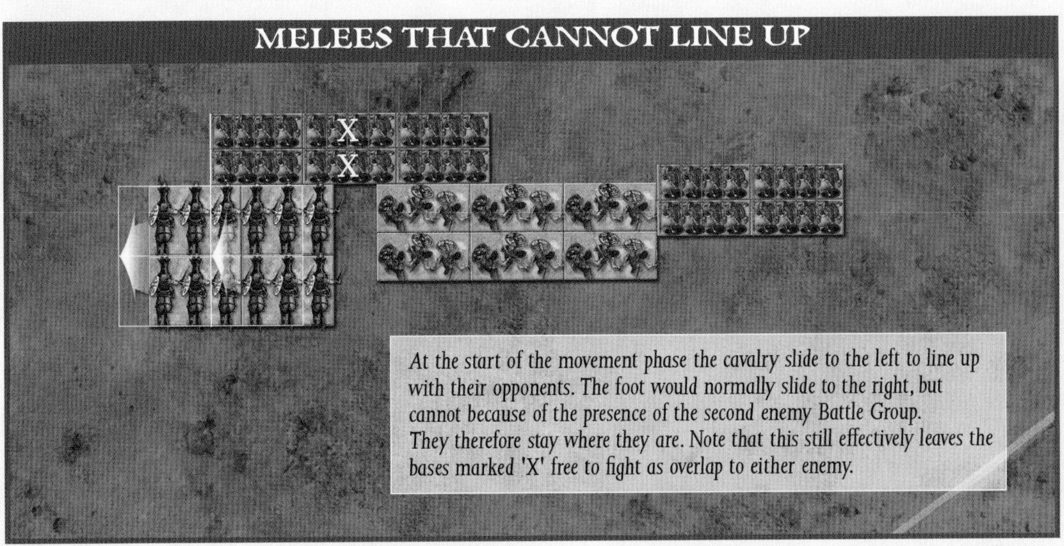

shortest distance to conform fights against it. If the distance is equal, their player chooses which fights.

Only the ends of a line of bases counting as "in front edge contact" can be overlapped, even if it is stepped forward. One enemy file can fight as an overlap at each end.

The battle of Crecy, 1346, by Graham Turner © Osprey Publishing Ltd. Taken from Campaign 71: Crecy 1346.

FIGHTING THE ENEMY IN TWO DIRECTIONS

A battle group only counts as fighting the enemy in 2 directions in melee if it has bases turned at 90 or 180 degrees to each other and it is in melee with different enemy battle groups on different facings. Note that this cannot happen as a consequence of a charge unless it was a legal flank or rear charge.

RESOLVING MELEES

See the **Combat Mechanism** section.

SACKING CAMPS

An unfortified camp contacted by an enemy battle group counts as immediately sacked, and no combat takes place.

A fortified camp is assumed to be defended by camp guards, who must be defeated before the camp can be sacked. For simplicity, this is dealt with as follows. In the melee phase of each turn, each enemy battle group in contact with the camp rolls one dice, the defenders none. Mounted troops need to roll a 6 and foot troops a 5 or a 6 to successfully sack a fortified camp. Quality re-rolls apply.

THE COMBAT MECHANISM

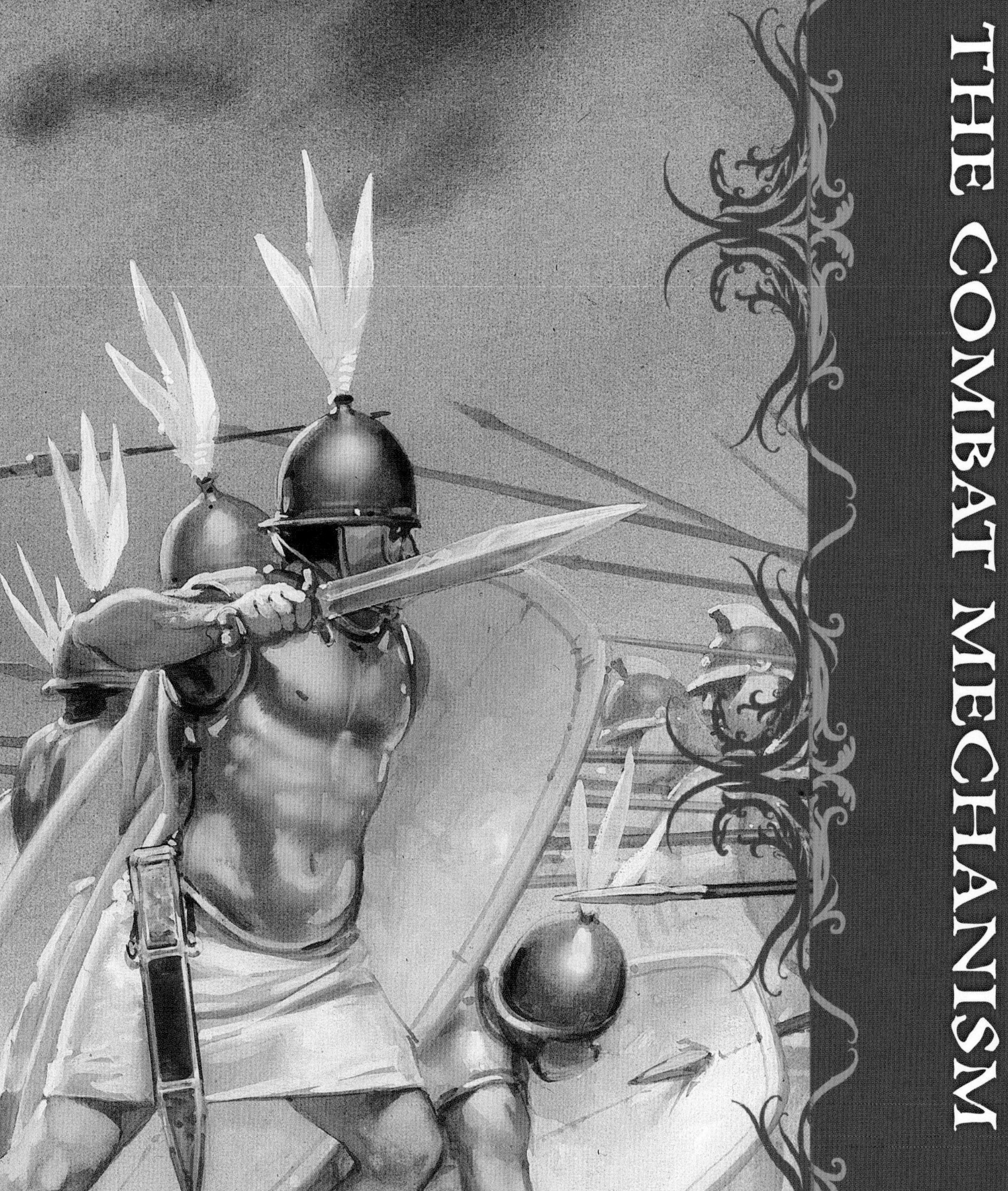

Roman infantry of Republican Rome, by *Angus McBride* © Osprey Publishing Ltd. Taken from *Men-at-Arms 291: Republican Roman Army 200–104 BC.*

Combat between unbroken battle groups, whether by impact, shooting or melee, uses the same combat mechanism. This always has the following sequence:

- Decide how many dice to roll.
- Roll dice to score hits and thereby decide (in close combat) who has "won" and "lost".
- Take cohesion tests.
- Take death rolls and remove any lost bases.
- Roll for commanders fighting in the front rank to see if they are lost. (In close combat only).
- Take cohesion tests for nearby battle groups seeing a battle group break or a commander lost.
- Make compulsory moves as a result of combat.

"Close Combat" is a general term for impact and melee combat. Once such combat has been joined, battle groups are deemed to be in close combat until one side breaks off, breaks or is destroyed (or a battle group fighting only as an overlap moves away).

TIP!

When rolling cohesion tests and death rolls, take them together by rolling 2 dice of one colour and one of another. It saves time.

DECIDING HOW MANY DICE TO ROLL

IN THE SHOOTING PHASE:

The shooting chapter specifies which bases are eligible to shoot. The number of dice to roll are as follows:

SHOOTING DICE		
Artillery (except when on battle wagons)	2 dice per base in effective range	
	1 dice per base outside effective range	
Medium Foot with Bow, Crossbow or Longbow (not Bow*)	1 dice per base of 1st shooting rank in effective range	
	1 dice per 2 bases of 2nd shooting rank or outside effective range	
Cavalry with Bow or Crossbow (not Bow*)	1 dice per base of 1st shooting rank	
	1 dice per 2 bases of 2nd shooting rank	
Chariots	1 dice per base	
Battle wagons	1 dice per base width from long edge only	
Light foot, Light horse or any troops with Javelins, Sling, Firearm or Bow*	1 dice per 2 bases in effective range	
	1 dice per 3 bases outside effective range	
DISRUPTED or DISORDERED	Lose 1 dice per 3	Dice loss for Disruption, Fragmentation, Disorder or Severe Disorder is not cumulative, but whichever is worst applies.
FRAGMENTED or SEVERELY DISORDERED	Lose 1 dice per 2	

DECIDING HOW MANY DICE TO ROLL
ALLOCATING COMBAT DICE
SCORING HITS – POINTS OF ADVANTAGE
ACCUMULATING HITS AND TAKING COHESION TESTS
SUPPORT SHOOTING IN THE IMPACT PHASE
COMMANDERS IN CLOSE COMBAT
FIGHTING BROKEN TROOPS
MOVEMENT OF BROKEN TROOPS AND PURSUERS
AN EXAMPLE OF CLOSE COMBAT

If the front rank of a battle group are not shooters, only the 2nd rank can shoot, but counts as the 1st shooting rank in determining the number of dice. Therefore, a battle group of 4 Islamic ghilman 2 wide and 2 deep, all archers, would shoot with 3 dice, whereas a battle group of 4 Byzantine cavalry, with 2 bases of archers behind 2 bases of lancers, would shoot with 2 dice. Battle wagons are treated as if they were 2 bases side by side when shooting.

IN THE IMPACT PHASE:

This is the initial clash as the charge goes in. The front ranks are the key troops at impact, with greater numbers being less important at this point. The question is, have the charging lancers broken into the front ranks of their foot opponents or have the foot stood firm?

Only bases coming into contact as a result of a charge in this impact phase fight. Combat between bases already fighting in the previous melee phase is not resolved until the next melee phase. If a new battle group charges into a battle group that was already in melee, there is an impact phase combat between the new charger and the bases it has just contacted. In the subsequent melee phase, all three battle groups will fight.

Turn any bases required to turn to face a flank or rear charge and proceed as follows: All bases that charge into front edge contact with enemy, or into front corner contact with an enemy edge, are eligible to fight. All enemy bases in contact with them are also eligible to fight. This includes bases contacted to their flank or rear which were unable to turn because they are already engaged to their front.

Both sides fight with the **same number of bases**, determined as follows:

- If both sides have an **equal** number of bases eligible to fight, all of them fight. As far as possible, these are paired off to fight, so that each base fights one enemy base. If it is possible to do this in more than one way, the active player chooses which.
- If the number of eligible bases is **unequal**, both sides fight with the **lower** number of bases. The side with the higher number of bases chooses which of his bases will not fight. His choice must leave every eligible enemy base paired off against one of his.

TROOPS ELIGIBLE TO FIGHT AT IMPACT

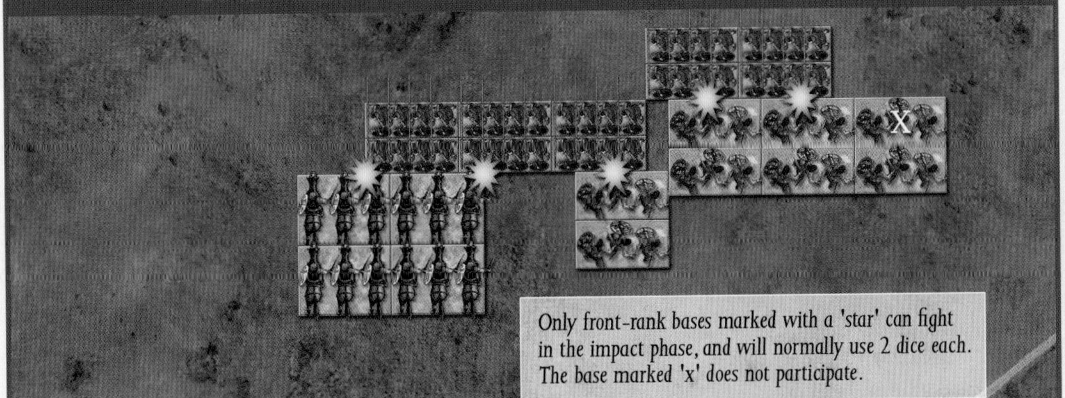

Only front-rank bases marked with a 'star' can fight in the impact phase, and will normally use 2 dice each. The base marked 'x' does not participate.

Note that if multiple battle groups are involved in an impact combat, the above rules apply to the whole combat. Battle wagons are treated as if 2 bases side by side when fighting on their long base edge, 1 base when fighting on their short base edge.

The number of dice to be rolled is as follows:

IMPACT PHASE DICE		
Scythed chariots		3 dice per front rank base
Battle wagons		2 dice per front rank base width
Other troops		2 dice per front rank base
Foot with bow, longbow, crossbow or firearm supporting medium or heavy foot of the same stationary battle group from a 2nd rank, or (bow only) from a 3rd rank.	Medium foot vs mounted or foot.	1 dice per 2nd or 3rd rank base behind a base in combat (one rank only). Use *Points of Advantage (POA)* as if shooting. (No dice against a flank or rear charge.)
	Light foot only vs mounted.	
REDUCTIONS		
Light foot or light horse	Lose 1 dice per 2 unless: • Light Foot versus Light Foot. • Light Horse versus Light Horse or Light Foot. • Any versus FRAGMENTED enemy.	
THEN		
DISRUPTED or DISORDERED	Lose 1 dice per 3	Dice loss for Disruption, Fragmentation, Disorder or Severe Disorder is not cumulative, but whichever is worst applies.
FRAGMENTED or SEVERELY DISORDERED	Lose 1 dice per 2	

IN THE MELEE PHASE:

In drawn out melees, a battle group's width and depth can be an advantage as it allows extra troops to be fed into the combat. Also troops in overlap positions and rear ranks that did not fight at impact can become involved in the combat:

- All bases whose front edge is in contact with enemy fight.
- An overlap fights against the same enemy base as the friendly base for which it provides an overlap. If able to provide an overlap on either side, its own player chooses which enemy base it fights.
- Rear ranks of an eligible troop type (see the combat dice table below) can fight if they belong to the same battle group as the front rank or overlap they are behind.
- The Melee Phase section above describes how to deal with melees if the battle groups have been unable to line up.
- A base contacted in front and flank and/or rear will now have more than one front rank enemy base fighting against it. It fights against its front edge opponent (even if it fought the impact round against a different base).

Battle wagons are treated as if 2 bases side by side when fighting on their long base edge, 1 base when fighting on their short base edge. When fighting on their long base edge, they count the file nearest the enemy as their front rank.

DECIDING HOW MANY DICE TO ROLL
ALLOCATING COMBAT DICE
SCORING HITS – POINTS OF ADVANTAGE
ACCUMULATING HITS AND TAKING COHESION TESTS
SUPPORT SHOOTING IN THE IMPACT PHASE
COMMANDERS IN CLOSE COMBAT
FIGHTING BROKEN TROOPS
MOVEMENT OF BROKEN TROOPS AND PURSUERS
AN EXAMPLE OF CLOSE COMBAT

MELEE PHASE DICE		
Elephants, knights, all chariots, artillery	2 dice per front rank base. No dice for rear rank bases of any type.	
Battle wagons	2 dice per front rank base width. No dice for rear rank bases of any type.	
Other Troops	1 dice per base in first 2 ranks	
Overlaps	As above	
REDUCTIONS		
Light foot or light horse	Lose 1 dice per 2 unless: • Light Foot versus Light Foot. • Light Horse versus Light Horse or Light Foot. • Any versus FRAGMENTED enemy.	
THEN		
DISRUPTED or DISORDERED	Lose 1 dice per 3	Dice loss for Disruption, Fragmentation, Disorder or Severe Disorder is not cumulative, but whichever is worst applies.
FRAGMENTED or SEVERELY DISORDERED	Lose 1 dice per 2	

TROOPS ELIGIBLE TO FIGHT IN MELEE

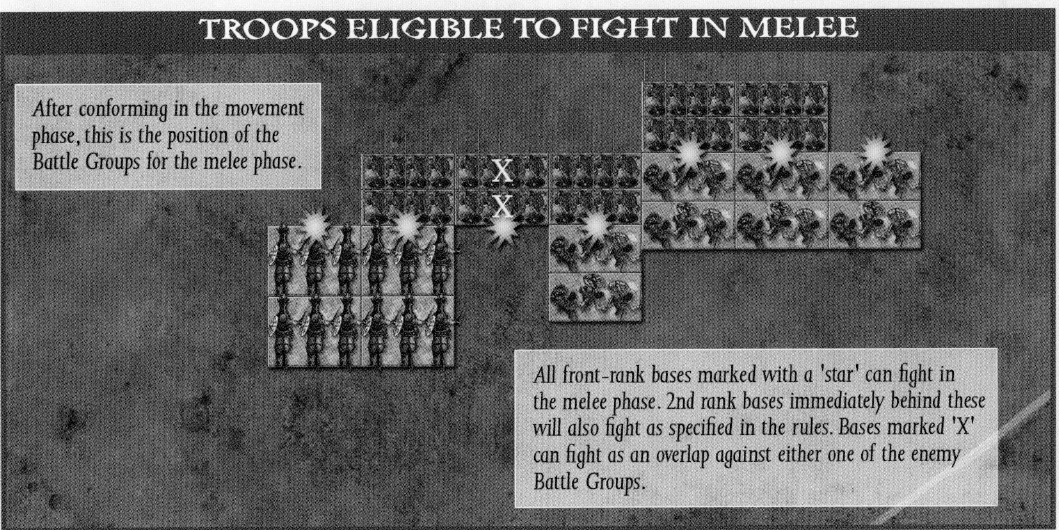

ALLOCATING COMBAT DICE

It is sometimes necessary to split up a battle group's combat dice, e.g. if it is fighting more than one enemy battle group, or if some bases are fighting on different *Points of Advantage* (POA):

- If a battle group is fighting against more than one enemy battle group, roll combat dice separately against each enemy battle group.
- If some bases have different POAs, roll separately for them.
- If more than one battle group is shooting at the same target, add the total number of bases to which a '1 dice per x bases' rule applies before calculating the number of dice to roll.

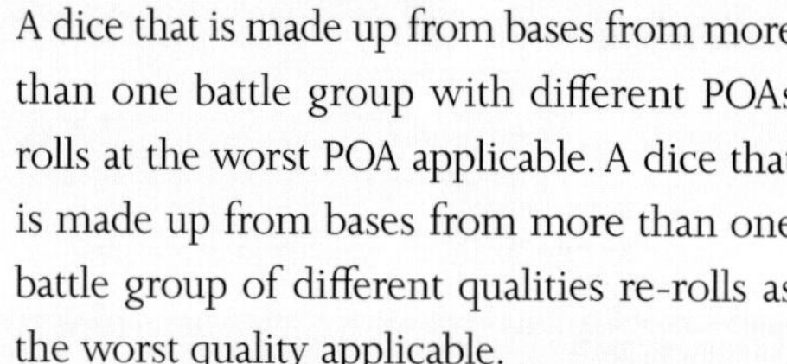

A dice that is made up from bases from more than one battle group with different POAs rolls at the worst POA applicable. A dice that is made up from bases from more than one battle group of different qualities re-rolls as the worst quality applicable.

- If a battle group which is losing shooting or close combat dice (due to DISRUPTION, FRAGMENTATION, DISORDER, SEVERE DISORDER or being light foot or light horse in close combat) is fighting against more than one enemy battle group, first determine the total number of dice the battle group should lose. Then apportion the lost dice, if possible, in proportion to the number of bases fighting each enemy battle group, leaving at least 1 dice (if possible) against each enemy battle group.
- Similarly, if fighting at different POAs against parts of the same enemy battle group, apportion lost dice, if possible, in proportion to the number of bases fighting each part of the enemy battle group, leaving at least 1 dice (if possible) against each part of the enemy battle group.

SCORING HITS – POINTS OF ADVANTAGE

If the numbers fighting in close combat are equal, a combination of troop type, armour, combat capabilities and situation will make all the difference. This could result in a finely balanced match, or an advantage (or big advantage) to one side or the other. In *Field of Glory*, rather than using numerical values, we use ***Points of Advantage*** (POAs for short) to see who has the upper hand. The roll required to score a hit depends on the "points of advantage" (POA):

- When shooting, a base will have its own overall POA.
- When in close combat, compare the overall POAs of opposing bases and take the difference as the net result. E.g. a base with two pluses fighting against a base with a single plus will be on a net plus one (+). Its opponent will be on a net minus one (-).
- If a base is fighting in close combat at a net +, the opposing enemy base fights at -. If a base is fighting in close combat at a net ++, the opposing enemy base fights at --.
- ++ is the maximum net advantage. -- is the maximum net disadvantage. Additional net POAs are ignored.
- In close combat, each front rank base uses its own POAs. Rear rank bases (except support shooters in the impact phase – see below) use the same net POAs as the front rank.
- Close combat POAs that require a minimum number of ranks only apply if all those ranks have the required capability.

The scores needed to get a hit are different for shooting and close combat as follows:

CLOSE COMBAT ROLLS TO HIT

(Quality re-rolls apply.)

ADVANTAGE	POA	MINIMUM SCORE TO HIT
Big advantage	++	3
Advantage	+	4
No advantage	No PoA	4
Disadvantage	-	5
Big disadvantage	- -	5

DECIDING HOW MANY DICE TO ROLL
ALLOCATING COMBAT DICE
SCORING HITS – POINTS OF ADVANTAGE
ACCUMULATING HITS AND TAKING COHESION TESTS
SUPPORT SHOOTING IN THE IMPACT PHASE
COMMANDERS IN CLOSE COMBAT
FIGHTING BROKEN TROOPS
MOVEMENT OF BROKEN TROOPS AND PURSUERS
AN EXAMPLE OF CLOSE COMBAT

SHOOTING ROLLS TO HIT

(Quality re-rolls apply.)

ADVANTAGE	POA	MINIMUM SCORE TO HIT
Big advantage	++	2
Advantage	+	3
No advantage	No PoA	4
Disadvantage	-	5
Big disadvantage	- -	6

TIP!

When shooting, it is usually easiest to roll all dice shooting at a single target together. Be careful to use different coloured dice if some troops have different POAs or re-rolls.

It now becomes obvious that the key to success is to make sure that you fight with + POAs. These can come from a base's troop type, armour, combat capabilities or the situation. Some of these may be advantages to the enemy, hence disadvantages to you. In the tables below POAs are listed as '+' when in a base's favour and '-' when not. Each '+' cancels a '-'.

SHOOTING POAS:

If shooting at a battle group that has mixed armour classes, the shooters' POAs are determined by the front rank armour class of the target, unless the shooting base is entirely behind a straight line extending the target battle group's rear edge. In this case use the rear rank's armour class to determine POAs.

SHOOTING POAS

Nearest rank of target is:		If shooting with:
Unprotected cavalry unless entirely 1 base deep	++	Longbow, bow, javelins or sling
Protected cavalry unless entirely 1 base deep	+	Longbow, bow, javelins or sling
Armoured cavalry unless entirely 1 base deep. Armoured knights.	+	Longbow
Cataphracts or heavily armoured knights	-	Bow, javelins or sling
Elephants	+	Any except bow or sling
Battle wagons	-	Any except artillery
Unprotected heavy or medium foot	+	Longbow, bow, javelins or sling
	-	Crossbow, firearm or artillery
Armoured foot	-	Any except longbow
Heavily armoured foot	-	Longbow, crossbow, firearm or artillery
	--	Bow, javelins or sling
Any other foot	-	Crossbow, firearm or artillery
Any	-	Any, if one or more of the following apply. (Count only one -): Shooting •in impact phase •to rear (LH or LCh) •at a battle group which is partly in close combat other than only as an overlap •by a battle group which is partly in close combat other than only as an overlap
In cover or behind field fortifications	-	Any except artillery

IMPACT AND MELEE POAS:

Battle wagons cannot defend fortifications.

IMPACT POAS			
Impact foot		++	against any foot
Impact foot		+	against any mounted, unless the foot are charging mounted shock troops
Any spearmen or pikemen if **not** charging		+	unless FRAGMENTED or SEVERELY DISORDERED or less than 2 ranks of spearmen or 3 ranks of pikemen
Pikemen or offensive spearmen if charging foot or non-shock mounted. Defensive spearmen if charging defensive spearmen		+	unless SEVERELY DISORDERED or less than 2 ranks of spearmen or 3 ranks of pikemen
Heavy weapon		+	against any foot
Foot with light spear		+	unless charging mounted shock troops
Mounted troops with light spear		+	against any troops if no other net POAs (other POAs cancel out)
Elephants		+	against heavy or medium foot, battle wagons or any mounted
Battle wagons		+	against any mounted except elephants
Only in *open terrain*	Knightly lancers	+	against any except elephants, scythed chariots, battle wagons or non-charging STEADY pikemen/spearmen
	Other lancers	+	against any except lancers, elephants, scythed chariots, battle wagons or non-charging STEADY pikemen/spearmen
	Heavy or scythed chariots	+	against any except skirmishers, lancers, elephants, battle wagons or non-charging STEADY pikemen/spearmen
	Mounted except elephants or scythed chariots	+	against any medium or light foot
	Extra for 4th rank of pikemen whether charging or not	+	unless FRAGMENTED
Charging flank or rear		++	**Net POA regardless of other factors**
Uphill or foot defending field fortifications or a riverbank		+	

Picture opposite: *The battle of Marathon, 490 BC, by Richard Hook © Osprey Publishing Ltd. Taken from Campaign 108: Marathon 490 BC.*

MELEE POAS			
Any one of….	Skilled Swordsmen	+	against any except elephants, mounted swordsmen or STEADY pikemen/spearmen
	Swordsmen	+	against any except elephants, swordsmen, skilled swordsmen or STEADY pikemen/spearmen
	Spearmen (at least 2 ranks)	+	unless FRAGMENTED or SEVERELY DISORDERED
	Pikemen (at least 3 ranks)	+	unless FRAGMENTED or SEVERELY DISORDERED
	Heavy Weapon	+	against any except skilled swordsmen or skirmishers. Also cancels enemy 'better armour' POA if any.
	Elephants	+	against heavy or medium foot, battle wagons or any mounted
	Heavy or scythed chariots	+	against any except skirmishers, elephants, battle wagons or STEADY pikemen/spearmen
	Artillery	-	
Extra for 4th rank of Pikemen in *open terrain*		+	unless FRAGMENTED
Better Armour (front rank)		+	against any except heavy weapon, elephants, chariots, artillery or battle wagons.
Fighting enemy in two directions		-	
Uphill or foot defending field fortifications or a riverbank		+	

ACCUMULATING HITS AND TAKING COHESION TESTS

Determine all of the hits inflicted by both sides before taking cohesion tests and death rolls. Place a dice behind each battle group to record the hits received. In close combat, use a separate dice for each battle group that inflicts hits, as you need to know who caused them in order to determine which battle groups (if any) lost the combat. By using this simple method you can easily keep track of multiple battle group combats. After all hits inflicted or received have been noted, take any outcome tests that are required. There is no need to record anything past this stage as there are no knock-on effects on unconnected combats.

A battle group has lost a close combat if the **total** number of hits it received from **all** of its opponents this phase is greater than the **total** number of hits it inflicted on **all** of its opponents this phase.

Next, take any ***cohesion tests*** or ***death rolls*** caused by shooting or combat (see **Cohesion Tests** and **Death Rolls**). If any battle group breaks, turn its bases around. It will rout at the end of the phase.

Cohesion tests are caused by shooting and combat in the following circumstances:

- Test a battle group after all shooting dice have been rolled if it suffered either of the following:
  - At least 1 shooting hit per 3 bases. (1 HP3B). See the **Glossary of Terms** for the full definition. Some troop types calculate HP3B differently and not all ranks count.
  - At least 2 shooting hits if shot at by artillery (whether or not the artillery scored the hits).
- Test a battle group after all close combat dice have been rolled if it lost an impact or melee close combat.

There are some additional reasons to test cohesion and these are covered in the **Cohesion Test** section.

SUPPORT SHOOTING IN THE IMPACT PHASE

Foot armed with certain missile weapons will attempt to inflict damage on enemy chargers by shooting over the ranks in front. This is represented by support shooting from a rank behind the one fighting in the impact phase and allows additional combat dice:

- The supporters must be medium or light foot armed with bow, longbow, crossbow or firearm (but not bow*).
- They must be supporting medium or heavy foot of the same stationary battle group.
- They must be supporting from a 2nd or 3rd rank, but not both. Only troops with bow can support from a 3rd rank.
- Support shooting by medium foot applies whether the charging enemy are mounted or foot. Support shooting by light foot only applies if the charging enemy are mounted.
- Irrespective of their weaponry, support

DECIDING HOW MANY DICE TO ROLL
ALLOCATING COMBAT DICE
SCORING HITS – POINTS OF ADVANTAGE
ACCUMULATING HITS AND TAKING COHESION TESTS
SUPPORT SHOOTING IN THE IMPACT PHASE
COMMANDERS IN CLOSE COMBAT
FIGHTING BROKEN TROOPS
MOVEMENT OF BROKEN TROOPS AND PURSUERS
AN EXAMPLE OF CLOSE COMBAT

shooters get 1 dice per supporting base. Light foot lose 1 dice per 2 dice as normal, so get 1 dice per 2 supporting bases, rounded up.

- Support shooters use shooting POAs. Note that there is a - POA for shooting in the impact phase. As in normal shooting, the POAs are **not** netted out against the opposing troops' POAs.
- The dice scores required to hit are as per shooting.
- Support shooting cannot be used against enemy charging the battle group in the flank or rear.

Roll dice for supporting shooters at the same time as your normal impact combat dice using different coloured dice to indicate which are which. Normal quality re-rolls apply. Hits count towards the total hits inflicted in the impact phase combat, and are treated as normal close combat hits. They never trigger a cohesion test for shooting hits.

COMMANDERS IN CLOSE COMBAT

Commanders can inspire their troops by fighting in the front rank. As you might expect, this carries significant personal risk. The commander's base is representative only and gets no dice in combat:

- A commander can be declared to be fighting in the front rank of a single battle group in close combat. This improves its fighting ability by enhancing its quality re-rolls on close combat "to hit" rolls. (See the *Battle Groups* section). The declaration is made before any close combat dice are rolled.
- A commander with the battle group, who is not declared to be fighting in the front rank, does not affect quality re-rolls and is not at risk of being lost.
- A commander declared to be fighting in the front rank is placed anywhere in the front rank in contact with the enemy (player's choice) to show that he is fighting. The base(s) he displaces is (are) placed behind him, but still fight as if they had not been displaced. Once declared as fighting in the front rank, the commander cannot leave the front rank of that battle group until it is no longer in close combat and no longer in contact with enemy routers.
- If a commander is fighting in the front rank of a battle group that suffers a total of 2 or more hits in close combat, the opposing player rolls 2 dice (no re-rolls) after post-combat cohesion tests and death rolls. If the commander's battle group lost the combat, the commander is lost if these total 11 or 12. If it won or drew the combat, he is lost if they total 12. A lost commander is removed from play, and the bases he displaced are put back into their previous position before measuring to see if any friendly battle groups are in range to test cohesion for seeing him lost (see the *Cohesion Tests* section below).
- A commander who is fighting in the front rank can only influence the complex move tests or cohesion tests of the battle group he is with. He cannot affect those of other friendly battle groups.

TIP!

Risking your commander in the front rank is a serious step and commits him for an unknown period of time, during which he is pretty preoccupied, losing his ability to control his other battle groups and putting him in real danger. However, it can turn a battle and the risk might just be worth it, especially if you need a quick break through or if things are getting desperate. The choice is yours!

FIGHTING BROKEN TROOPS

There is no explicit shooting or close combat against, or by, broken troops. Damage inflicted on broken battle groups is assessed in the joint action phase.

TIP!

An historical use of light troops was to pursue broken enemy troops and prevent them from rallying. This can be a very useful tactic in *Field of Glory*.

MOVEMENT OF BROKEN TROOPS AND PURSUERS

When a battle group breaks after shooting or close combat, or for any other reason, other nearby battle groups may have to take a cohesion test (see the **Cohesion Tests** section). This is done after all combats and post-combat cohesion tests, death rolls and rolls to inflict commander losses have been resolved, but before the broken troops are moved. Each newly broken battle group makes an **initial rout**, which, unless it is the result of being charged when fragmented, happens at the end of the phase. Winning battle groups may have to make an **initial pursuit**.

INITIAL ROUT

- Roll to determine the variable move distance adjustment.
- If a battle group breaks as a result of being charged when fragmented, shooting or while in close combat, it routs directly away from the enemy charging, shooting at or in close combat with it. If there is more than one such enemy, bisect the angle between them.
- If a battle group breaks in other circumstances, it routs towards its side's rear table edge, making wheels and/or turns as appropriate to end its move as close to the rear table edge as possible.
- If any obstructions would prevent completion of a routing battle group's move, adjust as per evade moves (see the **Impact Phase** section) to get past these, but not to avoid leaving the table. It must go round a fortified or enemy camp, but can pass through its own unfortified camp. If its path is obstructed by unbroken enemy that cannot be bypassed, the battle group is

DECIDING HOW MANY DICE TO ROLL
ALLOCATING COMBAT DICE
SCORING HITS – POINTS OF ADVANTAGE
ACCUMULATING HITS AND TAKING COHESION TESTS
SUPPORT SHOOTING IN THE IMPACT PHASE
COMMANDERS IN CLOSE COMBAT
FIGHTING BROKEN TROOPS
MOVEMENT OF BROKEN TROOPS AND PURSUERS
AN EXAMPLE OF CLOSE COMBAT

destroyed at the end of the phase.

- A commander who is with a battle group at the moment it breaks must rout with it once. Until the joint action phase he cannot leave the battle group and cannot influence any complex move tests or cohesion tests.
- Battle wagons and artillery never make a rout move. Instead, they are destroyed and removed from the table. Their opponents do not pursue.

INITIAL PURSUIT

- An unbroken battle group, all of whose close combat opponents (except those only fighting it as an overlap) have broken and routed this phase, always pursues unless:
  - It is foot who have broken mounted opponents, in which case:
    - Non-shock foot can choose to pursue mounted by passing a CMT.
    - Shock foot must pass a CMT not to pursue mounted.
  - It was fighting enemy in two directions.
  - It is battle wagons or artillery.
- If some of a battle group's close combat opponent's break, and some don't, it does not pursue unless it was fighting the unbroken enemy only as an overlap.
- Pursuers make a variable movement distance roll and adjust their move accordingly.
- Pursuers who remain in contact with routers at the end of an initial pursuit move inflict losses (bases are removed from the routing battle group) and may inflict commander losses, as detailed in the **Joint Action Phase** section.
- Initial pursuits obey the same rules as pursuits in the joint action phase for moving multiple pursuing battle groups, following routers, avoiding friends or encountering the table edge, terrain or fresh enemy. See the **Joint Action Phase** section.

COMPLEX PURSUIT MOVE

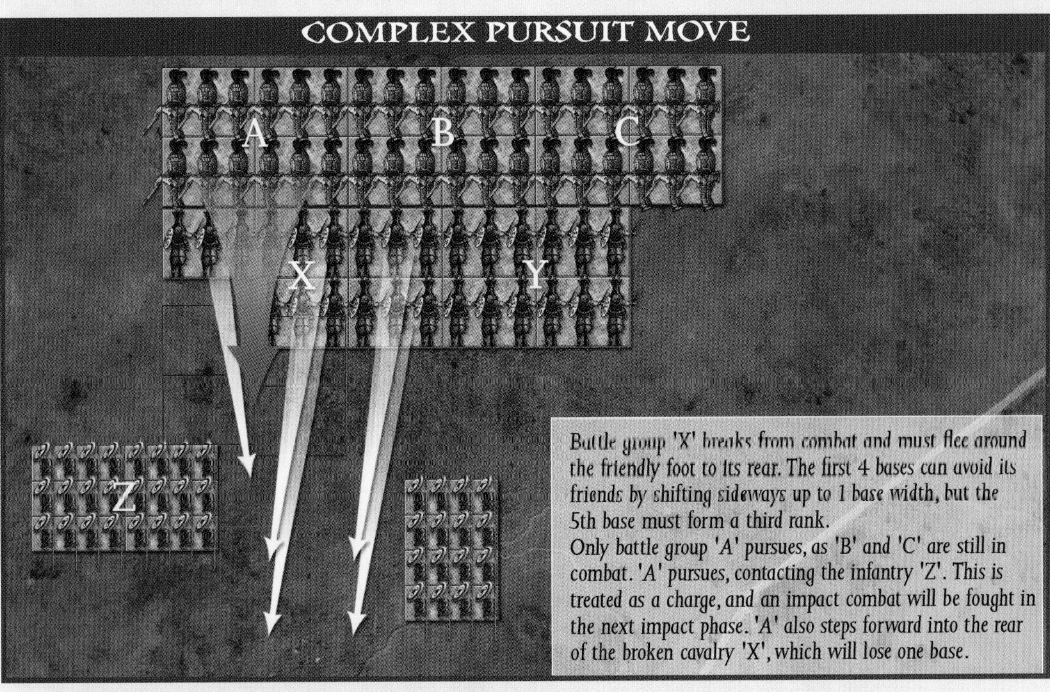

Battle group 'X' breaks from combat and must flee around the friendly foot to its rear. The first 4 bases can avoid its friends by shifting sideways up to 1 base width, but the 5th base must form a third rank.
Only battle group 'A' pursues, as 'B' and 'C' are still in combat. 'A' pursues, contacting the infantry 'Z'. This is treated as a charge, and an impact combat will be fought in the next impact phase. 'A' also steps forward into the rear of the broken cavalry 'X', which will lose one base.

AN EXAMPLE OF CLOSE COMBAT

Let's take a battle group of 12 bases of Gauls charging into a battle group of 8 bases of Roman legionaries from the late Republic. Both battle groups are deployed in two ranks and nobody else is involved. It is a straightforward head to head clash. The charge of the Gauls takes place in the impact phase.

The Gauls are classified as: *medium foot, protected, average, undrilled, impact foot, swordsmen.*

The Roman legionaries are classified as: *heavy foot, armoured, superior, drilled, impact foot, skilled swordsmen.*

A few comments on these classifications: Both have considerable impact when charging or receiving a charge, the Gauls through pure aggression, the Romans through the shock effect of a last minute volley of pila. Despite the Gauls being effective in melee against most troops, the Romans are even better. The Romans are of superior quality and will get to re-roll their 1s (see the quality re-rolls rules).

The Gauls have charged in, it's the impact phase combat resolution stage. In the impact phase dice table under "other troops", you find that both sides get **2 dice per front rank base** in contact. There are no overlaps in the impact phase, so even though the Gauls have more troops, this does not affect the situation yet. It is 8 dice versus 8 dice.

In the impact POA table, "impact foot" is a ++. Both sides have this POA, cancelling each other out. Neither side has a net POA advantage. The score needed to hit in the "Score to Hit" table for no POA is 4. (This is easy to remember with practice. It is 4 each when even, 4 v 5 for a +, and 3 v 5 for ++). Overall, at impact, the Romans have an edge through their re-roll, but not a great advantage.

The Gauls roll 6, 5, 4, 1, 2, 3, 5, 1, which gives them 4 hits on the legionary battle group. The Romans roll 3, 5, 2, 1, 3, 2, 6, 1. Alas, only 2 hits. But they have two 1s, and being superior, they can re-roll these. They roll 5 and 1. Only one more hit, for a total of 3. The final result is 4 hits on the Romans and 3 hits on the Gauls. **The Gauls have won the Impact phase, the Romans have lost.**

This is when it gets scary for the Republic. The Romans must now take a cohesion test. This is done by rolling 2 dice. The score to pass is 7. There are only a few modifiers in most circumstances. In this case, the modifiers are -1 for suffering >= 1

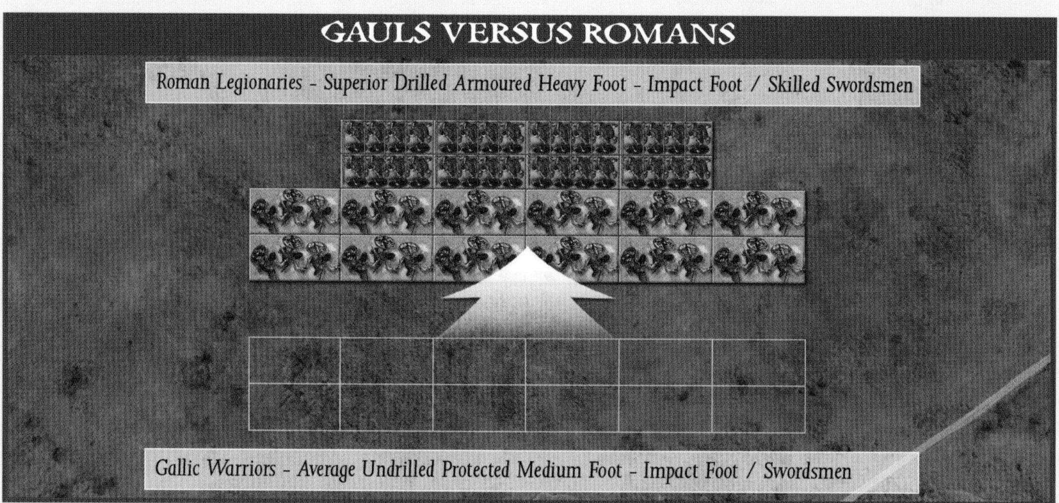

DECIDING HOW MANY DICE TO ROLL
ALLOCATING COMBAT DICE
SCORING HITS – POINTS OF ADVANTAGE
ACCUMULATING HITS AND TAKING COHESION TESTS
SUPPORT SHOOTING IN THE IMPACT PHASE
COMMANDERS IN CLOSE COMBAT
FIGHTING BROKEN TROOPS
MOVEMENT OF BROKEN TROOPS AND PURSUERS
AN EXAMPLE OF CLOSE COMBAT

hit per 3 bases and -1 for losing an impact phase combat versus impact foot. The Romans will subtract 2 from their roll. They roll 5, 3 for a total of 8, but the modifiers bring this down to 6. The factors are easy to remember. Usually it is either a -1 for a loss or -2 for a bad loss, and there are the few -1s that apply occasionally, such as for losing against impact foot or lancers in the impact phase.

The Romans therefore **fail** the cohesion test, though not badly enough to lose 2 cohesion levels. Even if they had scored 2 or less, they would not have dropped 2 cohesion levels because they only lost the combat by 1 hit. They drop one cohesion level from STEADY to DISRUPTED.

Each side then needs to make a death roll to decide if any bases are lost. This is straightforward. Roll more than the number of hits received to pass this test. If the battle group did not lose the combat (it inflicted as many or more hits than it received) then add 2 to the dice roll. Not losing combats is crucial. The losers get both a cohesion test and a much bigger chance of losing bases on the death roll. The Gauls get a +2 for winning and therefore only need to roll a 2 to pass, and do so with a 4. The Romans need 5, they roll 1 and lose a base. Note there are **no re-rolls** on **death rolls**, being superior does not help here. (The Romans were better at winning, but bled just as much when wounded).

There will be a break in the action now while the manoeuvre and shooting phases are played. We

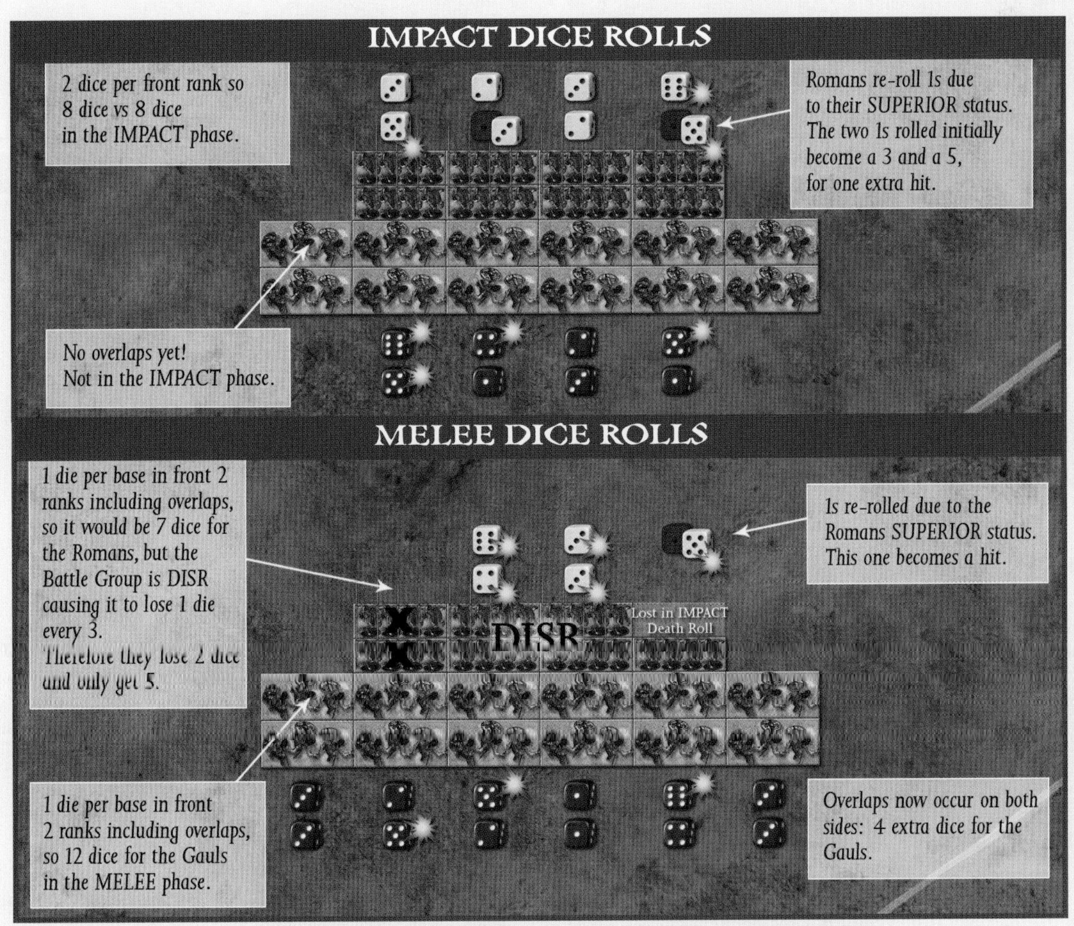

return to the fight in the melee phase. In the melee phase **each base in the first 2 ranks gets 1 dice**. Depth helps now, it had no effect in the impact phase. Further, overlaps now join the fight. The Gauls overlap the Romans on both sides. Everyone fights, with the Gauls getting a full 12 dice. The Romans have lost a base, so have 7 bases. This would be 7 dice if they were STEADY. However, they are DISRUPTED and lose 1 dice per 3, ending up with 5 dice to roll. (Consider the 7 as 3+3+1. Each complete three reduces to a two, giving 2+2+1.)

POAs in the melee phase are not the same as in the impact phase. This illustrates the impact-melee concept of the rules. The Gauls are as good as the Romans in the charge, but they are no match for the best Rome has to offer in the melee. Both equipment and training work to the Romans' advantage here. The Gauls are swordsmen (Sw), but the Romans are skilled swordsmen (SSw). The Romans get a + PoA for that. The Gauls get nothing. Swordsmen is not a + against skilled swordsmen (one of its few exceptions). Also, the Romans have better armour, which is very helpful in the melee giving another + POA. The Romans have a net 2 +s.

The 'to hit' rolls are very easy to remember. The Romans are on ++ (a double POA). They need only score a 3 to hit. The Gauls are on - - (a double POA against) and need to score 5 to hit. 12 dice needing a 5 versus 5 dice needing a 3. Those of you who like calculating odds will see that on average we should have 4 hits for the Gauls and 3 hits for the Romans, before re-rolls. The initial success of the Gauls is going to make this close. And so to the dice....

Gauls: 3, 3, 2, 5, 5, 2, 1, 1, 6, 4, 3, 3.

Romans: 6, 4, 3, 3, 1. They re-roll the 1 which comes up a 5.

The Gauls score 3 hits, but the Romans score 5. A turnaround for the Romans, they have won the melee phase. This time the Gauls must take a cohesion test. The Gauls suffered 5 hits to the Romans 3. The Gauls have a -1 as 5 hits is more than 1 per 3 bases, and a second -1 as they lost the melee by 2 or more hits, a bad loss. They also have a third -1 for being medium foot vs heavy foot in the open. They roll 2, 3 totalling 5. Subtracting 3 brings this down to 2, so they drop 2 cohesion levels, which is a disaster. They are now FRAGMENTED and will lose 1 dice in 2 for combat next time. With only half their original dice, they will be in trouble and unlikely to survive.

The death rolls. The Gauls took five hits, they need a 6 to pass as losers of a melee, and get it! The Romans need a 4, but get a +2 for winning, and roll a 1 to lose a base! The Romans must maintain their current frontage when removing the base. It is still going to be close. Next turn 6 Romans DISRUPTED (on 4 dice) will be against 12 Gauls FRAGMENTED (on 6 dice).

Gallic warriors prepare to charge

JOINT ACTION PHASE

Antcsignani in combat with Acheaen Cavalry, Acheaen War, 146 BC, by Angus McBride © Osprey Publishing Ltd. Taken from Men-at-Arms 291: Republican Roman Army 200–104 BC.

The final phase is a common phase in which various outcome moves are actioned. In addition, **both sides'** commanders get a chance to move to new positions and attempt to bolster or rally unsteady troops.

The order rarely matters, but the active player moves his troops first, or decides the sequence of events, should either side feel this is necessary.

OUTCOME MOVES IN THE JOINT ACTION PHASE

SCYTHED CHARIOTS

Scythed chariots that remain in front edge contact with unbroken enemy they fought this turn are removed from the table at the start of the joint action phase. This does not cause any cohesion tests.

BREAKING OFF

In historical battles, mounted troops often made repeated charges on steady enemy foot, falling back to regroup after each one. *Field of Glory* simulates this in the joint action phase when they pull back to prepare for their next charge:

- Mounted troops *fighting the enemy in 2 directions* do not break off.
- Elephants do not break off.
- Otherwise, mounted troops break off if at least half their close combat opponents are STEADY foot. (Counting only front rank bases in contact other than only as an overlap).

When breaking off, a battle group moves straight back. Move distance is not measured normally. Instead, the battle group ends the break off move separated from its opponent by a full normal move, facing them, in a permitted formation of the same frontage as before. It will thus be in

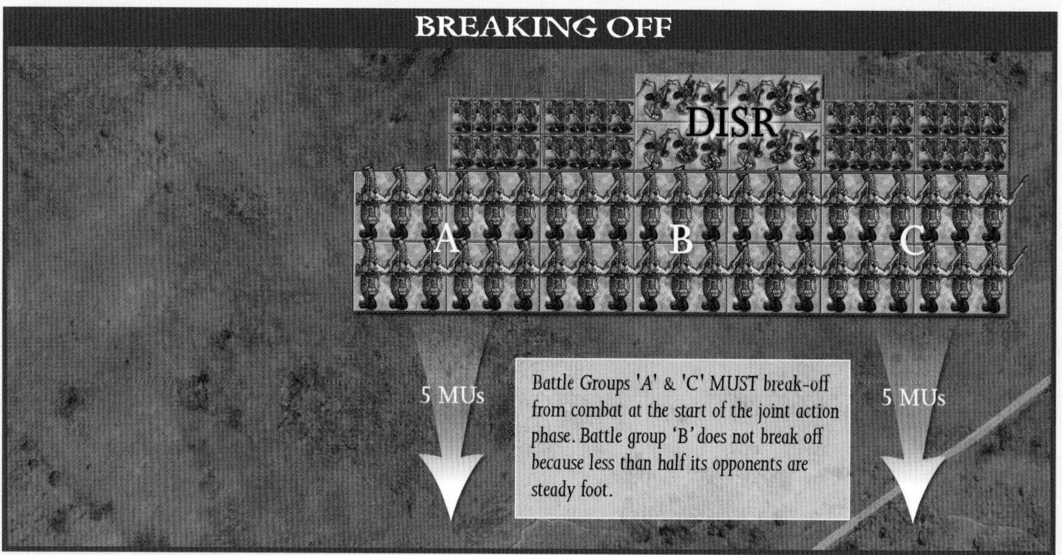

Battle Groups 'A' & 'C' MUST break-off from combat at the start of the joint action phase. Battle group 'B' does not break off because less than half its opponents are steady foot.

OUTCOME MOVES IN THE JOINT ACTION PHASE
COMMANDERS IN THE JOINT ACTION PHASE

position to charge the same enemy again in its next turn. The distance from the enemy is reduced in the following circumstances:

- If the move is blocked by a friendly battle group (even if of a type the breakers-off could normally interpenetrate) or camp, the battle group halts when it touches this.
- If the move would otherwise leave the table, the battle group halts when it touches the table edge.
- If the move is blocked by an enemy battle group or camp, the battle group halts 1 MU from this.
- If the move passes through terrain, the distance is reduced to the normal move distance in that terrain.
- If the move reaches terrain when the distance has already exceeded the normal move distance in that terrain, the battle group halts when it touches the edge of the terrain.

If, as a result, a battle group that should break off is unable to move back at least 1MU, it drops a cohesion level, the break off is cancelled, and the melee continues next turn.

STOPPING LOOTING

Once a camp is sacked, battle groups in contact with it must pass a CMT in the joint action phase to stop looting. If they succeed, they are free to move normally in their next turn. If all battle groups looting a camp stop looting, the camp is removed from the table.

ROUTERS AND PURSUERS

Broken troops (routers) and any pursuers move in every joint action phase as follows:

- Pursuers who remain in contact with routers must pursue unless they pass a CMT to stop pursuit. If they do so, they halt on the spot and can act normally next turn.
- Broken troops with enemy in contact at the start of this phase:
  - Move directly away from the enemy in contact, bisecting the angle if the enemy are facing in more than one direction.
  - Make a variable movement distance roll and adjust their move accordingly. Troops continuing their pursuit do the same.

Camp defenders guard against looters

- Broken troops not in contact with enemy make a normal distance move towards their side's rear table edge, making wheels and/or turns as appropriate to end their move as close to the rear table edge as possible.
- If any obstructions would prevent completion of a routing battle group's move, adjust as per evade moves (see the **Impact Phase** section) to get past these, but not to avoid leaving the table. It must go round a fortified or enemy camp, but can pass through its own unfortified camp. If its path is obstructed by unbroken enemy that cannot be bypassed, the battle group is destroyed at the end of the phase.
- Pursuers follow routers, wheeling if necessary to do so. They can contract frontage by dropping back bases if necessary to avoid friends.
- If more than one battle group is pursuing the same routing battle group, move the fastest pursuers first after rolling all VMD rolls. If the move distances are equal, the pursuer chooses which to move first.
- Pursuers who have lost contact with routers halt and can move normally in their next turn. They can choose to renew the pursuit by charging the routers again in their next impact phase. The routers are not allowed an extra move to escape. This represents the devastating effect of a determined pursuit. No combat is fought and damage is dealt with at the end of the next pursuit move as specified below.
- A pursuing battle group whose move would take any part of it off the table edge instead halts its move at the table edge.
- Pursuers can choose to stop at the edge of any terrain that would severely disorder any of their bases.

> **TIP!**
>
> Deciding whether to stop pursuing or to continue or renew the pursuit is often a difficult decision. Staying with the routers will certainly prevent them from being rallied, but sometimes there is more to be gained from leaving the pursuit to fight elsewhere.

- Pursuers normally contact any fresh enemy in their path. However, skirmishers can always choose to halt their pursuit 1 MU away from fresh enemy non-skirmishers, and other troops can do so if they pass a CMT. If they do so, all their front rank bases stop on that line.
- If pursuers contact fresh enemy in any phase, this is treated as a charge on the contacted enemy. These must immediately take a Cohesion Test if they are already FRAGMENTED unless the pursuers are light foot. Combat is adjudicated in the next impact phase. (Except that if contact occurred in the impact phase it is adjudicated in the same impact phase).
- Non-shock cavalry, camelry or light chariots entirely **1 base deep** or skirmishers that would be contacted by enemy pursuers in any phase can evade (unless they are already in close combat other than only as an overlap).
- Skirmishers that would be contacted by pursuing non-skirmishers in **open terrain** must pass a CMT not to evade (unless they are already in close combat other than only as an overlap).

REMOVING BASES FROM ROUTING BATTLE GROUPS

Pursuers who are in contact with a routing enemy battle group at the end of any pursuit move:

Pharaoh smites the Hittites at the Battle of Kadesh.

- Inflict 1 base loss on the routing battle group for each pursuing battle group in contact with it. No other combat occurs against routers.
- Can roll to kill the enemy commander if there is one with the routing battle group (whether or not he had been fighting in the front rank in any previous close combat). Roll 2 dice. If these total 10 or more, the commander is lost. Roll only once even if there is more than one pursuing battle group in contact with the routers.

REMOVING DESTROYED BATTLE GROUPS

At the end of the joint action phase, battle groups that are *auto-broken* or reduced to 1 base are destroyed and removed from the table. If the battle group was not already broken when this happens, this will trigger a cohesion test for nearby friendly battle groups as if it had broken. Leave it in place until this has been adjudicated.

COMMANDERS IN THE JOINT ACTION PHASE

MOVEMENT

Commanders of both sides can move once in the joint action phase. They cannot move a battle group with them.

BOLSTERING AND RALLYING TROOPS

Commanders of both sides can bolster or rally troops in the joint action phase. As battle groups deteriorate they drop down the cohesion ladder.

TIP!

Your decisions regarding your commanders in the joint action phase are some of the most important ones you will make in the game. Consider them carefully. It can be critical for a commander to be in the correct position next turn to influence a complex move test, modify cohesion tests if your troops are coming under pressure, or to fight in the front rank of a battle group that is about to be charged by the enemy. Bolstering your unsteady troops is vital in halting the deterioration of your army's fighting capability. Rallying routed troops could also save the day, but often you are faced with choosing the least worst option. These decisions often make the difference between an average player and a great one.

However, with encouragement from their commanders they can climb back up it. We call this bolstering when encouraging troops that are not yet broken and rallying when attempting to bring back a broken battle group.

The bolstering and rallying procedure is as follows:

- Battle groups cannot be bolstered or rallied if their Cohesion Level dropped in the current turn.
- Broken troops cannot be rallied if they are within 6 MUs of any enemy (excluding the enemy camp and commanders' bases).
- Otherwise a commander can attempt to bolster or rally a battle group that **he is with**. If it passes a cohesion test its cohesion level rises one level. If it fails, its cohesion level stays the same. (Cohesion level cannot drop when testing to bolster or rally.)
- Each commander can only attempt to bolster or rally one battle group in each joint action phase.
- When attempting to bolster or rally a battle group, only the commander with the battle group can apply his modifiers. (Thus the extra +1 for an IC only applies if he is the commander with the battle group).
- Only a commander in **line of command** can bolster or rally a battle group.
- A commander who attempts to rally a broken battle group does not have to rout with it if it fails the cohesion test.

TIP!

Bolstering troops is one of the most important functions of commanders. If no attempt is made to bolster a distressed battle group, its cohesion may drop further as the situation worsens. Pretty soon it will be too late, it will BREAK. This is particularly important when opposing armies engage in a prolonged shooting fight or an extended melee. If you leave the troops until they are broken before you attempt to rally them you are on a -3 when testing – so you will need a high score. Far easier to bolster troops when they are merely DISRUPTED.

BATTLE GROUP DETERIORATION

Clash of the Crusaders and Saracens, 1191, by Christa Hook © Osprey Publishing Ltd. Taken from Campaign 161: The Third Crusade 1191.

COHESION TESTS

Battle groups deteriorate primarily by failing **cohesion tests**. There are several reasons for a battle group to take a cohesion test:

FRAGMENTED TROOPS BEING CHARGED

- Test a FRAGMENTED battle group immediately if it is charged by enemy other than light foot. Battle groups contacted by enemy pursuers test as if being charged.

POST-COMBAT

- Test a battle group after all shooting dice have been rolled if it suffered either of the following:
  - At least 1 shooting hit per 3 bases. (1 HP3B). See the **Glossary of Terms** for the full definition. Some troop types calculate HP3B differently and not all ranks count.
  - At least 2 shooting hits if shot at by artillery (whether or not the artillery scored the hits).
- Test a battle group after all close combat dice have been rolled if it lost an impact or melee close combat.

SEEING FRIENDLY BATTLE GROUPS BREAK OR COMMANDERS LOST

- Test a battle group if a friendly battle group within 3 MUs breaks:
  - Immediately if a FRAGMENTED battle group breaks in response to being charged. Otherwise at the end of the current phase after resolving all combats, post-combat cohesion tests, death rolls and tests for inflicting commander losses.
  - Measure the distance before removing any lost troop bases. Test before the broken troops make their initial rout move.
  - Only skirmishers need test if the broken friends are skirmishers.
  - If an as yet unbroken friendly battle group is destroyed as a result of base loss(es) test as if it was broken, before it is removed from the table.
- Test a battle group if a commander in **line of command** is lost within 3 MUs:
  - At the end of the current phase after resolving all combats, post-combat cohesion tests, death rolls and tests for inflicting commander losses.
  - Measure from the nearest part of the battle group he was with, after removing his base and putting any troop bases he displaced back in their previous position.

BOLSTERING AND RALLYING

- Test in the joint action phase to bolster or rally a battle group with a commander (see *Joint Action Phase* section for details).

THE TEST

The cohesion test is a very simple pass fail test. Roll two dice and apply the adjustment factors in the table below.

The following rules also apply:

COMMANDERS AND COHESION TESTS

- Only one commander can affect a cohesion test – count whichever gives the best modifiers.
- A battle group in close combat can only count a commander who is with it.
- A commander with a battle group in close combat can influence other eligible battle groups unless he is fighting in the front rank.

MIXED BATTLE GROUPS

- Mixed battle groups of light and medium foot test as if entirely medium.
- Mixed battle groups of light and heavy foot test as if entirely heavy.
- Mixed battle groups of medium and heavy foot test as if entirely heavy.

MULTIPLE CAUSES

- If a battle group must test for multiple breaks due to charges, or multiple breaks or

COHESION TEST

Throw 2 dice (Quality re-rolls apply)

MODIFIERS

Battle group suffered at least 1 HP2B from shooting*	-1	Commander in ***line of command*** in command range if battle group is not in close combat, or with the battle group if it is in close combat.	+1
Battle group suffered at least 1 HP3B from close combat**	-1	Extra if he is an Inspired Commander	+1
At least 2 more hits received than inflicted in close combat**	-1	Battle group has ***rear support***	+1
Battle group has lost at least 25% of its original bases	-1	**Current Cohesion State**	
Non-skirmishers with ***threatened flank***.	-1	Disrupted or Severely Disordered	-1
More than 1 reason to test	-1	Fragmented	-2
Any one of… Any troops shot at by artillery or firearms* OR Any troops testing for having lost close combat even partly against elephants or scythed chariots** OR Medium foot testing for having lost close combat even partly against mounted troops or heavy foot in ***open terrain***** OR Any troops testing for having lost impact phase combat even partly against lancers** OR Foot testing for having lost impact phase combat even partly against impact foot**	-1	Broken	-3

* Only applies when testing as a result of shooting hits. The modifier for being shot at by artillery or firearms applies whether or not they scored the hits.

** Only applies when testing as a result of losing a close combat. The modifier for fighting specific enemy troop types applies whether or not these inflicted more hits on the battle group than it inflicted on them.

Other tests do not use these modifiers even if they occur in the same phase.

lost commanders at the end of the phase, it only tests once but with a -1 adjustment to the dice for "more than one reason to test".

TESTING MULTIPLE BATTLE GROUPS

- If several battle groups have to test at the same time for seeing friends break or commanders lost, their side's player decides which order to test them in. If further battle groups break as a consequence, those that have already tested do not have to test again. If pursuits result in the loss of a commander, battle groups that have already tested at the end of this phase for breaks/lost commanders do not have to test again.

IF THE FINAL SCORE IS...	
7 or more	• Rise one cohesion level if testing to bolster or rally the battle group. • Otherwise no change in cohesion level.
3, 4, 5 or 6	• Drop one cohesion level (ignore if testing to bolster or rally the battle group).
2 or less	• Drop two cohesion levels if: - Testing for losing a close combat in which the battle group received at least 2 more hits than it inflicted. - Testing for seeing friends break or commander lost. • Otherwise drop one cohesion level (ignore if testing to bolster or rally the battle group).

THE EFFECT OF COHESION LEVELS

COHESION LEVEL AND EFFECTS	
LEVEL	**EFFECT**
STEADY	All troops start the battle STEADY
DISRUPTED (DISR)	• -1 on all CMTs • -1 on all further cohesion tests • Battle group loses one dice per 3 in close combat or shooting • Non-shock battle groups must pass a CMT to charge or intercept
FRAGMENTED (FRAG)	• -2 on all CMTs • -2 on all further cohesion tests • Battle group can make a simple move to retire away from all enemy within 12 MUs but must CMT for any other move • Battle group loses 1 dice per 2 in close combat or shooting • Shock troops are no longer so • Battle group cannot charge or intercept • Battle group must take a cohesion test if charged by any troops except light foot
BROKEN	• Battle group makes a rout move in the phase in which it breaks, and in each subsequent joint action phase • -3 on cohesion tests to rally • 1 base removed for each pursuing enemy battle group in contact at the end of each rout move

COHESION TESTS
THE TEST
THE EFFECT OF COHESION LEVELS
DEATH ROLLS
BASE REMOVAL
AUTOBREAK

TIP!

The best way to develop a winning strategy in *Field of Glory* is to avoid taking cohesion tests! Minimise your risks by stacking combat modifiers in your favour and by preventing your opponent from concentrating shooting. Avoid the risk of panic spreading by keeping your supporting battle groups far enough back from the front line.

DEATH ROLLS

In addition to dropping cohesion levels, a battle group can also deteriorate by losing bases as a result of the death roll. This is a simple pass/fail roll on a single dice as follows:

DEATH ROLL
Roll 1 dice for the battle group. **(No re-rolls)**.
• Add +1 to the dice score if elephants, artillery or battle wagons.
• Add +2 to the dice score if the hits suffered were from shooting or the battle group won/drew a close combat.
If the score does not exceed the number of hits, remove a base.
If a base was removed, and there were more than 6 hits, deduct 6 from the hits and roll again for the remainder. (Use the same modifiers).

Thus, if losing a close combat, the roll needs to be more than the hits received. If being shot at or winning/drawing a close combat then no roll is required unless 3 or more hits are taken.

If a battle group must take a cohesion test as well as a death roll, the cohesion test is always resolved **before** the effect of the death roll. (This means that you can roll the dice together, but base losses that will result from the death roll do not affect the cohesion test modifiers).

EXAMPLE

A cavalry battle group suffers 9 hits from shooting. (Ouch!) Even if it scores 6 on its death roll, with +2 modifier its score could only reach 8, so it loses 1 base. It must deduct 6 from the total hits, leaving 3. It must now roll to score higher than this. As it has +2 modifier on its score (the hits are from shooting), it will lose another base only if it rolls 1 on the dice.

BASE REMOVAL

Bases removed as a result of failed death rolls or pursuits obey the following priorities for removal:

- **Shooting**: Nearest base to shooters.
- **Close combat**: Any front rank base facing the enemy battle group which inflicted most hits on the battle group.
- **Routing**: Furthest base from pursuers. (This is to prevent base removal from causing pursuers to lose contact).
- If bases are of equal priority, the battle group's owner chooses which to remove.
- If a battle group is in close combat with two or more enemy battle groups, do not remove a base that would leave any of the enemy battle groups (except those fighting only as an overlap) without a base to face (unless you run out of bases).
- If the base that should be removed has been displaced by a commander fighting in the front rank, remove the displaced base instead of the commander.
- If both players must remove bases, the active player does so second.

Other bases of the battle group immediately shuffle up to retain contiguity and fill vacated front rank positions. All vacated front rank close combat fighting positions (except overlaps) must be filled if the battle group has any bases available to do so. Non-front rank bases must be used if any are available, and can be from any part of the battle group. If not, front rank bases that are not in close combat or are only in close combat as an overlap must be used. If there are no such bases available, and there is a gap in the front rank, front rank bases in close combat must be shifted sideways to fill the gap. The player owning the battle group chooses which direction to shift, but if possible, it must leave at least one base in contact with each opposing enemy battle group (except those fighting only as an overlap).

AUTOBREAK

Battle groups automatically break immediately when they have lost a certain proportion of their original bases, so accumulated losses can get you in the end:

QUALITY	AUTOBREAK ON
Elite	> 60% lost
Superior	> 50% lost
Average	> 40% lost
Poor	> 30% lost

Battle groups below these break points cannot be rallied and are destroyed and removed from the table at the end of any joint action phase.

Battle groups with only one base left are also destroyed and removed from the table at the end of any joint action phase. Where a battle group has not already broken when this occurs, it will trigger a cohesion test for nearby friendly battle groups as if it had just broken.

VICTORY AND DEFEAT

Pictish raid on Hadrian's Wall, AD 360, by Wayne Reynolds © Osprey Publishing Ltd. Taken from Warrior 50: Pictish Warrior AD 297–841.

An army suffers an ***army rout*** if at the end of the current phase it has accumulated attrition points equal to the total number of battle groups it started with. Unless both sides suffer a simultaneous army rout, which is a draw, the enemy has achieved a **Decisive Victory**.

In stand-alone games the game is now over. In campaign or scenario games, additional rules may be provided to cover a retreat from the battlefield.

If playing to a time limit and neither army is broken at the pre-set time limit:

- A side that inflicted at least 4 more attrition points than the enemy and >= 3:1 gains a **Major Victory**.
- Failing that, a side that inflicted at least 3 more attrition points than the enemy and >= 2:1 gains a **Moderate Victory**.
- Failing that, a side that inflicted at least 2 more attrition points than the enemy gains a **Marginal Victory**.

If none of the above apply, the game is a draw.

Roman commander celebrates victory

SPECIAL FEATURES

Two regiments of Immortals, by Simon Chew © Osprey Publishing Ltd. Taken from Elite 42: The Persian Army 560–330 BC.

ELEPHANTS AND CAMELS

- Horses generally don't like camels or elephants, so Knights, cataphracts, cavalry, light horse and chariots are DISORDERED if they are less than 1 base width from elephants or camelry.
- Camelry are only so affected by elephants.
- Camelry treat soft sand as rough going, not difficult.
- Heavily armoured camelry otherwise move as undrilled cataphracts.
- Other camelry otherwise move as undrilled cavalry.
- Elephants cause a -1 modifier on the cohesion test when enemy lose a close combat against them.
- None of the the above applies to commanders depicted as camelry or on elephants.

Indian elephants trundle into battle

SCYTHED CHARIOTS

- Are shock troops.
- Get 3 dice per front rank base in the impact phase and 2 in the melee phase.
- Can never be part of a battle line.
- Can only make moves as permitted in the "charges" or "advances" sections of the simple and complex move chart.
- Cause a -1 modifier on the cohesion test when enemy lose a close combat against them.
- Are removed from the table at the start of

ELEPHANTS AND CAMELS
SCYTHED CHARIOTS
FIELD FORTIFICATIONS
PORTABLE DEFENCES
ORB FORMATION

the joint action phase if they remain in front edge contact with any unbroken enemy they fought this turn.

- Do not count towards their army's battle group count for attrition purposes and never count as attrition points when lost.

FIELD FORTIFICATIONS

- Except in scenario or campaign games, field fortifications (FF) are only allowed when permitted in our companion army list books and paid for.
- FF have a front and rear and these must be clearly identifiable.
- Troops count as defending a FF if they are in contact with its rear edge.
- The front edge of FF is treated as the front edge of a battle group defending them, including for measuring shooting ranges.
- Troops defending FF cannot be charged in flank/rear across the fortifications, and suffer no POA penalty for fighting in more than one direction across them. If not already facing the part of the fortification being attacked, the defending bases turn to face it and the rest of the battle group is shuffled up to maintain contact with the turned bases.
- Other than as above, troops defending FF never conform to enemy attacking across them.
- Undefended field fortifications do not impede movement of troops. (i.e. not sufficiently to be represented in the rules).

PORTABLE DEFENCES

- The most common type of portable defences (PD) are stakes.
- PD are only allowed when permitted in our companion army list books and paid for. They must be assigned to a specific battle group.
- A battle group carrying PD can place them (or pick them up) in the manoeuvre phase as a full complex move. Enough are carried to cover the front of the battle group when it is 2 bases deep. Stands depicting appropriate PD are placed on the table in the position of the front of the battle group. The battle group is shifted back to make room. The front edge of the PD is treated as the front edge of the battle group, including for measuring shooting ranges.
- Once placed, only that battle group can defend them. PD are treated as field fortifications when their defenders are in close combat against mounted opponents other than elephants, but give no advantage against foot, elephants or shooting.
- Troops defending PD never conform to enemy attacking across them.
- PD can only be picked up if there are no enemy within 6 MUs of the battle group.
- If the battle group moves away without picking up its PD, the PD markers are removed.
- A battle group that has placed and not picked up its PD cannot place more PD.

ORB FORMATION

- **Orb formation** is a special all round defensive formation permitted only to battle groups entirely of pikemen or spearmen.
- It is depicted by contracting the battle group to 2 files wide, and turning at least half the battle group's ranks to face the rear. The normal rules for a stationary contraction are used, except that it can be performed by undrilled troops, and the battle group must be shifted so that the centre of its front rank is in the same position as before. A battle group can only form ORB if it starts no more than 4 files wide.

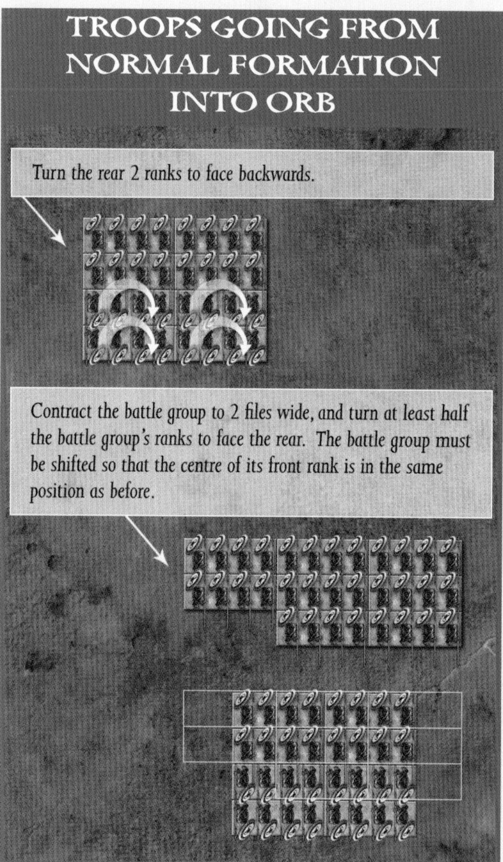

- A complex move test (CMT) must be passed to form or leave orb formation.
- A battle group cannot form orb formation unless there are unbroken enemy (excluding camp or commanders) within 6 MUs.
- A battle group cannot form or leave orb formation while in close combat.
- A battle group leaving orb formation can face any of its four edges as if making a 90 or 180 degree turn.
- A battle group in orb formation:
  - Cannot charge or intercept.
  - Can move 1 MU directly to front or rear in its side's manoeuvre phase.
  - Exerts no restricted area.
  - Never counts as charged in flank or rear and never turns to face enemy contacting its flank or rear. It never conforms to enemy in close combat.
  - Fights in any direction with one quarter of its bases, rounded up. Half of these, rounded up, count as front rank bases.
  - Cannot be overlapped.
  - Suffers no POA penalty for fighting in more than one direction.
  - Cannot fight as an overlap for another friendly battle group.
  - Cannot count any pikemen or spearmen POAs, but, if steady, counts as steady pikemen or spearmen for the purpose of determining enemy POAs.

REFERENCE SECTION

Battle of Thermopylae, 480 BC, by Richard Hook © Osprey Publishing Ltd. Taken from Elite 66: The Spartan Army.

SCALES

Tabletop wargaming requires a number of compromises to make our battle games enjoyable and to allow us to complete them in a reasonable period of time. This can of course work against us when attempting to recreate actual battles from history, but with a little care and preparation this is easily overcome. For normal club or competition games we are constrained by time, table space and our opponent's available armies. Love it or hate it, the modern phenomenon of wargaming anachronistic battles allows players to research and paint up armies from any location and time frame covered by the rules without worrying about the availability of historical opponents. The minute we do this, we compromise literal figure scales, e.g. to make a "what if" battle between a Viking force and a Persian army work, we need to adjust the scale of the armies, as historically the Vikings could never field a force anywhere near the size of a Persian army. This is where our companion army list books and points values come into play and allow any combination of opposing armies to work. Obviously the approach differs for historical re-fights, and also for campaigns.

In *Field of Glory*, the troop scale can be taken as **averaging** very approximately 250 men per base, but in practice we recommend ignoring this and treating each army as a coherent whole, representing whatever full-sized army its prototype usually fielded. Our companion army list books are specifically designed to create the correct SHAPE and feel of each army, allowing a good historical representation of how it fought. The rules generally assume that these lists are being used.

FIGURE SCALE

The rules are compatible with all figure scales from 2mm to 28mm. All distances and ranges given in the rules are the same regardless of figure scale. Base sizes are listed below. The size

A Viking Shieldwall

for 15mm scale figures is shown first, followed by the size for 25/28mm scale figures in square brackets. For scales smaller then 15mm it is recommended that the base sizes for the 15mm scale are used, simply add more figures to the base for visual effect. The base widths are standard for all bases. Base depths are always a compromise in tabletop armies and have been chosen to suit the size of the figures rather than the actual depth of the formation.

The number of men represented by each base will depend on the size of battle being fought. Each base can be assumed to represent a body of troops in a battle formation of 3 to 5 ranks with most battle groups being deployed 2 bases deep (6 to 10 ranks). Each base has a number of figures giving a visual representation of the formation that the battle group would most likely use.

The figures used should be an accurate representation of the troops they depict. This will assist your opponent to see at a glance what troops he is facing. In all games, but more especially tournament games, players must fully explain their troops at deployment or when asked.

Command bases are an exception to the figure scales. They are not fighting units, and are only used to indicate the location of the commanders on the battlefield. They do not add to the base count of any battle group they are with. Commanders are mounted on a single stand of a maximum 40mm [60mm] square or on a smaller stand of a suitable size for their troop type. They need not contain the same number of figures as their equivalent troop type, but must be easily identifiable as a commander, even when adjacent to a similarly armed combat battle group. Commanders' bases can therefore be as extravagant as you like.

An Egyptian army gathers at the oasis

GROUND SCALE

The ground scale used is defined by effective bow range. The choice of scale is again a compromise and has been made with a view to making movement distances and missile ranges sufficient to ensure that players are faced with enough decision making to keep the game interesting while still maintaining a reasonable simulation of historical march rates and shooting distances.

All distances are specified in movement units (MUs). One movement unit, or MU for short, is either 25mm or 1 inch, as agreed by the players or decided by tournament organisers.

TIME SCALE

Each pair of game turns represents a varying amount of time on the battlefield, sufficient to encompass the majority of discrete battlefield actions. It also allows a reasonable period of time for battle groups to regroup during pauses in the action. The mass of minutiae that occur during battle are absorbed and incorporated into the cohesion, movement and combat mechanisms. Each turn represents a phase of battle rather than a fixed amount of time.

BASE SIZES

Troop bases must be rectangles. For 15mm scale figures the width of all bases is 40mm. For 25/28mm scale figures the width is always 60mm. The depth varies according to troop-type. The following tables show measurements for 15mm scale models. The 25/28mm scale equivalent is in brackets. Each base represents a body of men. The number of figures per base and the base depths are as follows:

BASE SIZES		
Troop Type	**Figures per base**	**Depth of base: 15mm [25/28mm]**
Heavy foot	4	15mm [20mm]
Medium foot	3 or 4	20mm [30mm]
Light foot	2	20mm [30mm]
Mob	5-8	30mm [40mm]
Cavalry	3	30mm [40mm]
Light horse	2	30mm [40mm]
Camelry	3	30mm [40mm]
Knights	3	30mm [40mm]
Cataphracts	3 or 4	30mm [40mm]
Chariots	1	40mm [80mm]
Elephants	1	40mm [80mm]
Artillery	1	40mm [80mm]
Battle wagons	1	80mm [120mm]
Commander	As required*	40mm [60mm] or less
Fortifications	Models of the defences	15mm [20mm]
Supply camp	This will be a selection of tents, wagons etc. It is a rectangle 120mm [180mm] by 80mm [160mm]. It can be fortified if allowed in the army list.	

* Commanders will normally be depicted as one of their troop types. This is specified in the companion army list books. It is acceptable to use a slightly different number of figures to make the commander, his bodyguard and standard bearers easily distinguishable.

USING TROOPS BASED FOR OTHER SYSTEMS

As long as the correct base widths are adhered to, it is fine to use troops based for other rules systems. Modification to comply with *Field of Glory* may require a little ingenuity. For example:

- Single-based figures can be "blue-tacked" on to temporary bases of the correct width.
- Lesser numbers of figures per base can be used if the figures or the stands they are attached to are too large to fit the normal number on our standard base widths.
- Base depths can be larger than standard if the figures or the stands they are attached to are too large to fit on our standard base depths.
- Some bases from some other systems may need to be placed side by side and treated as two bases one behind the other.

There are any number of other temporary fixes. If both players have troops based to the same system they can be used, as long as all bases are the same width.

TROOP TYPES IN DETAIL

The troop types in these rules are defined by their battlefield behaviour rather than their physical appearance or equipment alone. For example, the term "heavy foot" is used to describe all infantry troop types that fight shoulder to shoulder in close formation. There are a number of individual troop-types and these are described in the table overleaf.

ARMOUR

The following is a guide to the characteristics of the armour classes in *Field of Glory*. A number of considerations have been taken into account when determining the armour classes specified for historical troops in our companion army list books, e.g. where the various ranks in a battle group are armoured differently, or where individuals have a variety of armour levels, the troops are classified according to their average functional armour level. Reflecting significant differences between armour levels of different troop-types within the same historical period has sometimes outweighed rigid adherence to standard descriptions.

COMBAT CAPABILITIES

Field of Glory is function-based. The mere possession of a weapon is not sufficient to qualify for a combat capability. For example, ghilman (ghulam) cavalry were primarily horse archers, so get bow capability but not lancers capability, even though some were armed with lances. Conversely, Sarmatian heavy cavalry were armed with lance and bow, but preferred to charge rather than use their bows in battle, so get lancers capability but not bow capability.

Similarly, Burgundian feudal men-at-arms in the later 15th century were recorded by contemporaries as being incompetent in the use of their lances. Therefore they are not credited with a lancers capability even though they carried lances.

TROOP TYPE	REF	DESCRIPTION
Heavy Foot	HF	Foot troops who fight in close formation. These include most line-of-battle infantry.
Medium Foot	MF	Foot troops capable of fighting in close formation, but less reliant on formation for their fighting style, and hence better suited than heavy foot to fighting in rough terrain. They are capable of fighting alongside heavy foot in the open, but less able to resist a mounted charge and less resilient in a losing fight.
Light Foot	LF	Foot troops who fight in a dispersed formation. They are classified as **skirmishers** when in battle groups entirely of light foot.
Mob	Mb	Untrained rabble, usually of low morale, fighting as a disorganised mass. They may be equipped with only peasant weapons or may have been hastily equipped with proper weaponry but not trained to use it effectively. They are treated as Medium Foot in all respects except that they are based differently.
Knights	Kn	European Medieval knights. They ride knee to knee on heavy horses, and rely on a devastating charge. They often fight in less depth than other mounted troops. Usually only a proportion of the troops are actual knights, with the remainder being sergeants and/or retainers.
Cataphracts	Ct	Ancient cavalry covered from head to foot in armour, with similar protection for their horses. They ride in close formation at a slower speed than most other cavalry. They are very well protected from missiles and their armour gives them an edge in an extended melee.
Light Horse	LH	Lightly equipped horsemen specialising in skirmishing, usually with missile weapons. They are classified as **skirmishers**.
Cavalry	Cv	Most other mounted troops fall into this category. They are capable of skirmishing or of forming a solid body to shoot or charge. They are not classified as skirmishers.
Camelry	Cm	Camel-mounted troops. They are treated as cataphracts if heavily armoured, otherwise as cavalry, but they have less difficulty with movement over sand. Camelry disorder horses.
Elephants	El	Indian or African elephants, whose strength is breaking into solid lines of enemy troops. Elephants disorder horses.
Heavy Chariots	HCh	Chariots with 3 or 4 crewmen.
Light Chariots	LCh	Chariots with 2 crewmen. Capable of charging or skirmishing. They are not classified as skirmishers.
Scythed Chariots	SCh	Chariots with scythes and spears attached to the structure. Driven into the enemy ranks as a terror weapon.
Light Artillery	LArt	Small bolt shooters or organ guns. Moveable to a limited extent on the battle-field. Treated as foot.
Heavy Artillery	HArt	Heavy bolt-shooters, stone throwers or bombards. Intended more for sieges than for field battles and immovable once set up. Treated as foot.
Battle Wagons	BWg	Horse or ox drawn wagons, usually with missile-armed crew on board. Treated as foot. Not very manoeuvrable, so always count as undrilled.

GLOSSARY OF ARMOUR CLASSES		
Description	**Phase**	**Distinctive features**
Heavily Armoured	Shooting, Melee	Metal armour almost entirely covering the body. Horses mostly barded, at least for front ranks.
Armoured	Shooting, Melee	Metal armour at least for the head and thorax – combined, in the case of foot, either with a substantial shield or with additional metallic protection. Horses may or may not be armoured – if armoured, usually with leather or textile armour. Also cavalry with extensive non-metallic armour for man and horse.
Protected	Shooting, Melee	With a minimum of at least a moderate sized shield and/or leather or textile armour. Foot with a limited degree of metallic protection but lacking shields. Also mixed battle groups of unamoured and armoured men resulting in an equivalent average level of protection.
Unprotected	Shooting, Melee	Lacking armour and without or with only small or flimsy shields.

Some foot spearmen were the main offensive arm of their army; others adopted a defensive posture and a role of supporting their army's mounted troops. We accept the view that this was not due merely to circumstances, but to different tactical doctrines, and hence these troops are treated differently under the rules. Other troops armed with spears were not organised sufficiently to form any sort of concerted spear phalanx and merely had spears because they were cheap weapons, so are not credited with either "spearmen" capability. They may instead have a "light spear" capability or no combat capability at all.

Many troops had swords as secondary weapons, but the "swordsmen" capability only applies to those who were happy to engage in close combat and used swords (or equivalent) as their primary close combat weapon. "Skilled swordsmen" capability is given only to those with the highest skill and training with the sword.

The capabilities available to each historical troop type are specified in our companion army list books. Allocation of capabilities inevitably has a subjective element. In *Field of Glory* we have based our decisions on the most recent evidence available to us. The emphasis is always on establishing the historical role of each troop-type, especially when fighting contemporary opponents. It should therefore be accepted that the descriptions below are not prescriptive and are for use only in *Field of Glory*.

Capabilities are situational and may not result in a point of advantage in every combat.

TRAINING

The allocation of "drilled" to a troop type can be subjective. Where written evidence of training manuals exists, giving descriptions of how units should manoeuvre, troops are classified as drilled. In other instances, historical accounts give indicators of how troops fought.

FORTIFICATIONS

TYPE	REF	DESCRIPTION
Field Fortifications	FF	Temporary earthworks or other obstacles used to enhance defensive positions.
Portable Defences	PD	The most common type of portable defences are stakes.

GLOSSARY OF COMBAT CAPABILITIES

Capability	Phase	Description
Bow	Shooting	Specialist foot bowmen or horse archers. (Excluding crossbowmen or Medieval longbowmen).
Bow*	Shooting	Foot or cavalry making effective use of bows but only as a subsidiary weapon. Example: Lithuanians. Also cavalry trained to fight in shallow mixed formations of lancers and bowmen, with only a few ranks armed with bow. Example: Some Byzantine cavalry. Troops with Bow* capability use the same POAs as those with Bow capability, but shoot with less dice.
Crossbow	Shooting	Foot or mounted troops armed with crossbows.
Firearm	Shooting	Foot or mounted troops armed with handguns or naphtha bombs.
Heavy Artillery	Shooting	Heavy artillery such as heavy bolt-shooters, stone-throwers or bombards.
Heavy Weapon	Impact, Melee	Troops armed with pole arms or 2-handed swords, axes or rhomphaia. Examples: Dacian falxmen, Anglo-Danish huscarles and most dismounted Later Medieval knights.
Impact Foot	Impact	Foot relying on a fierce charge to disrupt the enemy at impact. Examples: Gauls and Visigoths. Foot relying on a barrage of heavy throwing weapons to disrupt the enemy at impact. Examples: Roman legionaries and Spanish scutarii.
Javelins	Shooting	Light foot or light horse skirmishers with javelins. Example: Numidians.
Lancers	Impact	Mounted troops specialising in charging with lance. Examples: Hellenistic xystophoroi, Sarmatians, Ostrogoths, Byzantine lancers and Medieval knights.
Light Artillery	Shooting	Light artillery such as light bolt-shooters or organ guns.
Light Spear	Impact	Foot armed with light spear or javelins, whether thrust or thrown, but not trained to fight as a concerted offensive or defensive spear phalanx. Mounted troops armed with light spear or javelins, whether thrust or thrown. NB: Troops with "Light Spear" do not count as "Spearmen".
Longbow	Shooting	Foot armed with Medieval longbows.
Pikemen	Impact, Melee	Foot armed with long 2-handed pikes and forming a concerted pike phalanx. Most such troops are also armed with swords – the Pikemen melee POA already takes this into account. They never use "Swordsmen" POA.
Sling	Shooting	Foot armed with slings.
Spearmen	**Defensive Spearmen**	Spearmen accustomed to adopting a defensive stance, repelling all enemy attacks, and often acting primarily in the role of supports for the army's mounted troops. Examples: Byzantine, Arab and most Medieval spearmen.
	Offensive Spearmen	Spearmen accustomed to adopting an aggressive phalanx formation, with the aim of attacking and defeating enemy foot. Example: Greek hoplites.
The two categories of spearmen behave differently in the Impact phase but identically in the Melee phase. The term "**spearmen**" is used to apply to both offensive and defensive spearmen. It does not refer to "light spear", this is a separate category described above. Most spearmen are also armed with swords – the spearmen melee POA already takes this into account. Spearmen never use "swordsmen" POA.		
Skilled Swordsmen	Melee	Foot using swords as their primary weapon and trained to a very high standard of swordsmanship. Examples: Early Imperial Roman legionaries and later Samurai.
Swordsmen	Melee	Foot using swords as their primary weapon, often supplemented by javelins or other throwing weapons. Examples: Samnites, Gauls and Franks. Foot equipped with swords or equivalent weapons as secondary weapons, but ready and willing to fight hard hand-to-hand when required. Example: English longbowmen. Mounted troops equipped with swords, maces or horseman's axes and ready and willing to fight hand to hand when required. Examples: Most non-skirmisher mounted troops and most steppe nomads.

TERRAIN DESCRIPTION, VISIBILITY AND COMBAT EFFECTS	
CLEAR	
Open (O)	An open area of ground offering no impediment to movement. Full visibility.
UNEVEN	
Open Fields (OFl)	An area of cultivated land, either open or only divided by shallow irrigation or drainage ditches.
Broken Ground (BG)	A mostly open area, with some rocks and/or scrub
ROUGH	
Brush (B)	An area mostly covered by substantial brush or rocks or by small gullies or boggy ground. LF wholly inside are only visible within 4 MUs.
Enclosed Fields (EFl)	An area of cultivated land divided by walls, hedges or deep irrigation or drainage ditches. Counts as cover for bases wholly inside. LF wholly inside are only visible within 4 MUs
Plantation (P)	An area lightly covered with fruit or olive trees, or other managed woodland with little undergrowth. Counts as cover for bases wholly inside. Troops wholly inside are only visible within 4 MUs. Troops inside can only shoot in 1 rank. Troops beyond a plantation cannot be seen.
Gully (G)	A gully is a depression in the ground. It is too uneven to provide any uphill advantage but can conceal troops. Troops in a gully are only visible from outside within 1 MU. Troops in a gully can see outside.
DIFFICULT	
Forest (F)	Dense woodland or jungle. Counts as cover for bases wholly inside. Troops wholly inside are only visible within 2 MUs. Troops inside can only shoot in 1 rank. Troops beyond a forest cannot be seen.
Vineyards (V)	A cultivated area of vines, usually planted in straight lines. Counts as cover for bases wholly inside. LF wholly inside are only visible within 4 MUs.
Marsh (M)	A very boggy area, which may include small ponds with occasional trees and shrubs. LF wholly inside are only visible within 4 MUs.
Soft Sand (SS)	An area of soft sand and some low sand dunes. LF wholly inside are only visible within 6 MUs. Camelry count it as Rough.
Village (Vg)	An area of buildings and sheds with a road passing through it. Counts as cover for bases wholly inside. Troops wholly inside are only visible within 2 MUs. Troops inside can only shoot in 1 rank.
Steep Hill (SH)	A steeply sloping hill which gives a close combat advantage to those higher up the slope. Troops on such a hill can shoot over troops below them. Troops beyond a crest line are only visible within 1 MU. Steep hills are always difficult, whether clear or covered by broken ground, brush, plantation, vineyards, forest or a village.
IMPASSABLE	
Impassable (I)	An area of extremely steep hills or a quarry, or a lake etc. No troops can enter. Any troops forced into it are destroyed.
SLOPES	
Gentle Hill (GH)	A gently sloping hill which gives a close combat advantage to those higher up the slope. Troops on such a hill can shoot over troops below them. Troops beyond a crest line are only visible within 1 MU. Slopes can be clear, uneven (if covered by broken ground), rough (if covered by brush or plantation) or difficult (if covered by vineyards, forest or a village).
LINEAR	
Road (Rd)	A single base wide road or track that must pass through or touch a village if there is one, and must connect 2 different table edges, no more than one of them a short edge. The maximum length of the road is 60 MUs.
Coastline (C)	Extends up to 6 MUs in from the short table edge – May be the bank of a major river or the sea. Impassable to troops.
River (Rv)	Up to 4 MUs wide, entirely within 6 MUs of the side edge. The placing side dices for its difficulty when putting it down. 1 = uneven, 2,3 = rough, 4,5 = difficult, 6 = impassable. Troops can only move within 45 degrees of straight across. The river cannot have more than 2 bends.

TERRAIN PIECE SIZES

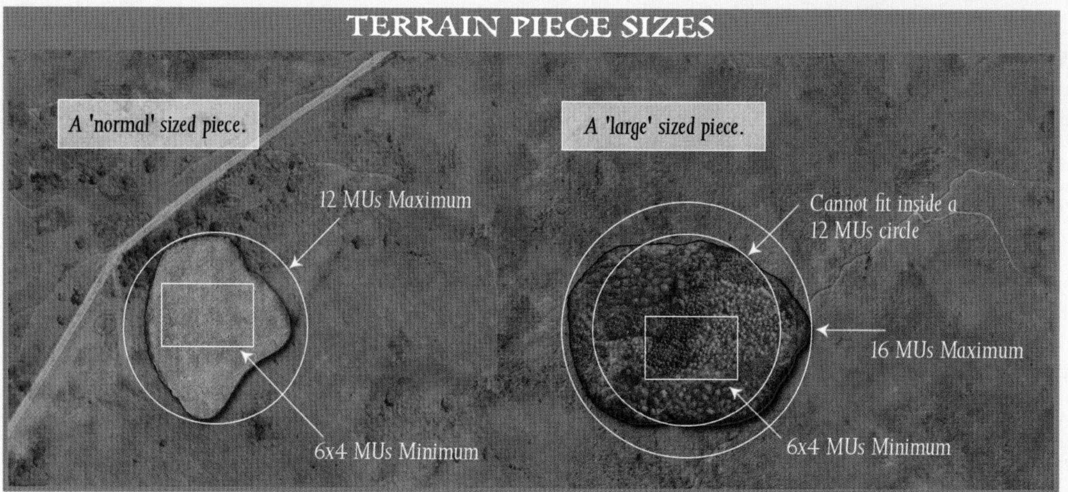

VISIBILITY EFFECTS

Terrain blocks line of sight beyond the visibility distances specified above. In some cases light foot can see out but not be seen. If they shoot, however, they become visible to the battle group shot at, who can then shoot back.

DISORDER EFFECTS

If a battle group's formation could not function well due to its situation (such as in terrain, part way through an interpenetration, or near camelry or elephants) it is DISORDERED or SEVERELY DISORDERED and therefore vulnerable. The terrain causing disorder or severe disorder for various troop types is shown in a table in the General Movement Rules section. The effects are listed in the table below:

- Only bases that are currently at least partly in the situation are affected.
- Bases not in the situation do not suffer penalty, so a long line of spearmen may be disordered at one end and unaffected at the other.
- If any part of a battle group is DISORDERED or SEVERLY DISORDERED, it makes complex move tests (CMT) as if entirely so. If it finds itself in combat, only those bases affected suffer any penalties.
- Lost combat dice for DISORDER or SEVERE DISORDER are **not** cumulative with dice loss for DISRUPTION or FRAGMENTATION. Only one state applies - whichever is worst.
- Heavy Artillery are assumed to be in prepared positions and therefore are not disordered by terrain.

Disorder effects are temporary and recover immediately that the cause is no longer present:

- Terrain effects cause DISORDER or SEVERE DISORDER to some troops. Bases at least partially in the terrain are affected. The effect ceases when they leave it.
- The elephants and camelry effect ceases when they are no longer within the disordering distance.
- The partial interpenetration effect ceases when the battle group moves again and clears the battle group it was passing through.

TERRAIN GRADE	EFFECT
NO EFFECT	
DISORDER	Does not count as STEADY
	-1 on complex move tests.
	Lose 1 dice per 3 for shooting and close combat.
	No cohesion test penalty.
SEVERE DISORDER	Does not count as STEADY
	-2 on complex move tests.
	Lose 1 dice per 2 for shooting and close combat.
	-1 on cohesion tests.

APPENDIX 3: GLOSSARY OF TERMS

<:
Less than.

<=:
Less than or equal to.

>:
Greater than.

>=:
Greater than or equal to.

Active Player:
The player whose turn it currently is.

Advance:
A move listed in the ***Advances*** section of the Simple and Complex Moves table. It must result in at least part of the battle group ending further forward than its original front edge.

Army Rout:
An army suffers an army rout if at the end of the current phase it has suffered Attrition Points equal to or greater than its initial number of battle groups.

Attrition Points:
Attrition points are received for various adverse events. If sufficient attrition points are accumulated, the army routs. See the ***Playing the Game*** section.

1 Base Deep:
Cavalry, camelry or light chariots are considered to be "entirely 1 base deep" for the purpose of evading or being shot at if their battle group is entirely in a single rank of bases. This represents a formation in which smaller troops of cavalry separated by gaps dash around harassing the enemy.

Note that two battle groups each entirely 1 base deep but one behind the other still count as 1 base deep for the purpose of evading or being shot at.

Better Armour:
Heavily armoured is best, then armoured, followed by protected and lastly unprotected.

Chariots, elephants, artillery and battle wagons have no armour class. No enemy counts "better armour" against them, and they don't count "better armour" against any enemy.

Charge Range:
A battle group is in charge range if it can make a

"legal" charge contact (See the **Impact Phase** section) within its normal move distance.

Close Combat:

"Close Combat" is a general term for impact and melee combat. Once such a combat has been joined, battle groups are deemed to be in close combat until one side breaks off, breaks or is destroyed (or a battle group fighting only as an overlap moves away).

Impact and melee phase combat use the close combat mechanisms. An exception is that rear support shooting in the impact phase uses the shooting mechanisms to determine the number of hits.

Cohesion Test:

A test taken to see if adverse events cause a battle group to drop down the Cohesion ladder. See the **Battle Group Deterioration** section.

Column:

A battle group is a column if its formation is entirely 1 base wide. This is the only formation that can be "kinked" – kinking at the point at which its front base wheeled to change direction.

Command Range:

The distance at which commanders can influence troops – i.e. control battle lines and affect complex move tests and cohesion tests. This is:

- Inspired commander (IC): 12 MUs.
- Field commander (FC): 8 MUs.
- Troop commander (TC): 4 MUs.
- Command range is measured from the nearest point on the commander's base.
- A C-in-C or sub-commander can influence any troops except allied troops.
- An ally commander can only influence troops that are part of his own allied contingent.

Complex Move Test (CMT):

A test taken to see if a battle group or battle line can make a complex move as defined in the Simple & Complex Moves Table. See the **General Movement Rules** section.

Cover:

Plantation, forest, village, vineyards, enclosed fields. These give cover to bases wholly within them.

Death Roll:

A test taken to see if hits cause base losses. See the **Battle Group Deterioration** section.

Defending a Riverbank:

For a base to count as defending a river bank in close combat, the following must all apply:

- The entire fighting edge of the base must be facing the river and not in it.
- At least part of the fighting edge of the base must be within 1 MU of the river.
- The enemy front rank base must be at least partly in the river.

1 Dice per x Bases:

"1 dice per x bases" = 1 dice per full x bases, i.e. round dice down.

1 Dice per x:

"Lose 1 dice per x" = Lose 1 dice per full x dice, i.e. round dice up.

Field Fortifications:

Temporary earthworks or other obstacles used to enhance defensive positions. See the **Special Features** section.

Fighting enemy in 2 directions:

A battle group only counts as fighting enemy in 2 directions in melee if it has bases turned at 90 or 180 degrees to each other and it is in melee with different enemy battle groups on different facings. Note that this cannot happen as a consequence of a charge unless it was a legal flank or rear charge.

File:
A single front rank base and all the bases of the same battle group lined up behind it.

HP2B (Hits per 2 bases) & HP3B (Hits per 3 bases):
1 HPxB = 1 hit per x bases in the battle group, except that:

- Elephants and artillery count front rank bases only, but each counts as 2 bases.
- Battle wagons count the bases from one rank or file, whichever is the greater number. Each base counts as 2 bases.
- Other troops count all bases in the front 3 ranks only.
- Commanders' bases do not count.

Line of Command:
The C-in-C and sub-commanders are considered in line of command for all troops in the main army, but not for any allied troops. Ally commanders are not in line of command for troops other than their own contingent.

Movement Units (MU):
All distances are specified in Movement Units (MUs). Each MU is either 25mm or 1 inch, as agreed by the players or decided by tournament organisers.

Non-Skirmishers:

- All troops other than light foot or light horse.
- Mixed battle groups including heavy or medium foot as well as light foot.

Open Terrain:
The whole battle-field apart from areas of uneven, rough, difficult or impassable terrain counts as "open terrain".

POAs and Cohesion Test modifiers only applying "in open terrain" do not count:

- If the base claiming the POA or causing the Cohesion Test modifier even partly enters uneven, rough or difficult terrain.
- If attacking or defending fortifications or a riverbank.

Overlap:
See the ***Manoeuvre Phase*** and ***Melee Phase*** sections.

POA - Points of Advantage:
POAs are combat advantages arising from troop type, armour, combat capabilities and situational factors. Troops often have different POAs in the different phases: Impact Phase, Shooting Phase and Melee Phase. See the *Combat Mechanism* section.

Portable Defences:
See the ***Special Features*** section.

Quality Re-rolls:
The mechanism by which the effect of troop quality is represented. See the ***Battle Groups*** section.

Rear Support:
A battle group can claim rear support if it has steady friendly non-skirmishers of equal or better quality to its rear, but only if all of the following apply:

- The number of such bases at least partly directly to the battle group's rear must be at least half the original total number of bases in the supported battle group.
- The supporting bases must all be within 8 MUs of the rear of the battle group if they are foot, 12 MUs if they are mounted.
- The supported battle group must be at least partly in front of a straight line extending the front edge of the supporting bases.
- There are no enemy troops even partly between the battle group claiming rear support and the bases giving rear support.
- The bases giving rear support are not part of a battle group that is in close combat.

Battle wagons cannot claim rear support.

Restricted Area:
The area ahead of a battle group in which enemy movement is restricted in the manoeuvre phase. A battle group's Restricted Area is the rectangle directly in front of the battle group to a distance of 2 MUs. See the ***Manoeuvre Phase*** section.

Scythed Chariots:
See the ***Special Features*** section.

Shock Troops:
- Any mounted with lancers capability, except light horse
- Heavy chariots
- Scythed chariots
- Foot with impact foot capability
- Foot with offensive spearmen capability
- Foot with pikemen capability.

They do not count as shock troops while Fragmented.

Skirmishers:
- Light foot in battle groups entirely of light foot.
- Light horse.

Supply Camp, Sacking:
See the ***Melee Phase*** section.

Terrain Sizes:
Normal pieces: Each must be so sized and shaped that both of the following apply:
- A 4 x 6 MU rectangle can be fitted entirely within its footprint.
- Its entire footprint can be fitted within a 12 MU diameter circle.

Large pieces: Each must be so sized and shaped that all of the following apply:
- A 4 x 6 MU rectangle can be fitted entirely within its footprint.
- Its footprint cannot be entirely fitted within a 12 MU diameter circle.
- Its entire footprint can be fitted within a 16 MU diameter circle.

Threatened Flank:
A battle group of non-skirmishers has a threatened flank if either of the following apply:
- There are enemy non-skirmishers capable of charging the battle group's flank/rear in their next turn.
- Any part of the battle group is less than 6 MUs from any table edge. It makes no difference which way the battle group is facing.

Uphill:
Unless a hill has clearly defined peaks or ridge crests, it is considered to have a single peak at the most central point of the terrain piece. A base is uphill if it is standing entirely on a hill, and the nearest peak or point on a ridge crest is behind a straight line extending its front edge. If both bases have their front edge touching a peak or ridge crest, or if both would count uphill using the above definition, then neither counts as uphill.

Variable Movement Distance:
See the ***General Movement Rules*** section.

Within:
At or closer than.

Zone of Interception (ZOI):
The zone ahead of a battle group where it can intercept an enemy charge. A battle group's Zone of Interception (ZOI) is the rectangle directly in front of the battle group to a distance of 2 MUs if foot, 4 MUs if mounted troops. In the ZOI battle groups of some troop types have the option of making interception charges. See the ***Impact Phase*** section.

APPENDIX 4: SET UP RULES

The wargame may be an historical re-creation, a scenario or part of a campaign. Various factors will determine the setup for such battles and it is likely that the opposing armies will be unequal. Parts of the following set-up rules covering items already decided can therefore be ignored.

In contrast, for tournaments, typical club or pick up games, players will most likely be on a level footing. This type of game does not take into account events preceding the battle and only requires each player to supply an army (possibly anachronistic) to a fixed total points value. A later appendix describes how to use the information contained in our companion army list books to work out the composition of your army. These books give details of literally hundreds of accurately researched historical armies.

In multi-player games each side has one player designated to carry out the set-up procedure for his side.

ORDER OF MARCH

Prior to set up, players design their armies to a fixed total points value in accordance with the constraints specified in our companion army list books. Each player writes down an "order of

Defending the pilgrims, by Christa Hook © Osprey Publishing Ltd. Taken from Warrior 33: Knight Hospitaller (1) 1100–1306.

A Roman Army deployed

march" listing the army's battle groups in the order in which they will be deployed on table. The army's total initiative modifier, and the number of battle groups in each deployment batch, as described below, must also be noted.

SETTING UP THE GAME

The following sequence of events precedes play:

- Dice for pre-battle initiative.
- Terrain choice and placement.
- Deploy camps, field fortifications and ambush markers.
- Record outflanking marches.
- Deploy battle groups.
- Commit to dismounting.
- Deploy commanders.
- The player who **lost** the initiative roll begins the game as the active player in the first turn.

PRE-BATTLE INITIATIVE

From the dawn of time successful generals have endeavoured to bring the enemy to battle in a place of their choosing, whether as an invader, such as Henry V at Agincourt, or in defence of their own territory, such as the Parthian commander Surena at Carrhae. Often they achieved this through better battlefield intelligence, by employing fast moving mounted troops to scout out their opponents and determine their strengths and weaknesses. This generally gave them the initiative in the forthcoming battle. In *Field of Glory* we reflect this by allowing the general who has gained this initiative to select the overall terrain type, reflecting the likelihood that he will have a greater influence on choosing the battlefield. His opponent also starts deploying first, revealing his initial dispositions, and makes the first move, which to some degree shows his hand. However,

PRE-BATTLE INITIATIVE MODIFIERS	
+2	C-in-C is an inspired commander
+1	C-in-C is a field commander
+1	The army has 10-24 bases of cavalry, light horse, camelry or light chariots, excluding commanders
+2	The army has more than 24 bases of cavalry, light horse, camelry or light chariots, excluding commanders

TIP!

Choosing and positioning terrain is a very important aspect of your pre-battle planning. You want the terrain to favour your army and inconvenience the opposing army: e.g. mounted armies might prefer to fight on the open steppes, whilst armies with an advantage in light or medium foot will look for rough or uneven ground where they will have the advantage.

just as in reality, a good opponent will devise his own tactics to counter these disadvantages.

An army's total initiative modifier is pre-calculated and included in its order of march. At set up each player rolls a d6 and adds its total initiative modifier. If the total scores are equal, roll again. The high scorer has pre-battle initiative.

TERRAIN CHOICE

Each army list in our companion army list books specifies a set of territory types characteristic of those typically found in the army's homeland. The player gaining the initiative chooses a territory type from those available to either army. Terrain is then chosen and placed according to this territory type.

The table below shows the terrain pieces available in each territory type. The maximum number of allowed pieces of each type is shown, followed by the compulsory minimum in brackets. Both players make their terrain selections from the row relating to the territory type chosen by the player with pre-battle initiative.

A **river** or a **coast** counts as 1 piece but 2 selections. A **road** counts as 1 piece and 1 selection.

Other terrain pieces come in 2 sizes:

- Normal piece: A 4 x 6 MU rectangle can be fitted entirely within its footprint. Its entire footprint can be fitted within a 12 MU diameter circle.
- Large piece: A 4 x 6 MU rectangle can be fitted entirely within its footprint. Its footprint cannot be entirely fitted within a 12 MU diameter circle. Its entire footprint can be fitted within a 16 MU diameter circle. A large

TERRAIN SELECTION MAXIMUM(COMPULSORY)

TERRITORY TYPE	Open	Uneven		Rough				Difficult						Impass	Variable		
		OF	BG	B	EF	P	G	F	V	M	SS	SH	Vg	I	GH	Rd	Rv/C
DEVELOPED	2	3			3(1)	2	1		3			1	(1)		2	1	1
AGRICULTURAL	2	4(2)			3	1	1		2			1	1		2	1	1
HILLY			3	3(1)		1	1	2		1		3(1)	1	1	3	1	1
WOODLANDS				2		2	1	4(2)		2		1	1		2	1	1
STEPPES	4(2)		4	2			1								1		
MOUNTAINS				2		1	1	1		1		4(2)	1	2		1	1
TROPICAL				2				4(2)		2		1	1	1	1	1	1
DESERT	2		2	2			1				4(2)	1		1	1	1	

piece counts as 2 selections and as 2 towards the maximum of that type, unless it is one of the two compulsory pieces. Compulsory pieces can be chosen as either size.

A **hill** can be clear or can be wholly or partly covered with one of either **broken ground**, **brush**, **plantation**, **vineyards**, **forest** or a **village**. It counts as the number of selections for its size. The covering does not count as extra selections. However, both the hill and the covering each count towards the maxima (and minima) of their respective types.

Only the player with pre-battle initiative can choose a **river**, a **coastline**, or a **village**. He cannot choose both a **river** and a **coast**.

The player with initiative selects one of the two compulsory pieces, and must choose a **village** if the territory type is Developed. The other player must select the other compulsory piece. A covered hill can be chosen as a compulsory piece only if either of the following apply:

- Hills are compulsory.
- Hills are permitted and the covering is compulsory and of at least normal size.

The player with initiative then makes from 2 to 4 other selections from the list of available terrain. The total pieces of any type, together with any compulsory features of that type, cannot exceed the maximum of that type.

The other player then makes from 2 to 4 other selections from the list of available terrain. He cannot select any pieces that, together with those already chosen by both players, would exceed the maximum of that type.

All terrain selection is made before **any** are placed on the table.

TERRAIN PLACING SEQUENCE

The order in which terrain is placed is as follows:

1. The player with initiative places any **river** or **coast**.
2. The player with initiative places any **village** (including any integral hill).
3. The player with initiative places his **compulsory item**.
4. The other player places his **compulsory item**.
5. The player with initiative places any **open area**(s).
6. The other player places any **open area**(s).
7. The player with initiative places his remaining pieces.
8. The other player places his remaining pieces.
9. **Open area** pieces are removed from the table.

No piece can be placed (prior to adjustment) closer than 4 MUs to any other piece except:

- Any piece can be placed closer than 4 MUs to a coast, river or road.
- A road can be placed closer than 4 MUs to any piece and can pass through a village, but (for aesthetic reasons) not through other terrain pieces.
- A road must pass through or touch a village if there is one.

The use of open areas is to restrict the placing of other terrain.

The whole of the battlefield counts as open, except where terrain pieces are placed.

TERRAIN PLACING DICE ROLLS

The placing player rolls to determine where on the table a piece is to be placed. The other player makes an adjustment roll, which may allow the placement to be amended or negated.

The placement roll:

1 = Touching the long edge – opponent's half.
2 = Touching the long edge – own half.
3 = Touching a side edge or coast – opponent's half.
4 = Touching a side edge or coast – own half.
5 = Anywhere over 8 MUs from edges – opponent's half.
6 = Anywhere over 8 MUs from edges – own half.

The initial placement roll is not required for **rivers, coasts** or **roads**.

The adjustment roll is made after each terrain feature is placed:

0–2 = No change permitted.
3,4 = Can slide the piece up to 6 MUs in any direction.
5 = Can either slide the piece up to 12 MUs in any direction or pivot the piece on one point through any angle.
6+ = Can remove the piece entirely.

Modify the dice roll by:

-1 if the piece is a **compulsory** terrain item
+1 if it is **impassable** or a **river** or **coast**.

Rivers and **coasts** can be removed, but not slid or pivoted.

When a piece "slides" it must maintain its angle of placement relative to the table edges. To pivot, fix any point on the edge of the terrain piece and rotate the piece around this point. A piece cannot be slid or pivoted off table, nor to overlap another terrain piece.

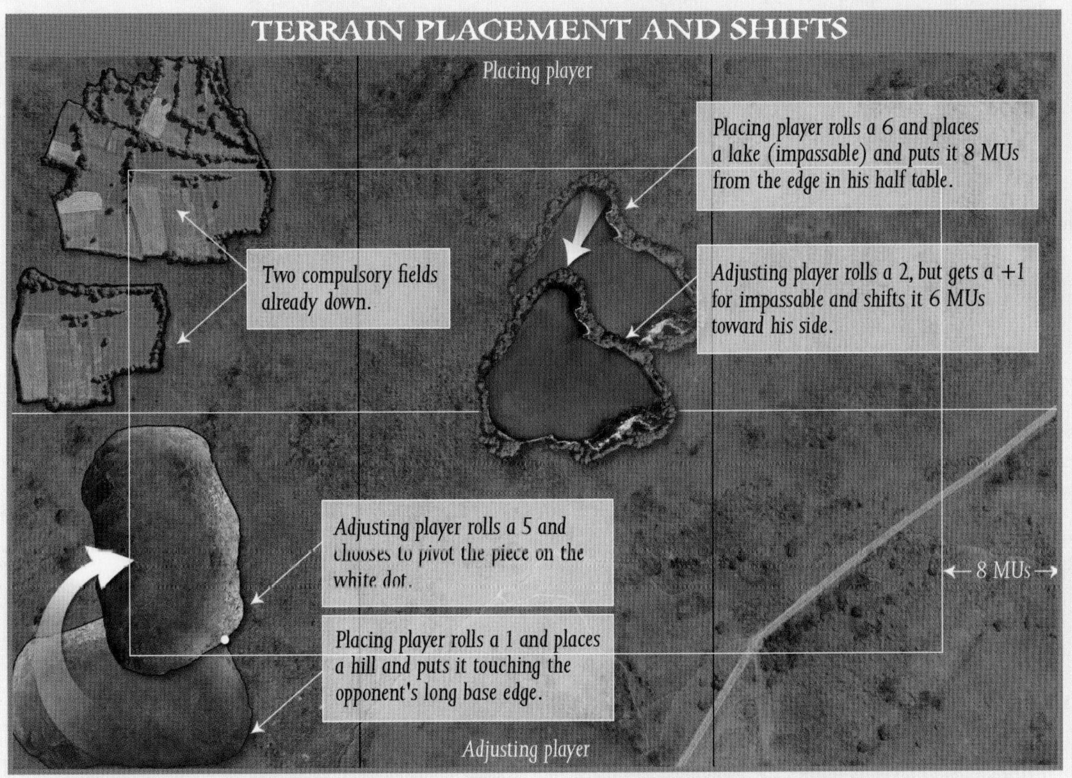

FIELD FORTIFICATIONS, SUPPLY CAMPS AND AMBUSHES

The player without the initiative deploys any field fortifications anywhere up to 10 MUs from his side's rear table edge, or 15 MUs if in the central third of the table's width. He deploys his supply camp anywhere up to 10 MUs from his side's rear table edge, or anywhere completely behind his field fortifications if he has placed any. The supply camp cannot be placed in impassable terrain or a river, nor in a position surrounded on more than two sides by impassable terrain. Finally, he places any ambush markers.

The player with initiative then does the same.

In equal-points games, field fortifications and fortified camps must be paid for with army points – see ***Appendix 5***.

AMBUSHING

The player with pre-battle initiative can place ambushes up to half way across the table from his side's rear table edge, in the two outer thirds of the table's width. The other player can place ambushes up to 18 MUs forward from his side's rear table edge, in the two outer thirds of the table's width.

Ambushes must not be visible from any part of the enemy deployment area for skirmishers (even if the enemy have no skirmishers). Battle groups can only ambush in terrain they could move in.

Ambushes are made by placing "ambush markers" as follows:

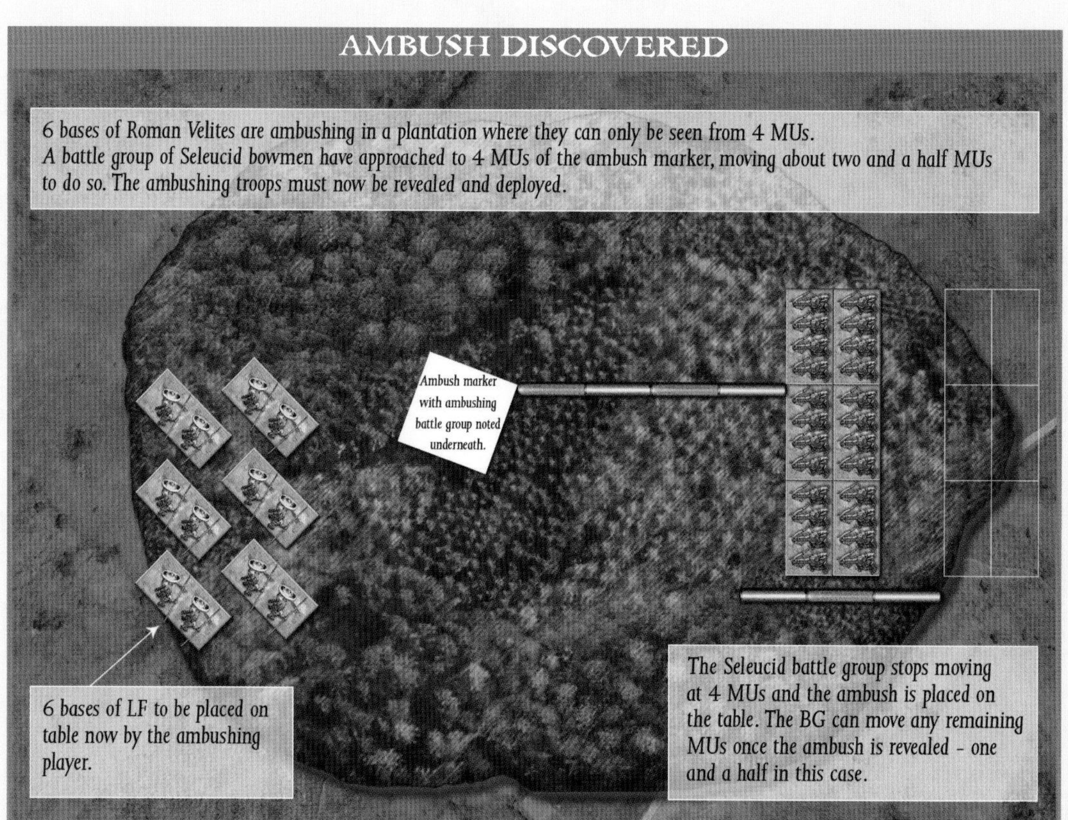

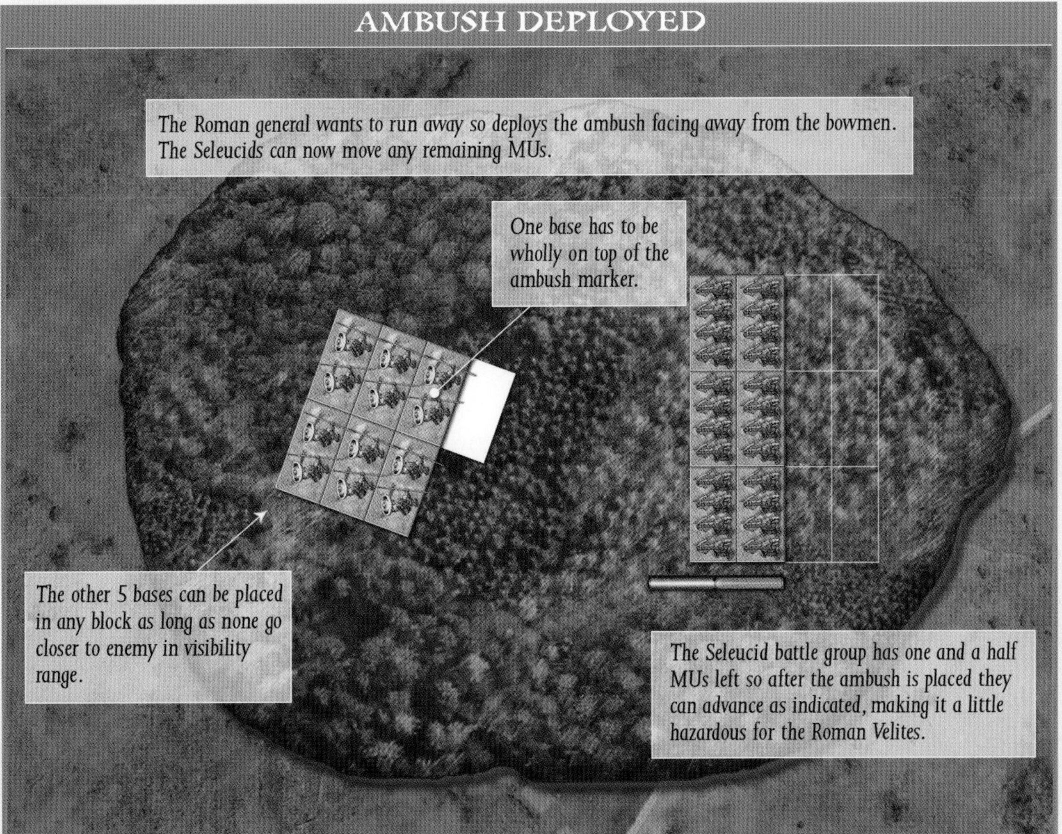

- Each side can place up to 3 ambush markers on the table. An ambush marker is a 40mm square in 15mm scale, 60mm in 25/28 mm scale. The player must clearly identify (by noting on the bottom of the marker) the single battle group from his order of march that this represents, and any commander who is to accompany it. Alternatively the marker can be left blank as a "dummy marker" to confuse the enemy.
- If any enemy come within visibility range of the marker, the ambush (or its non-existence) is immediately revealed.
- When an ambush is revealed, place a base entirely on top of the ambush marker and then deploy the battle group around this base. It can face any of the edges of the ambush marker, and can be in any legal formation. A commander who was ambushing with it must be placed in legal contact with it. No base can be placed closer than the first base to any enemy battle group to which it would be visible. A base that cannot be properly placed for any reason is lost. The enemy can then complete their move, unless it was a second move and they are within 6 MUs of the ambushers.
- Either player can reveal an ambush at any time in his own turn. He need not move the battle group to do so, but must place it on table in the correct position.

OUTFLANKING MARCHES

Many accounts of historical battles describe attempts by one side or the other to gain a tactical advantage by sending a force on a wide outflanking manoeuvre in the hope of catching the enemy by surprise and arriving on their flank at a crucial point in the battle. If successful this could often turn the battle. This tactic is possible in *Field of Glory* and therefore:

- Each army's C-in-C can choose to send up to two off-table outflanking marches, one on each flank. These are noted down before deployment, specifying on which flank they will arrive (relative to his own army).
- Each outflanking march must include a single commander and between 1 and 3 battle groups. The C-in-C cannot flank march.
- An allied commander can only make an outflanking march with troops from his own allied contingent and must take his whole contingent.
- Battle wagons, artillery and scythed chariots cannot be sent on outflanking marches.
- An outflanking march normally arrives anywhere on the specified side table edge (but see below).

The player testing for the arrival of his outflanking marches rolls two dice for each such march at the beginning of each of his turns and consults the table below:

When a flank march successfully dices to arrive:

- The controlling player must immediately declare which flank the outflanking march is on and the number of battle groups it includes.
- Unless both armies have an outflanking march on that flank (see below), the outflanking battle groups and commander arrive in any legal formation in the manoeuvre phase of the controlling player's

OUTFLANKING MARCH ARRIVAL TEST	
Roll two dice for each outflanking march. (No re-rolls).	
Modifier	
+1	If the flank march is led by a field commander
-1	If the outflanking march includes medium or heavy foot
Score	**Result**
9 or less	Roll again next turn.
10 or more	Success – see below

STRAGGLING TEST	
On the turn when the outflanking march should arrive, roll two dice for each battle group to see if it is straggling. Straggling battle groups will not arrive in time for the battle.	
Modifier	
+1	Drilled troops or skirmishers
-1	Medium or heavy foot
A battle group is straggling (and will not arrive) if it scores less than 5. Quality re-rolls apply.	

next turn, anywhere on that flank's side table edge. All battle groups must be in command range of their commander at the end of their first move on to the table.

- The player rolls now for each battle group to see if any are straggling.
- Straggling battle groups are assumed to be delayed sufficiently that they will not arrive in time for the battle. Each straggling battle group counts as 1 attrition point for the purposes of army defeat. If all the battle groups of an outflanking march are straggling, the commander is also assumed to be straggling.
- If both armies have an outflanking march on that flank:
  - The side with more battle groups, excluding those entirely of light foot or light horse, drives the other back.
  - If equal, the side with more battle groups of all types drives the other back.
  - If still equal, both sides are driven back.
  - A driven back flank march arrives in the manoeuvre phase of its side's **next turn** following either side's successful dicing for arrival on that flank. It arrives on the side table edge up to 12 MUs from its army's rear table edge. Each battle group arrives in any legal formation and makes a full double move on to the table perpendicular to the table's side edge, ending its move facing away from that table edge. This counts as its full normal movement for the turn. It does not have to be in command range of its commander.
  - If not themselves driven back, the enemy arrive in the manoeuvre phase of the following turn, using the normal rules for arrival (see above), except that they too must arrive in the same 12 MUs of the side table edge.
  - Both sides are subject to the normal rules for straggling, but this is not tested for until after determining which side is driven back.
- Battle groups within 6 MUs of the point of arrival of enemy flank marchers obey the following rules:
  - Unless already in close combat, artillery and battle wagons are destroyed and removed from the table, their crews having fled and dispersed. (This does not cause friends to take a cohesion test).
  - Supply camps are assumed to have been sacked, even if fortified.
  - Unless already in close combat, other types make an evade move perpendicularly away from the side table edge, even if of a type not normally able to evade. They do so as if evading in the direction of a charge from that direction (see the ***Impact Phase*** section).
- Arriving flank marchers (whether arriving normally or driven back) measure their move from the side table edge. Their first move must be perpendicular to the table edge. Normal restrictions on second moves apply to those arriving normally. Any battle groups that cannot fit onto the table this turn must arrive in their side's next turn or the first turn thereafter when space is available. They have no effect on enemy within 6 MUs.

DEPLOYING BATTLE GROUPS

The total number of battle groups in the army is divided into 4 deployment batches **as evenly as possible**, with larger numbers allocated to the earlier batches (e.g. 8 becomes 2-2-2-2, 9 becomes

3-2-2-2 and 15 becomes 4-4-4-3). The size of these batches is noted in the order of march.

All battle groups except those in ambush or on an outflanking march are deployed in the order listed in the order of march. The number of battle groups to be deployed in each batch is pre-determined as above. Battle groups in ambush or on an outflanking march are omitted, and the next battle groups in the order of march must be deployed instead. Thus the correct number of battle groups must be deployed in each batch, until all visible on-table battle groups have been deployed. As a result, there may be no battle groups left to deploy in the last batch.

Other than when in ambush, skirmishers can be deployed anywhere up to 15 MUs forward from their side's rear table edge and other battle groups anywhere up to 10 MUs from the side's rear table edge, or anywhere completely behind their own field fortifications (if any). Exceptions: No troops can be deployed in impassable terrain or a river. Heavy artillery cannot be deployed in difficult terrain. Other troops cannot be deployed in terrain in which they have no movement allowance.

The deployment sequence is as follows:

- The player **without** pre-battle initiative deploys his first batch of battle groups.
- The player with initiative then deploys his first batch of battle groups.
- The players continue alternately deploying their second, third and fourth batches.

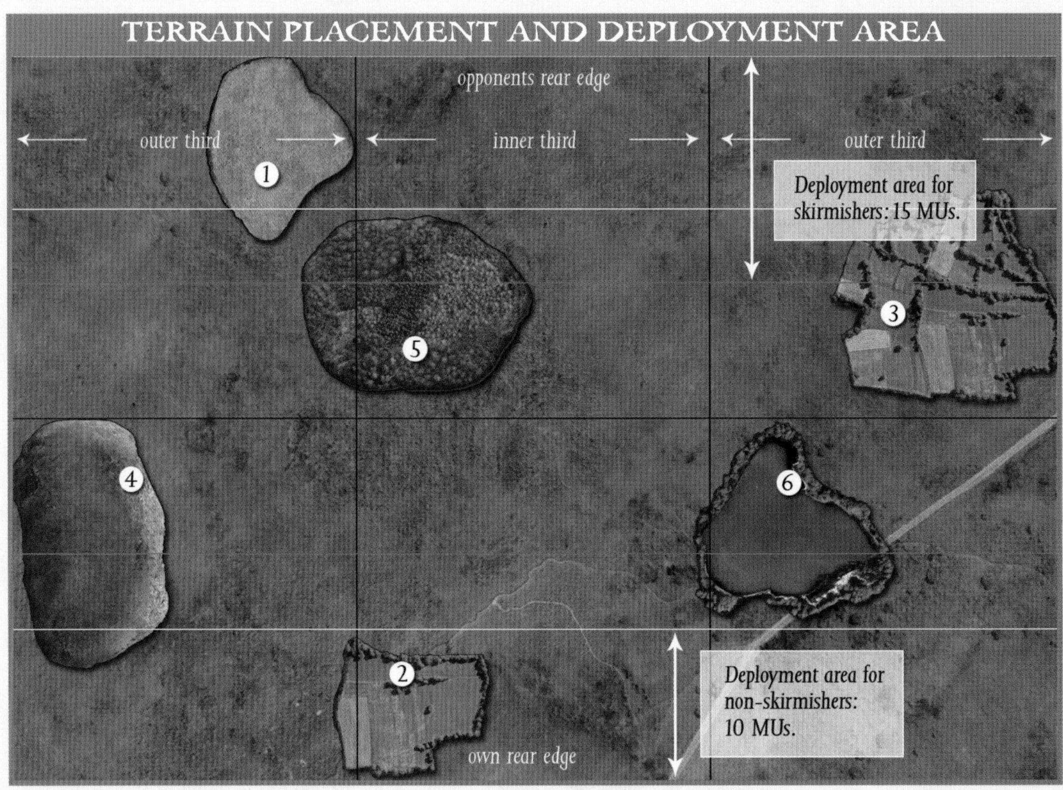

The troop types of all battle groups must be fully defined to your opponent as they are placed on the table.

DEPLOYING MOUNTED TROOPS DISMOUNTED

Mounted battle groups are only allowed to dismount if any of the following apply:

- Their list in our companion army list books indicates that they are permitted to dismount.
- The enemy have placed field fortifications (not portable defences).
- The enemy have deployed battle wagons.

A battle group of mounted troops can only dismount at the following times:

- When it is first deployed on the table.
- Immediately after all non-ambushing on-table battle groups have been deployed by both sides. The player without initiative decides first.
- When its ambush is revealed. (But only if it was noted as dismounted on the ambush marker).

Unless otherwise specified in our companion army list books, each base dismounts as its nearest foot equivalent:

- The dismounted troop-type is as listed in the table below.
- Dismounted charioteers are treated as protected. Other dismounted troops have the same armour class as when mounted.
- The dismounted weapon capabilities are the same as when mounted (except that lancers are treated as offensive spearmen). Mounted bows have the range of foot bows when dismounted.

DEPLOYING COMMANDERS

Commanders, except those in ambush or on an outflanking march, are positioned after both armies have deployed all visible on table battle groups. The player without initiative deploys his commanders first. Commanders can be deployed anywhere up to 15 MUs forward from their side's rear table edge.

TROOP TYPE	REF	DESCRIPTION
Knights	Kn	Dismount as heavy foot
Cataphracts	Ct	Dismount as heavy foot
Cavalry	Cv	Dismount as medium foot
Light horse	LH	Dismount as light foot
Camelry	Cm	Dismount as medium foot
Heavy chariots	HCh	Dismount as protected medium foot
Light chariots	LCh	Dismount as protected medium foot
Scythed chariots	SCh	Cannot dismount
Elephants	El	Cannot dismount

Chinese Emperor in his battle chariot reviews his troops

APPENDIX 5: ARMY COMPOSITION AND THE POINTS SYSTEM

In historical re-fights or campaign battles, the armies are determined by actual battle accounts or by the campaign scenario. However, for one-off battles that provide a reasonable opportunity for either player to win, a points system can be very useful. To achieve balance, the more effective the troops, the more each base costs in points. The recommended total points value for a singles game of about 2 to 4 hours is between 600 and 800 points. We suggest 800 points for 15mm singles tournament games and 650 points for 25/28mm.

Each base has a basic cost determined by its type, armour and quality. There is an addition if it is composed of drilled troops other than light foot or light horse. This is the left hand side of the table. The right hand side details the extra costs to be added for combat capabilities.

To calculate the cost of your battle groups, take the basic cost from the table, add the additional cost for drill and combat capabilities, then multiply the total by the number of bases in the battle group. An easier way is simply to look up the cost of each base in our companion army list books.

Points costs for portable defences and field fortifications are per base frontage. See the **Special Features** section for the restrictions on bases using portable defences.

POINTS VALUES	BASIC COST				
Commanders (-10 pts if ally)	80 (IC)	50 (FC)	35 (TC)		**Extra if Drilled unless LF or LH**
Quality	**Elite**	**Superior**	**Average**	**Poor**	
Foot BGs					
Heavily Armoured	15	12	9		2
Armoured	13	10	7	5	1
Protected	9	7	5	3	1
Unprotected	6	5	4	2	1
Artillery - Heavy			20		-
Artillery - Light			15		2
Battle wagons			14	8	na
Battle wagons with light artillery			20	14	na
Mounted BGs					
Knights - Heavily Armoured	24	20	15		3
Knights - Armoured	20	17	13		2
Cataphracts	18	15	11	8	2
LH, Cv or Cm - Armoured	16	13	9	6	1
LH, Cv or Cm - Protected	11	9	6	4	1
LH, Cv or Cm - Unprotected	9	7	5	3	1
Heavy Chariots	20	17	13		2
Light Chariots	17	14	10		1
Scythed Chariots	-	-	15		na
Elephants			25		na
Specials					
Fortified Camp				24	na

COST OF COMBAT CAPABILITIES	
Foot (Multiply cost by 3 for battle wagons)	
Swordsmen	1
Skilled swordsmen	2
Offensive Spearmen	2
Defensive Spearmen	1
Impact foot	1
Heavy Weapon	2
Longbow	2
Bow, Bow* or Crossbow	1
All other weapons	0
Mounted	
Swordsmen	2
Lancers	1
Light Spear	1
Bow	3
Bow* or Crossbow	2
Javelins or Firearm	1
Camelry	+2
Defences – per base frontage	
Portable Defences	3
Field Fortifications	3

The cost of a commander is reduced by ten points if he is the commander of an allied contingent.

Supply camps are compulsory but cost no points unless fortified. They are not battle groups.

When choosing an army it is recommended that players reference one or more of the companion army list books published to accompany these rules. A few opening lines from an example army list are shown overleaf.:

The list fully describes the bases available to the army by type, armour, quality, training, and combat capabilities. The list also states how many bases are allowed in each battle group and how many bases there should and can be in the army.

COMMANDERS

Each army must have a commander-in-chief and 1 to 3 subordinate or allied commanders. Allied commanders are only available if specified by the army lists, either from the same or more commonly from other lists. An allied commander can only affect battle groups of his own contingent and these can only be affected by him.

LATER CARTHAGINIAN										
Territory Types: Agricultural, Developed										
C-in-C	Inspired Commander/Field Commander/Troop Commander						80/50/35	1		
Sub-commanders	Field Commander						50	0-2		
	Troop Commander						35	0-3		
Troop name	**Troop Type**				**Capabilities**		**Points per base**	**Bases per BG**	**Total bases**	
	Type	Armour	Quality	Training	Shooting	Close Combat				
Core Troops										
Gallic or Spanish cavalry	Cavalry	Armoured	Superior	Undrilled	-	Light Spear, Swordsmen	16	4	0-4	4-12
	Cavalry	Protected	Superior	Undrilled	-	Light Spear, Swordsmen	12	4-6	0-12	
Numidian or Spanish light cavalry	Light Horse	Unprotected	Average	Undrilled	Javelins	Light Spear	7	4-6	6-12	

EXAMPLE

The Numidian or Spanish light cavalry on the last line cost a basic 5 points. Adding 1 for javelins capability and 1 for light spear capability makes a total of 7 points per base. They must be in battle groups of 4 or 6 costing 28 or 42 points respectively. Any combination of battle groups of 4 and 6 can be chosen, but the army must have between 6 and 12 bases in total of Numidian and Spanish light cavalry.

BATTLE GROUP COMPOSITION

All troops are organized into battle groups. Battle groups must comply with the following restrictions:

- If using our companion army list books the number of bases in a battle group must correspond to the range specified in the list.
- Each battle group must initially comprise an even number of bases. The only exception to this rule is that battle groups whose army list specifies them as ⅔ of one type and ⅓ of another, can comprise 9 bases if this is within the battle group size range specified by the list.
- If using our army lists, a battle group can only include troops from one line in a list, unless the list specifies a mixed formation by indicating fractions of the battle group to be of types from two lines. e.g. ⅔ spearmen, ⅓ archers.
- All troops in a battle group must be of the same quality and training. When a choice of quality or training is given in a list, this allows battle groups to differ from each other. It does not permit variety within a battle group.
- Unless specifically stated otherwise in an army list, all troops in a battle group must be of the same armour class. When a choice of armour class is given in a list, this allows battle groups to differ from each other. It does not permit variety within a battle group.
- Elephants and artillery can only be in battle groups of 2 bases each.

APPENDIX 6: CHOOSING, PAINTING AND USING YOUR ARMY

How do you choose your army? The best answer is to pick an army that interests you as you will find it much easier to research and paint. The complete set of companion army list books that accompany *Field of Glory* contain over 250 different armies. They all have their own strengths and weaknesses so which you choose is largely a matter of personal preference.

If your preference is to fight against historical opponents, you will find that the armies in our companion army list books are designed to give relatively balanced battles, allowing a reasonable chance of victory for most armies. If your group of friends prefer to fight only within historical and geographical sub-periods, you will be well advised to choose from armies that fought against several of your available opponents. In most sub-periods this should still allow you plenty of choice.

If you intend to fight non-historical opponents in tournaments, beware that in anachronistic battles some armies can have an Achilles' heel which might make them a risky bet. Only through experience and trial and error will you be able to spot this.

TIP!

Beware of selecting an army that contains predominately one troop type. This can lead to a one dimensional battle plan that is easy to predict and therefore counter.

Knights prepare for battle

The most important thing is to choose an army that interests you and suits your preferred style of play. In *Field of Glory* you have almost limitless choice. If you like to have maximal control, you should choose well drilled troops. If you enjoy defeating the enemy by sheer ferocity and weight of numbers, and consider manoeuvre effete, you might want to try an army of undrilled shock troops. If it amuses you to run rings around the enemy and shoot him to death, you could try a horse archer army with plenty of mobility. You might even fancy trying out some of the more exotic armies packed with elephants, camels, scythed chariots, naphtha bombers or battle wagons. The choice is yours.

Another important factor when considering how to get started is the potential to use some troops in a variety of different armies; e.g. light foot and other support troops were often armed and equipped similarly and it is therefore possible to use them in a wide selection of armies, especially if they are from the same region. Hoplites are another good example as they can be used in many Classical armies.

Pooling these sorts of troop types will give you much greater flexibility when building your collection and also provides an easy way of trying out new armies before you splash out and buy them. However, you have to be careful not to overdo this as can easily be demonstrated by looking at the Romans.

At first glance, Roman armies may appear to vary little, but in fact their appearance and equipment changed substantially over time, so you will need to decide which period the army you are collecting is from, from the very start, although even here an element of flexibility is possible; e.g, Late Roman legionaries can be used in a Dominate or Foederate Roman, or Early Byzantine army without raising any eyebrows.

Roman legions' last stand.

Carthaginian Cavalry

Even in the later periods there is still opportunity for "morphing" Knights and much of the infantry from the same approximate period in Western European medieval armies are particularly interchangeable in this way. From the above, it can be seen that a little research can pay big dividends.

The flip side to interchangeability is that there is no finer sight on the wargames table than an accurately presented and painted army. You will undoubtedly identify with your army more closely if all the figures are correct and you have researched the shield patterns, flags and commanders' names. To field the army of one of history's great generals such as Alexander the Great, Hannibal, Alexius Comnenus or Vlad the Impaler (Dracula) certainly gives a boost to a player's morale. It can also save you from endless alchemical attempts to produce an invincible army by juggling the army lists instead of by perfecting your tactical skills.

Before buying, think about the weaknesses that the army may have in terms of a lack of terrain capable troops or other disadvantages against likely opponents. An army of all mounted troops might look good on paper, and will be effective on an open table, but may find things much more difficult if fighting in heavy terrain. Some armies are one dimensional, others are more balanced, your choice is almost infinite.

Eventually, having chosen which army you intend to field, think about its strengths and weaknesses and try to design an order of battle that will maximise your strengths. Most armies have a set of core troops that will to a large extent dictate your battlefield tactics and fighting doctrine. Structure your army in such a way that the battle groups will support each other. Try to imagine how the army will look when it is deployed. If your plan is to swarm the wings don't put all your troops in large unmanoeuvrable battle groups, but if you intend a heavy frontal slog the size and resilience of larger battle groups might be useful.

Finally, make sure you have enough commanders of the right type to suit your style of play. Remember that commanders can be used to control the troops or they can also be used to lead a head-on charge to victory. Again, the choice is yours!

TACTICAL ADVICE FOR BEGINNERS

The most important lesson that a beginner has to learn is that he should have a plan. Almost any plan is better than no plan at all. A good plan, however, is the first step to victory. It should take into account the layout of the battlefield, the relative strengths and weaknesses of the opposing forces and the enemy's likely actions. If you misjudge, you will find it difficult to change your plan or redeploy, so best get it right first time if possible.

Ask yourself how your army differs from that of the enemy. Who has the best close combat infantry? If it's you, plan your attack around them, but if it's the enemy, you will need to avoid or delay contact with them. Who has the best rough/difficult terrain infantry? If you do, you can use terrain to secure your flanks and create outflanking opportunities. However if it's the enemy, you should plan to avoid such terrain. Who has the best cavalry? If you do, you may be able to carry out sweeping manoeuvres on his flanks but if he does, or if his army greatly outnumbers yours, you will need to avoid being outflanked yourself.

Does the enemy have any troops that are certain to give you problems, have you enough skirmishers to delay their advance? Does the enemy have shock troops? Can you break them up or draw them out of formation before the decisive impact? Screen your own shock troops from the enemy, for you can be sure he will be trying to do the same to you.

It is not always necessary to attack immediately, but if you adopt a defensive position, don't rely on your opponent attacking where you want him to. Few opponents will co-operate by making a suicidal attack on an impregnable position. If you adopt a rigid defence, a clever opponent

The Saxon host defend Senlac Ridge at the battle of Hastings.

Carthaginian elephants support the front line.

will concentrate his main attack on your weakest point while demonstrating against the rest of your battle line to keep it occupied. He may concentrate shooting on part of your line until its cohesion fragments before charging your demoralised troops. A defensive stance followed by a pre-planned counter-attack can be more effective.

It is often effective to attack on one wing while skirmishing or defending on the other. Obviously the attacking wing should contain heavy troops and the refused wing should contain troops capable of skirmishing or be in a secure defensive position. If your refused wing looks as if it is in danger, do not be tempted to siphon off troops from your attacking wing to bolster it. All this is likely to do is ensure that your main attack peters out. If you are playing in a larger game with several players on each side, make sure that you give control of the refused wing to a defensively minded player. Some players are unable to restrain themselves from attacking whatever the situation, often with disastrous results. Similarly, avoid giving command of your attacking wing to an over-cautious player.

You should try to keep your plan and your deployment as simple as possible, with most of your troops deployed in battle lines under the control of your commanders. This will allow you to make double moves in the early part of the game and prevent the majority of your troops from being overlapped or attacked in flank. You should avoid leaving gaps in your line, unless you have supporting battle groups to protect your flanks.

If you plan a wide, on-table, outflanking move, this should be led by a commander. Or you might try an off-table outflanking march, as these can be very effective. The danger is that it may arrive too late or never at all. Ambushes can also be effective, but do not be tempted to ambush in every piece of terrain just because you can. Such stratagems should be part of your overall plan.

Troops held back behind the front line can give rear support to the front line troops and can act as reserves to plug a hole or exploit an opportunity. The Byzantines reckoned to have ⅔ of their troops in the front line and ⅓ in a second line. A central reserve of good quality mobile troops can be used to achieve a crucial advantage at the point of decision if employed in the right place at the right time.

An army with a second line as reserves will obviously occupy less frontage than an army deployed in less depth, creating a risk that you might be outflanked. However, terrain can be used to secure flanks, and failing this your flank reserves should be suitably positioned to counter any enemy outflanking manoeuvre. This flexibility and ability to deal with all eventualities can be contrasted with the rigidity of the army deployed on too wide a front, which has no counter to an enemy breakthrough and will find it difficult to compensate for any deficiencies in its original plan.

Roman ballista prepare to unleash hell before the cataphracts attack.

One possible exception to the above general rule might be armies largely consisting of horse archers, who cannot expect to win a frontal contest and must therefore attempt to outflank the enemy on one or both flanks. They may still benefit from keeping a strong reserve and even if this leave gaps in their line, the enemy will find it difficult to exploit this without breaking up their own formation, which in turn may present opportunities for the horse archers to concentrate their shooting or to attack flanks.

A good tactic to delay the enemy is to rush forward with your skirmishers (light horse or light foot) to obstruct his path and prevent him making second moves. They can then fall back slowly in front of the enemy, evading if charged. Remember, however, that light foot are vulnerable to mounted troops in the open and may not be able to evade far enough to get away. They may be better able to delay the enemy if deployed in ambush in terrain ready to spring out at the appropriate moment.

Flank attacks, especially by non-skirmishers, can be overwhelming, so you must avoid enemy getting behind the flanks of your battle groups. Conversely, if you can manage to outflank the enemy the battle should be all but won.

A commander fighting in the front rank of a battle group will greatly improve the odds in close combat, but there is a risk of losing the commander. On balance, the benefit usually outweighs the risk if the combat is otherwise at least equal, or if the result of the combat is critical. However, once committed, the commander cannot be used to rally other troops or influence their cohesion tests or complex move tests until the close combat is over. You pay your money and you take your chance!

King Arthur and his warriors defend the pass

PAINTING MINIATURES FOR THE BEGINNER

by Joseph A. McCullough

"**Any** paint job is better than **no** paint job."
wargamer axiom

As a professional painter, I would love to say that painting miniatures takes huge amounts of talent and years of practice, but in fact, neither statement is true. With just a little patience and a few tips on the basics, anyone can paint good-looking miniatures. The following guide serves as a brief introduction to the five important steps between taking your miniature out of the package and getting it onto the wargaming table.

CLEANING

Before you begin painting, carefully examine your miniature for "flash" and "mould lines." Flash are little bits of excess metal left over from the casting process. Most of the time, they can be easily trimmed off with a sharp modelling knife. Mould lines are raised ridges created by a slightly imperfect fit of the two halves of the mould. Take a small metal file and lightly file them away. At this point, it is probably a good idea to wash your miniature, making sure it is completely dry before moving on to priming.

PRIMING

Normal paint does not like to stick to metal. If you do paint directly onto a metal figure you will soon find the paint flaking off. Because of this, it is necessary to prime your miniature. Primer usually comes in aerosol cans and can be purchased at any game or model shop. Most figure painters use black or white primer, but beginners will probably want to use black as it helps to hide mistakes.

To prime, stick the figure on a temporary base with either blue-tack or a bit of PVC glue. Hold

Cleaning

Priming

Painting

the can of primer about a foot away from your miniature. Using quick spurts, lightly coat the miniature on every side. Be careful not to apply too much, or the primer will clump and the figure will lose detail. It is likely that the primer will not get into every little crevice on the figure. That's fine. After the primer dries, you can touch up the missed areas with a bit of watered-down black paint applied with a paintbrush.

PAINTING

Now that your figure is primed, you are ready to begin painting. These days, almost everyone uses acrylic paints as they dry in seconds and can be cleaned with water. *Foundry*, *Games Workshop*, *Vallejo*, and *Reaper Miniatures* all put out nice sets of acrylic paints designed especially for miniatures. Some craft paints also work well. Paintbrushes can be bought at any art store. Just get some cheap ones to start. Once you've decided which brush sizes suit your painting style, you can go back and get the expensive ones.

At this point, painting a miniature can be as simple as applying the appropriate colour to each section of the figure. However, there are three simple techniques that can really add definition to your figures. The first of these is called dry-brushing and is especially useful for painting metal items such as armour and swords. To use dry-brushing, dip your brush into the appropriate colour, then wipe off most of the paint on a bit of newspaper. When the paint stops making marks on the newspaper, lightly brush over the area you want to paint. The paint will cling only to the raised areas of the miniature giving a nice shading effect. The results of this technique are most easily viewed on the chain mail on the Roman Auxiliary, but I also used it for the helmet and spearhead.

A second technique that can help bring your figures to life is layering. Layering involves painting an area in a dark base colour and then painting over it with lighter shades of the same colour. These lighters shades can be created by adding a bit of white paint to the base colour. The key to this technique is to leave the original base colour showing in the recesses and around the edges to create areas of shadow. In theory, you

can use as many layers as you want, each one a little lighter and covering just a little less area than the previous shade. Most painters these days use three layers, the final layer, often called a "highlight" being only applied to the most raised edges of a figure. I have used two layers on the flesh areas, the blue tunic, and the moustache of the Roman Auxiliary.

The final technique that you might want to use is called inking. For this you can buy special inks or just used slightly watered-down paint. To ink a figure, paint the chosen area your preferred colour, then paint the ink into the recesses. This is the quickest way to achieve shading. It is also the messiest. Be careful how much ink you put on your brush as too much will run all over your figure. I used inking on the beard of the Viking holding the axe.

As you paint your first few figures, don't worry too much about staying perfectly within the lines. One of the great advantages of painting figures for the wargaming table is that the detail on individual figures is much less important than the look of a unit as a whole.

SEALING

After you have completed painting your figure, you should seal it. This will help keep the paint from rubbing off your figures as they are handled. Sealer (or varnish) comes in cans just like primer and should be available at all the same places. It comes in two varieties, matt and gloss. Matt gives a more drab, realistic finish. Gloss gives the figures a shiny look. Pick whichever suits your taste. To seal the figures, hold the can at least a foot away and spray with gentle spurts. It is better to let the sealer float down onto the figure than to spray it directly on. Warning – if you spray sealer onto the figure at very short range, you are likely to melt the paint off the miniature.

BASING

The last step in painting your miniatures is basing. The size of base you need depends on the game you are playing and the type of figure you are a painting (see Appendix 1 for the appropriate bases sizes in *Field of Glory*). Numerous bases are available commercially, or bases can be constructed out of balsa wood or plastic card. Glue

Sealing

Basing

your figure to the base using superglue, then paint the base in a neutral ground colour appropriate for your figure, usually green or brown.

Although you could leave the base here, most people like to add some kind of basing material, either tiny rocks, flocking, or a combination of both. Flocking is the name for the finely ground fake grass often used for model railroads. Basing material is applied by spreading a thin layer of PVC glue over the base and then dipping the base in the sand or flocking.

Once the base is dry, your figures are ready to go!

FACES

The hardest part of any miniature to paint is the face. However, when painting a figure as part of a unit, it is not worth worrying too much about the detail. Paint the face as you would the rest of the flesh, using a couple of layers or maybe some light inking. If you are feeling bold, you can try to paint a white slit with a black dot. Otherwise, just go with a black dot or even just dark eye sockets. At a distance of more than a foot or so, no-one one is going to be able to tell.

CONTRAST

Although historical figures are usually painted to mimic historic uniform colours, and Osprey books are a perfect reference for this, it is worth giving a quick thought to the use of contrast. Because they are small, it is often hard to distinguish details on miniatures. By using contrasting colours next to each other, it brings out the detail, and creates a more visually appealing figure.

Take a look at the Medieval Swiss Command Unit. The central figure uses a dark purple next to black, which causes the two colours to slightly blend together and obscures the detail. The figures to either side demonstrate the benefits of contrast.

(All miniatures supplied by Foundry. Joseph A. McCullough has been painting miniatures for twenty odd years, the last ten professionally. You can view more of his work at his website www.josephamccullough.com)

Inking

Contrast

APPENDIX 7: EXAMPLES OF UNUSUAL SITUATIONS

The rules already cover what to do in different situations but for ease of reference we include here diagrams and descriptions for a number of reasonably common and apparently complicated situations. You will also find explanations and details, along with scoring ideas for competition organisers and much more at www.fieldofglory.com.

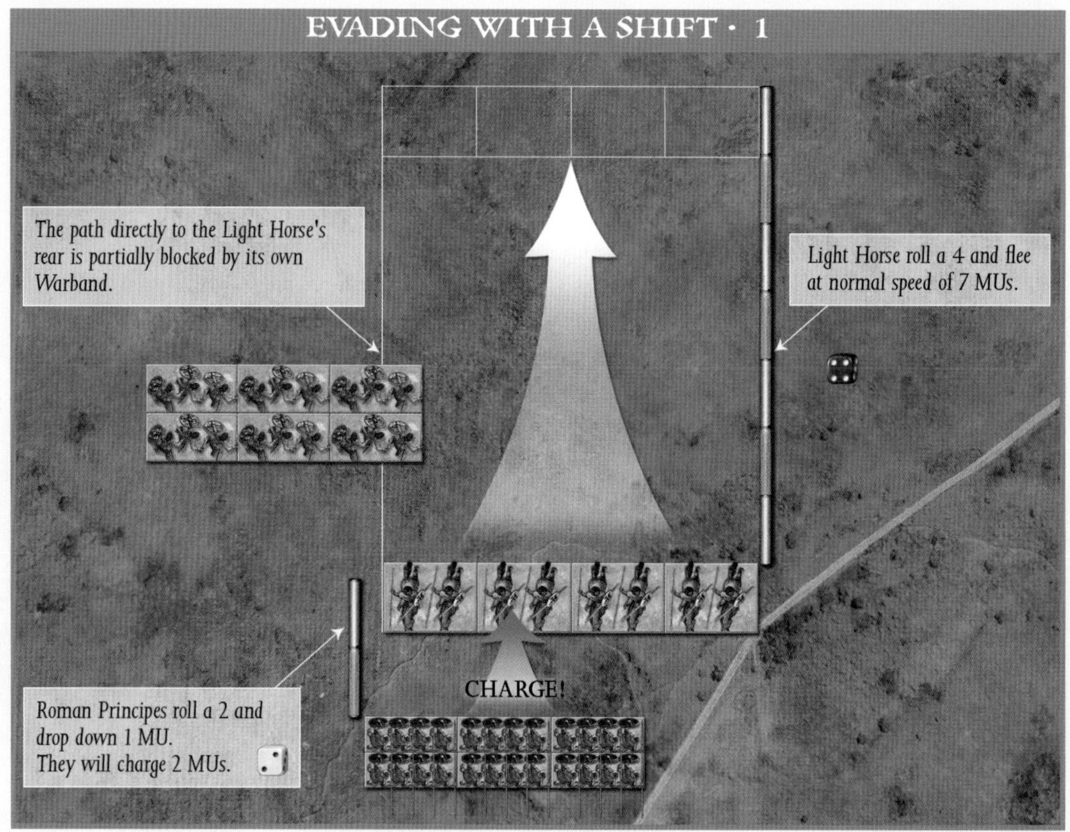

EVADING WITH A SHIFT · 2

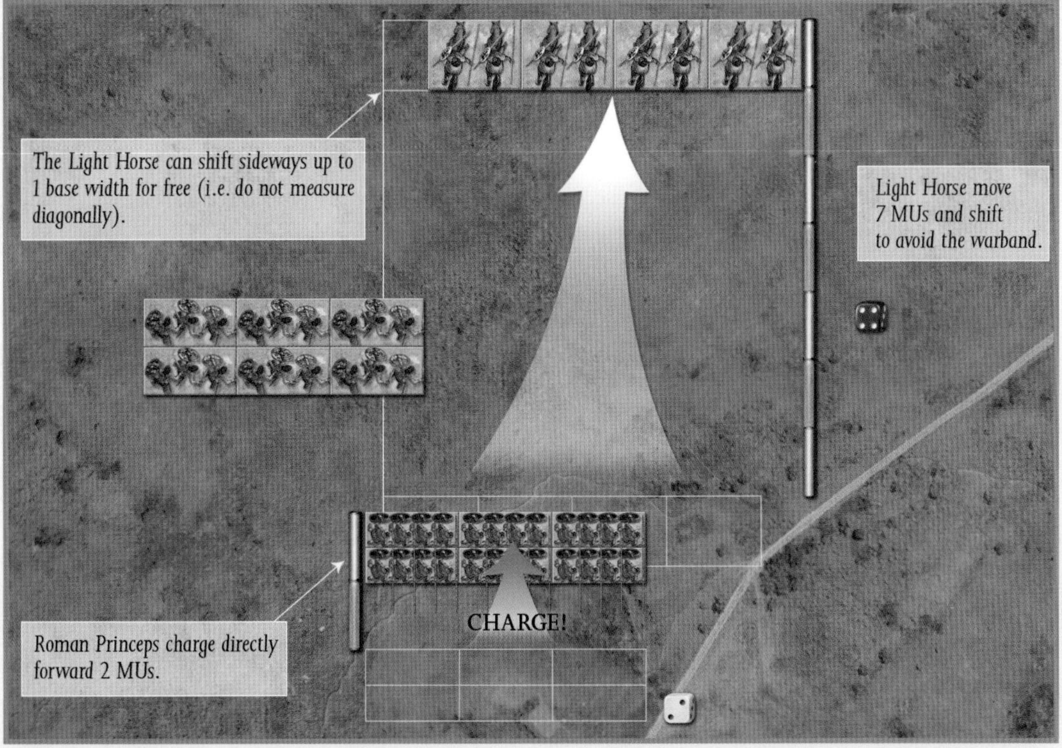

The Light Horse can shift sideways up to 1 base width for free (i.e. do not measure diagonally).
Light Horse move 7 MUs and shift to avoid the warband.
CHARGE!
Roman Princeps charge directly forward 2 MUs.

BURSTING THROUGH WHEN EVADING · 1

The Numidians roll first and get a 1 - they have to evade through the friendly Gallic Warband Battle Groups.
The Numidian Light Horse here have nowhere to go since they can only slide one base width, which isn't enough to clear either Warband Battle Group.
CHARGE!
Roman Princeps roll a 5 and will thunder forwards 4 MUs hitting anything in the way.

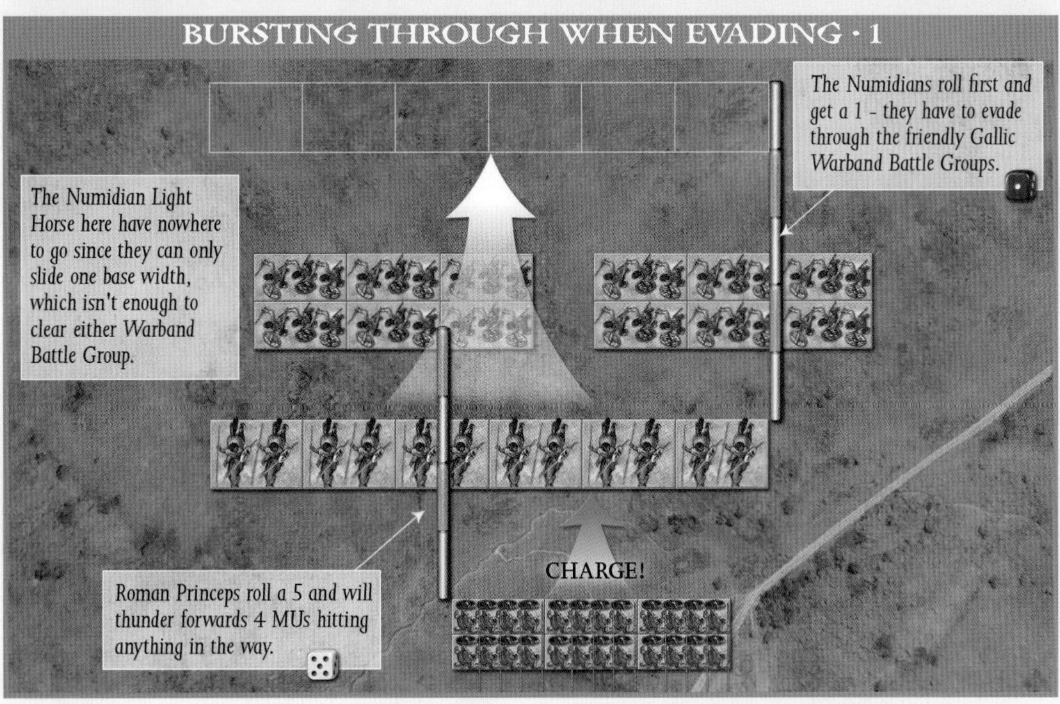

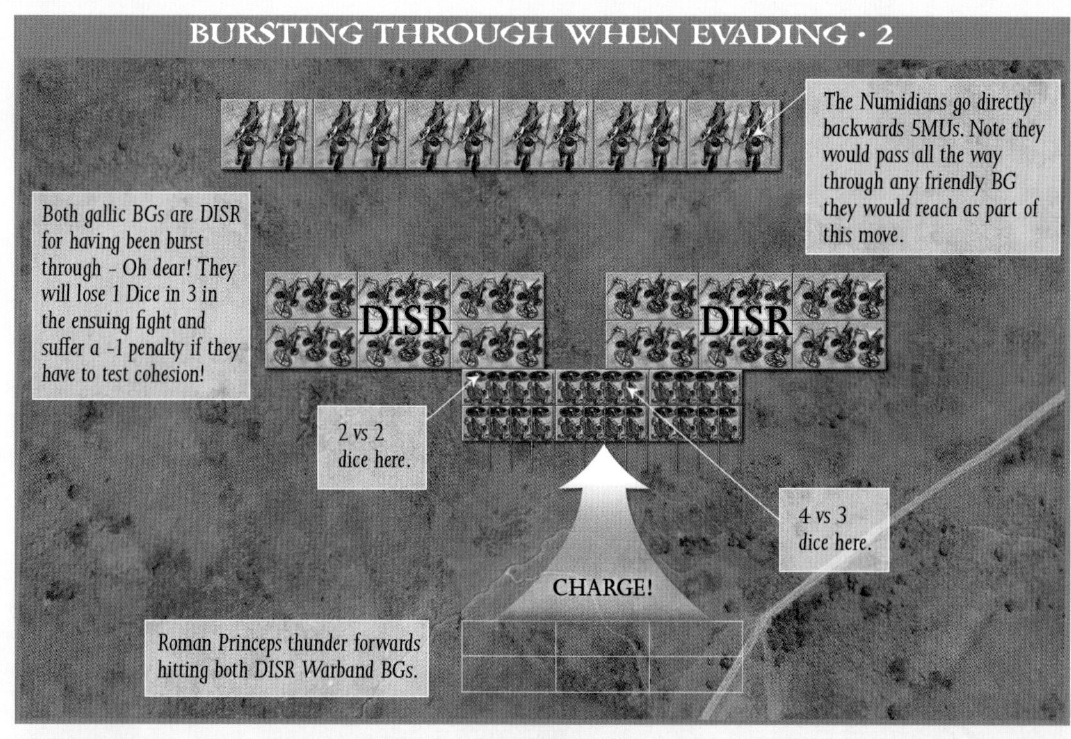
BURSTING THROUGH WHEN EVADING • 2
The Numidians go directly backwards 5MUs. Note they would pass all the way through any friendly BG they would reach as part of this move.
Both gallic BGs are DISR for having been burst through - Oh dear! They will lose 1 Dice in 3 in the ensuing fight and suffer a -1 penalty if they have to test cohesion!
DISR
DISR
2 vs 2 dice here.
4 vs 3 dice here.
CHARGE!
Roman Princeps thunder forwards hitting both DISR Warband BGs.

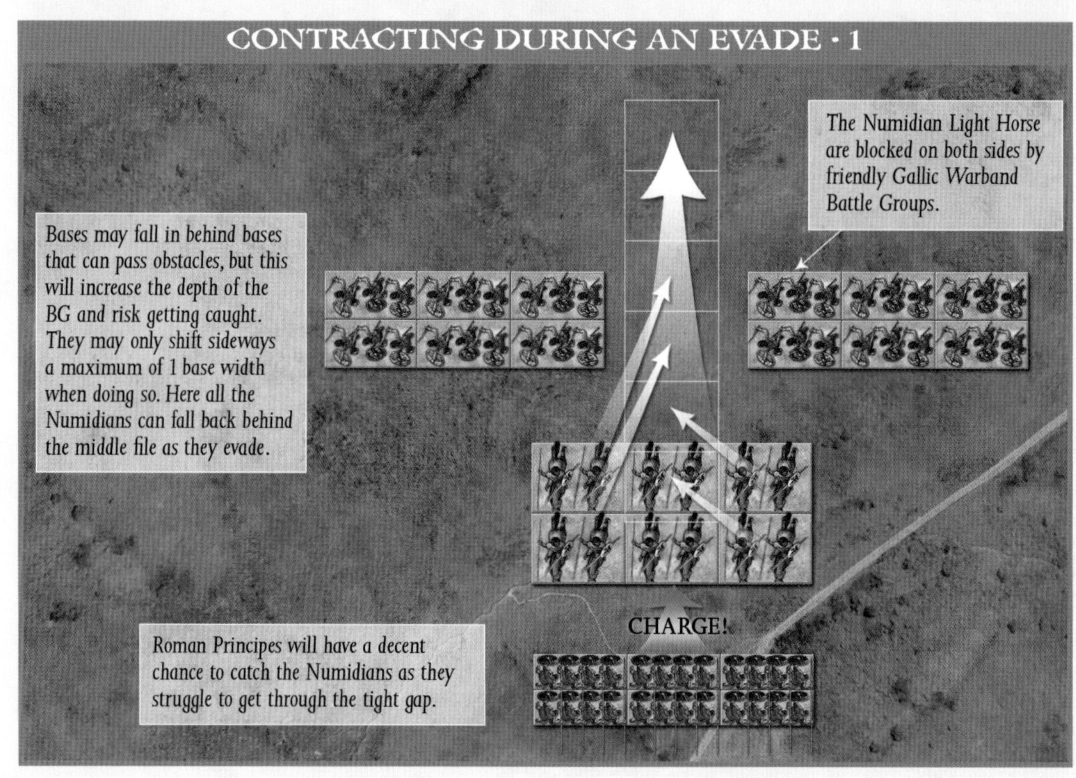
CONTRACTING DURING AN EVADE • 1
The Numidian Light Horse are blocked on both sides by friendly Gallic Warband Battle Groups.
Bases may fall in behind bases that can pass obstacles, but this will increase the depth of the BG and risk getting caught. They may only shift sideways a maximum of 1 base width when doing so. Here all the Numidians can fall back behind the middle file as they evade.
CHARGE!
Roman Principes will have a decent chance to catch the Numidians as they struggle to get through the tight gap.

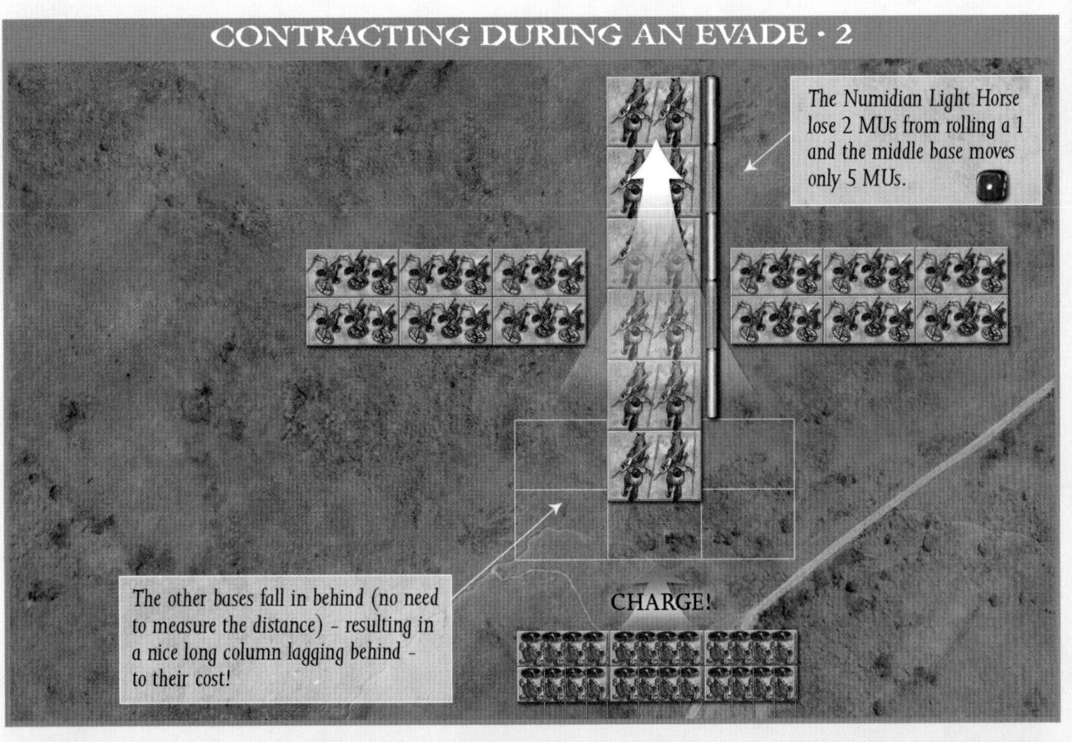
CONTRACTING DURING AN EVADE · 2
The Numidian Light Horse lose 2 MUs from rolling a 1 and the middle base moves only 5 MUs.
The other bases fall in behind (no need to measure the distance) - resulting in a nice long column lagging behind - to their cost!
CHARGE!

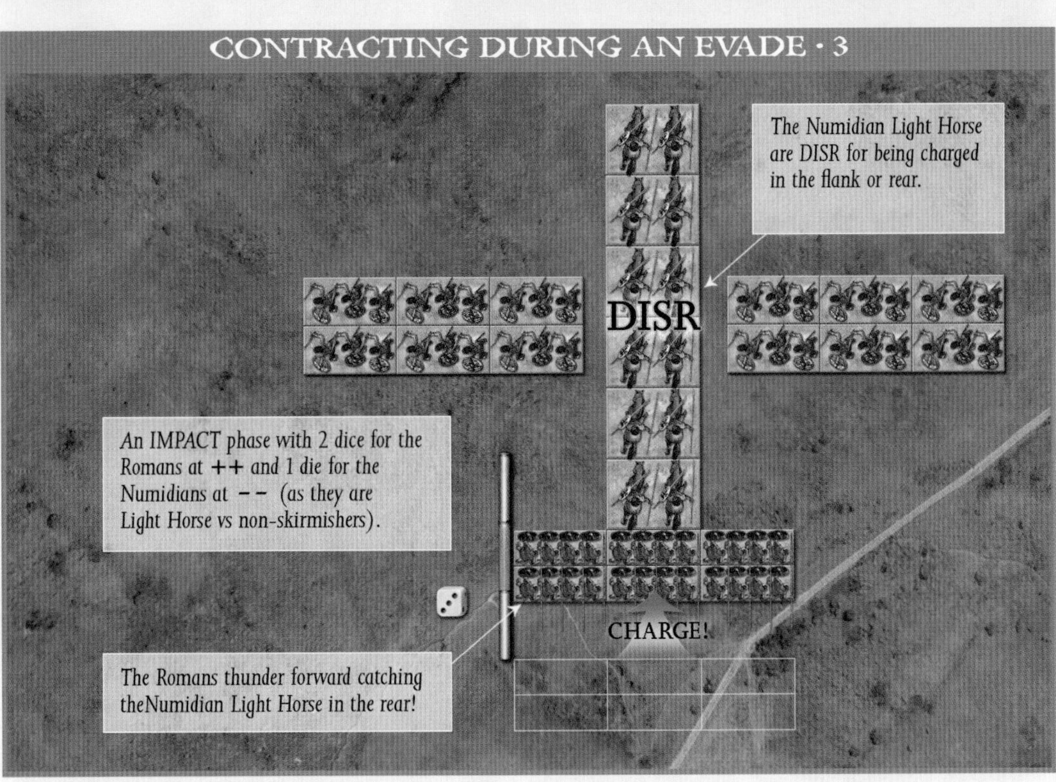
CONTRACTING DURING AN EVADE · 3
The Numidian Light Horse are DISR for being charged in the flank or rear.
DISR
An IMPACT phase with 2 dice for the Romans at ++ and 1 die for the Numidians at -- (as they are Light Horse vs non-skirmishers).
CHARGE!
The Romans thunder forward catching theNumidian Light Horse in the rear!

COMPLEX EVADE · 1
This Warband BG is in the way in either case, but easier to avoid with a 90 degrees turn.
CHARGE!

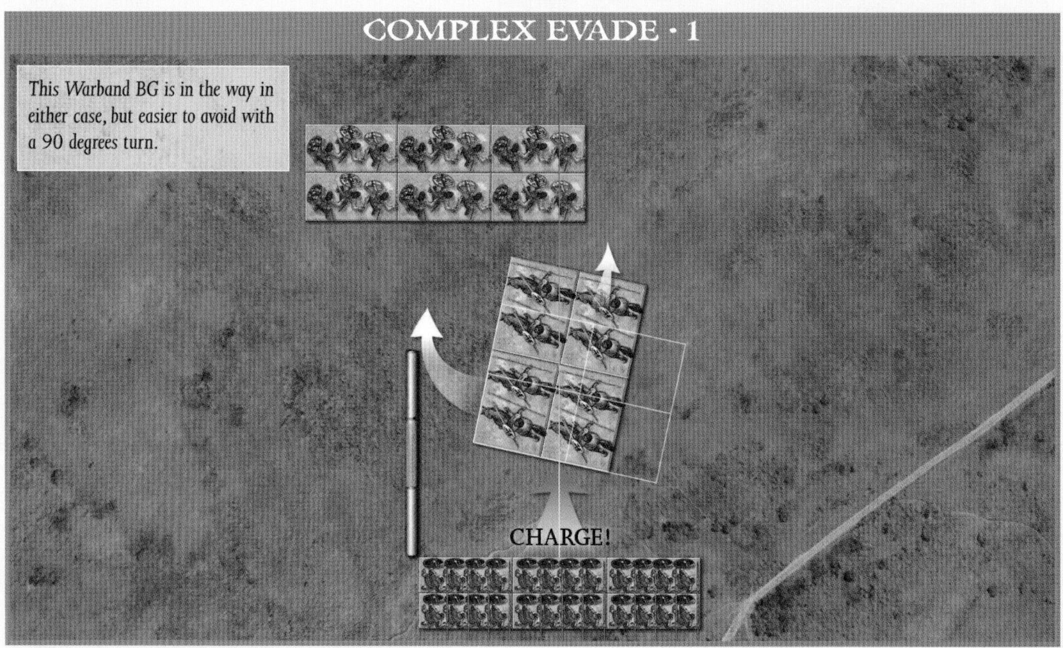

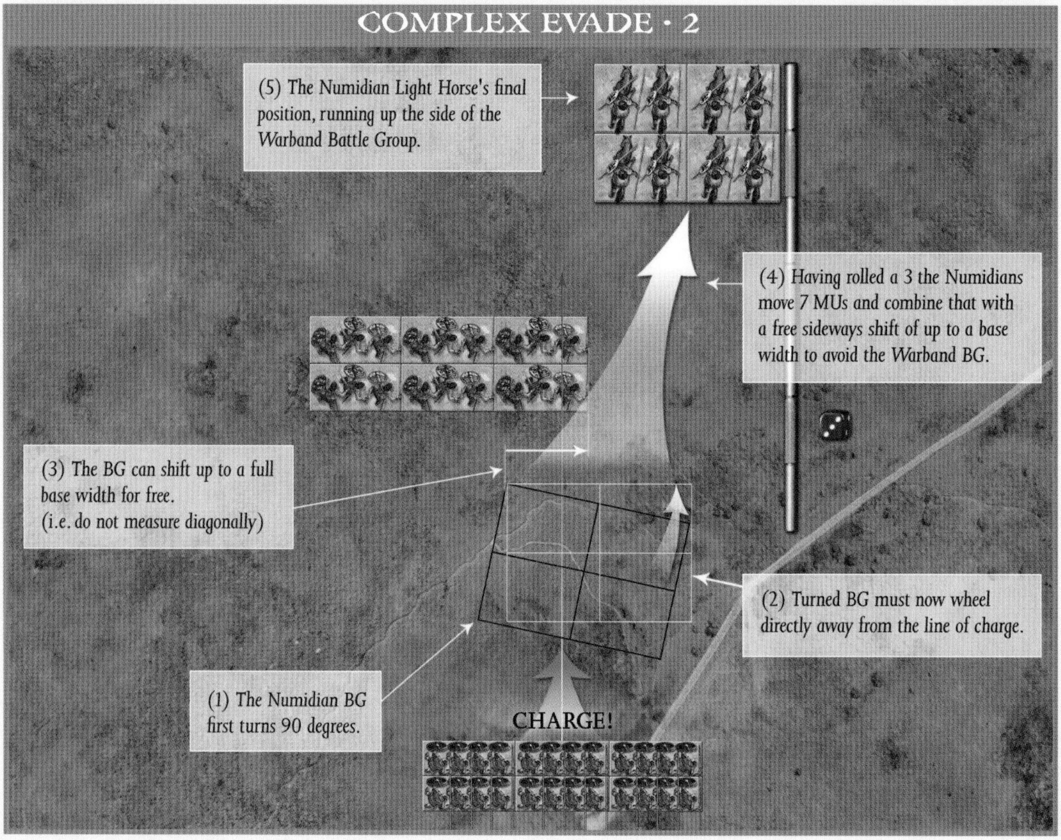

COMPLEX EVADE · 2
(5) The Numidian Light Horse's final position, running up the side of the Warband Battle Group.
(4) Having rolled a 3 the Numidians move 7 MUs and combine that with a free sideways shift of up to a base width to avoid the Warband BG.
(3) The BG can shift up to a full base width for free.
(i.e. do not measure diagonally)
(2) Turned BG must now wheel directly away from the line of charge.
(1) The Numidian BG first turns 90 degrees.
CHARGE!

TURNING WHEN CHARGED IN FLANK · 1

This BG hits the front corner and presses forward.
It will fight with 1 base.

The Legionaries drop to DISR due to being hit in the flank. They only drop once even though there are two separate contacts.

DISR

This BG has wheeled to get more bases in contact and presses forward.
It will fight with 2 bases.

This BG charges directly ahead, hits the rear corner of the Roman BG and presses forward.
It will fight with 2 bases.

TURNING WHEN CHARGED IN FLANK · 2

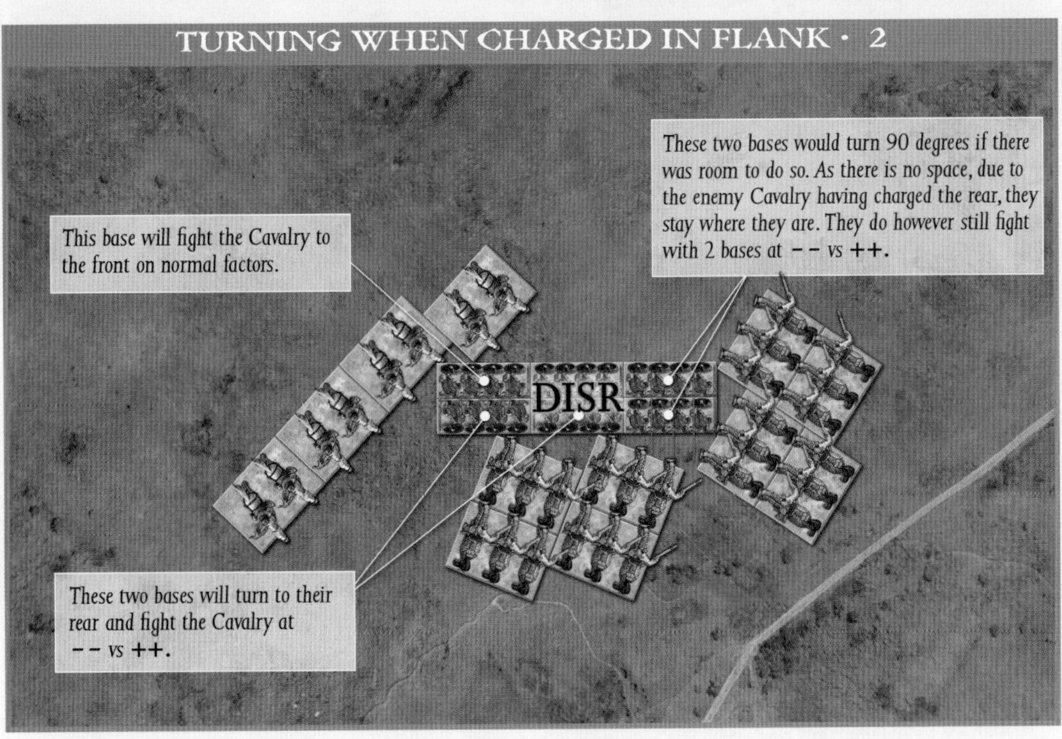

APPENDIX 8: FULL TURN SEQUENCE

The complete and detailed order of play in each turn is shown below. In many turns some of these items will be irrelevant, but you will quickly get used to this and learn when they apply and when they don't. In your first few games it's worth checking the order as you go.

FULL TURN SEQUENCE
1) IMPACT PHASE
Roll for arrival of outflanking marches Declare all charges. CMT for skirmishers or missile foot wishing to charge non-skirmishers. CMT for shock troops wishing to avoid charging. CMT for skirmishers not wishing to evade non-skirmishers. Resolve cohesion tests for FRAGMENTED troops being charged. If they break: Resolve cohesion tests for seeing them break. Make their initial rout move. Make interception charges. Make evade moves. Resolve cohesion tests for FRAGMENTED troops being charged as a result of intervening friends evading. If they break: Resolve cohesion tests for seeing them break. Make their initial rout move. Make charge moves. Troops contacted by flank or rear charge (except non-skirmishers by skirmishers) drop 1 Cohesion level. Resolve impact combats. Resolve post-combat cohesion tests, then death rolls, then roll to inflict commander losses. After the above is completed for all combats, resolve cohesion tests for seeing friends break or commanders lost. Make initial rout moves for troops broken this phase (other than FRAGMENTED troops that broke when charged). Make initial pursuits. Remove bases if pursuers remain in contact at the end of the rout move. Roll to inflict commander losses. Resolve cohesion tests for seeing commanders lost.
2) MANOEUVRE PHASE
Reform battle groups and conform troops in close combat to enemy. Feed additional bases into existing melees. Make normal movement for each battle group or battle line individually and move commanders. CMT if required as each battle group or battle line moves.
3) SHOOTING PHASE.
Resolve shooting – both sides shoot. Resolve post-shooting cohesion tests, then death rolls. After the above is completed for all shooting, resolve cohesion tests for seeing friends break. Make initial rout moves for troops broken this phase. Make initial pursuits. Remove bases if pursuers remain in contact at the end of the rout move. Roll to inflict commander losses. Resolve cohesion tests for seeing commanders lost.
4) MELEE PHASE
Resolve melee combats. Resolve post-combat cohesion tests, then death rolls, then roll to inflict commander losses. Assault fortified camps. After the above is completed for all combats, resolve cohesion tests for seeing friends break or commanders lost. Make initial rout moves for troops broken this phase. Make initial pursuits. Remove bases if pursuers remain in contact at the end of the rout move. Roll to inflict commander losses. Resolve cohesion tests for seeing commanders lost.
5) JOINT ACTION PHASE. BOTH SIDES
Remove scythed chariots if so specified. Make break-offs. CMT to stop pursuing or looting. Move commanders. Commanders attempt to bolster or rally BGs but only those whose cohesion level did not drop this turn. Move routers & pursuers. Remove bases if pursuers remain in contact at the end of the rout move. Roll to inflict commander losses. Resolve cohesion tests for seeing commanders lost. Remove any battle groups that are autobroken or reduced to 1 base.

ABOUT OSPREY PUBLISHING

Osprey Publishing is a leading publisher of illustrated military history. Over 1,300 titles in print provide the definitive resource for both established military enthusiasts and a wider audience with a general interest in military history. Osprey publishes a number of series chronicling human conflict on the ground, at sea and in the air from ancient times to the present day, covering a full range of perspectives on every major war and warrior group in history.

SELECTION OF RELATED ANCIENT AND MEDIEVAL OSPREY TITLES

ANCIENT

BTO	027	The Roman Army of the Punic Wars 264–146 BC
CAM	007	Alexander 334–323 BC
CAM	036	Cannae 216 BC
CAM	108	Marathon 490 BC
CAM	174	Pharsalus 48 BC
CAM	182	Granicus 334 BC
CAM	188	Thermopylae 480 BC
ELI	007	The Ancient Greeks
ELI	039	The Ancient Assyrians
ELI	042	The Persian Army 560–330 BC
ELI	066	The Spartan Army
ELI	155	Roman Battle Tactics 109 BC–AD 313
MAA	046	The Roman Army from Caesar to Trajan
MAA	069	The Greek and Persian Wars 500–323 BC
MAA	093	The Roman Army from Hadrian to Constantine
MAA	121	Armies of the Carthaginian Wars 265–146 BC
MAA	148	The Army of Alexander the Great
MAA	283	Early Roman Armies
MAA	291	Republican Roman Army 200–104 BC
MAA	373	The Sarmatians 600 BC–AD 450
NVG	089	Greek and Roman Artillery 399 BC–AD 363
NVG	119	Bronze Age War Chariots
WAR	030	Celtic Warrior
WAR	050	Pictish Warrior AD 297–841
WAR	101	Roman Auxiliary Cavalryman
WAR	120	Hittite Warrior

MEDIEVAL

CAM	009	Agincourt 1415
CAM	013	Hastings 1066
CAM	066	Bosworth 1485
CAM	071	Crécy 1346
CAM	078	Constantinople 1453
CAM	102	Bannockburn 1314
CAM	132	The First Crusade 1096–99
CAM	138	Poitiers 1356
CAM	154	Acre 1291
CAM	161	The Third Crusade 1191
ELI	003	The Vikings
ELI	009	The Normans
ELI	019	The Crusades
MAA	085	Saxon, Viking and Norman
MAA	089	Byzantine Armies 886–1118
MAA	099	Medieval Heraldry
MAA	111	The Armies of Crécy and Poitiers
MAA	113	The Armies of Agincourt
MAA	144	Armies of Medieval Burgundy 1364–1477
MAA	145	The Wars of the Roses
MAA	166	German Medieval Armies 1300–1500
MAA	171	Saladin and the Saracens
MAA	200	El Cid and the Reconquista 1050–1492
MAA	231	French Medieval Armies 1000–1300
MAA	287	Byzantine Armies AD 1118–1461
MAA	317	Henry V and the Conquest of France 1416–53
MAA	337	French Armies of the Hundred Years War
MAA	409	The Hussite Wars 1419–36
WAR	005	Anglo-Saxon Thegn AD 449–1066

OSPREY SERIES KEY

Battle Orders (BTO): Command and organizational structures of major forces on campaign.

Campaign (CAM): Great battles of history, with analysis of the command, strategies, tactics and combat resources of the opposing forces.

Elite (ELI): Combat history, uniforms and equipment of military units and larger forces.

Men-at-Arms (MAA): Uniforms and equipment of the world throughout history.

New Vanguard (NVG): Design, development, construction and operational history of the machinery of war.

Warrior (WAR): Daily lives of fighting men through their own eyes, covering recruitment, training, weaponry, equipment and experiences in and out of combat.

For more information on these and other Osprey books visit www.ospreypublishing.com.

ABOUT SLITHERINE SOFTWARE LTD

Slitherine Software is the leading developer and publisher of historical strategy games on PC, console and the tabletop. Slitherine's reputation is built on the blend of realism and accuracy combined with great gameplay. Slitherine's games have sold hundreds of thousands of copies and have been translated in 15 languages.

All these games and more are available to download from www.slitherine.com

INDEX

References to illustrations are shown in **bold**.

advances 41, 45
see also charges; stepping forwards
ambush markers 75
ambushes **142**, 142–143, **143**
archers see bowmen
armies 12
armies, starter 32–34
armour, levels of 14–15, 127, 129
army, choosing 151–153
army, using 154–157
army composition and points system 148–150
artillery 15, 41, 57, 71, 73, 74, 75, **80**, 82
attrition points 37
autobreak 116

bases 12, 22, 72–73, **73**, **86**, 86, 116, 126–127
see also commanders: bases
battle group deterioration 112–116
see also cohesion tests; death rolls
autobreak 116
base removal 116
cohesion levels, effect of 114–115
battle group disorder **26**, 26, 40–41, 132–133
battle group quality (quality re-rolls) 24, 99
battle groups 9–10, 22
already in contact but not committed to close combat 76–78
bursting through 48–49, **49**, 67, **163**, **164**
composition 150
deploying 145–147
destroyed, removing 109
friendly, seeing them break or commanders lost 112
routing, removing bases from 108–109
battle lines **30**, 30
board 12
bowmen **18**, **62**, **64**, **84**, 91, **142**, **143**
breaking off 61, **106**, 106–107
bursting through 48–49, **49**, 67, **163**, **164**
Byzantines 91, 156

camels 120
camp defenders **107**
camps **19**, **20**, 22, 78, 88, 142
Carthaginian army **15**, 16, **23**, **24**, **33**, 33, **61**, **153**, **155**
Carthaginian Wars **105**, 150
cavalry, light see horse, light
charge contact, 'legal' 52, 53
charges 47
declaration of 52
interception 37, **62**, 62–64, **63**
possible responses to 61–68
receiving **61**, 61–62
and responses, sequence of 68
charging, formation changes when **54**, 54
charging attempts when disrupted or fragmented 60
charging with battle groups **53**, 53
charging to contact 54, **55**
charging a flank or rear 55–57, **57**
charging with missile-armed foot troops 60
charging skirmishers 60
chariots **10**, 15, **28**, 30, 37, 41, 82, 106, **109**, 120–121, **148**
cohesion levels 24–25, **25**, 114–115
cohesion tests 80, 90, 98, 100, 102–103, 108, 112–114, 115
columns 23
combat, close 90, **102**, 102–104, **103**
base removal 116
commanders in 90, 99–100
conforming to the enemy in 70–71, **72**
rolls to hit 94
and shooting **84**, 84
combat, resolving 68
combat capabilities 14, 16, 17, 127–128, 130
combat effects 131
combat mechanism 90–104
see also cohesion tests; Points of Advantage
combat, close, example of **102**, 102–104, **103**
commanders in close combat 24, 90, 99–100
dice, combat, allocating 93–94
dice, deciding how many to roll 90–93
fighting broken troops 100
hits, accumulating 98
movement of broken troops and pursuers 100–101, **101**
support shooting in impact phase 98–99
command, line of 29
command range 28, 30
commanders **9**, 28–29, 70, 149
bases 28, 49–50, 125
choosing 153
in close combat 90, 99–100
and cohesion tests 113
deploying 147
in joint action phase 109–110
movement of 49–50
pre-battle initiative 138–139
complex move test (CMT) 41, 42–43, **49**, 52, 58, **59**, 59, 60, 63, 64, 75, 101, 107, 108, 122
conforming to the enemy in close combat 70–71, **72**
contact, charging to 54, **55**
contact, 'legal' charge 52, 53
contact with enemy 75–76, 78
contractions **46**, 46, **164**, **165**
Crécy, battle of (1346 AD) 34, **87**
Crusaders **111**

death rolls 80, 90, 98, 103, 104, 115
defeat 118
defences, portable (PD) 121, 129
design philosophy 9–10
dice 12
see also cohesion tests; Points of Advantage
combat, allocating 93–94
death rolls 80, 90, 98, 103, 104, 115
deciding how many to roll 90–93
re-rolls 24, 99
terrain placing rolls 140–141, **141**
distance measurement 12

elephants 8, **9**, **15**, 15, 30, **65**, 106, **120**, 120, **155**
evade moves 37, 47, 58, 64, **65**, 66–68, **67**, **68**
complex **166**
contracting during **164**, **165**
turning 90 degrees to **66**, 66–67
evading, bursting through when **163**, **164**
evading with a shift **162**, **163**
expansions **46**, 46

fighting the enemy in two directions 23, 71, 78, 88
figure scale 124–125
fire, arc of 81, 82, **83**
flanks, charging 55–57, **57**
formation changes when charging **54**, 54
formations 23
see also orb formation
fortifications, field (FF) 121, 129, 142

Gauls **14**, 16, **17**, 62, **64**, **102**, 102–104, **103**, **104**, **162–167**
ghilman troops 16, 91, 127
ground scale 126

history, period of interest 17
hits, accumulating 98
hits, scoring see Points of Advantage – scoring hits
horse, light **47**, **62**, **64**, **65**, **67**, **68**, 82, 91, 150, **162–167**

impact phase 37, 52–68, 102
see also charges, possible responses to
charge contact, 'legal' 52, 53
charges and responses, sequence of 68
charging a flank or rear 55–57, **57**
charging attempts when disrupted or fragmented 60
charging to contact 54, **55**
charging with battle groups **53**, 53
charging with missile-armed foot troops 60
declaration of charges 52
dice rolls 91–92, **103**
formation changes when charging **54**, 54
fragmented, being charged when 61
resolving combat 68
skirmishers charging 60
stepping forwards 54–55, **56**, **64**
support shooting in 98–99

troops eligible to fight **91**, 91
troops who cannot charge 57
troops who may charge without orders 58–59, **59**
impact POAs 96
initiative modifiers, pre-battle 138–139
Interception, Zone of (ZOI) **62**, 62
interception charges 37, **62**, 62–64, **63**
interpenetrations **47**, 47–48, 67

joint action phase 37, 38, 106–110
see also outcome moves in joint action phase
commanders in 109–110

knights **22**, **137**, **151**

lancers **48**, **59**, 91
line of sight 82, **83**, **84**
"Little Wars" 8
looting, stopping **107**, 107

manoeuvre phase 37, 70–78
bases, feeding more, into existing melee 72–73, **73**
battle groups in contact but uncommitted to combat 76–78
conforming to the enemy in close combat 70–71, **72**
moving into contact with enemy 75–76, 78
reforming 70, **71**
restricted area **74**, 74
second moves 75
march, order of 137–138
melee, feeding more bases into existing 72–73, **73**
melee phase 37–38, 86–88, 103–104
see also combat mechanism
bases eligible to fight in **86**, 86
dice rolls 92–93, **103**
fighting the enemy in two directions 71, 78, 88
melees that cannot line up 86–87, **87**
overlaps 86
sacking camps 88
troops eligible to fight 92, **93**
melee POAs 97
men-at-arms **13**, 128
movement and shooting 81
movement rules, general 40–50
see also complex move test; moves; turns; wheeling
advances 41
bursting through friends 48–49, **49**, 67
commanders, movement of 49–50
contractions and expansions **46**, 46
interpenetrations **47**, 47–48, 67
move, variable, distance (VMD) 47, 68
move distances and disorder 40–41
moving from an overlap position 50
moving through friendly troops 47–49
shifting **45**, 45
troops leaving the table 50
movement units (MU) 12
moves 41, 42, 43
compulsory 23
see also compulsory move test
variable 46–47

orb formation 23, 56, 71, 74, **122**, 122
outcome moves in joint action phase 106–109
breaking off **106**, 106–107
chariots, scythed 106
looting, stopping **107**, 107
pursuers 107–109
removing bases from routing battle groups 108–109
removing destroyed battle groups 109
routers 107–108
outflanking marches 144–145
overlap positions 45, 50, 70, 74, 75–76, 86

painting miniatures 158–161
phases 37–38
see also individual phases
pikemen 26
pilgrims **137**
playing the game **36**, 36–37
points, attrition 37
Points of Advantage (POA) 57, 86, 93, 94, 102, 104
scoring hits 94–97
close combat rolls to hit 94
impact POAs 96
melee POAs 97
shooting combat rolls to hit 95
shooting POAs 95, 99
points system and army composition 148–150
pursuers/pursuits 47, 100–101, **101**, 107–109

quality (skill levels) 14, 15, 17, 24
quality re-rolls (battle group quality) 24, 99

ranges 81
rear, charging 55–57, **57**
receiving the charge *see* evade moves; interception charges
reforming 70, **71**
requirements 12
restricted area **74**, 74
Roman army **32**, 32, **56**, **61**, **62**, **63**, **67**, **138**, **152**
ballista **156**
cavalry **14**, **15**
commander **118**
hastati **14**, **26**, 26
infantry of Republican Rome **89**
legio ii Parthica **29**
legionaries 15–16, **17**, **21**, 62, **72**, **102**, 102–104, **103**, **167**
praetorians **29**, **31**
principes **59**, **64**, **71**, **162–166**
velites **71**, **142**, **143**
rout, army 37, 118
rout, initial 100–101
routers 107–108
routing, base removal 116
routing battle groups, removing bases from 108–109

scales 124–127
set up rules 137–147
setting up a game 36
shifting **45**, 45, **162**, **163**
shooting phase 37, 80–84
arc of fire 81, 82, **83**
dice, deciding how many to roll 90–91
line of sight 82, **83**, **84**
movement and shooting 81
overhead shooting 82, **83**
ranges 81
shooting and close combat **84**, 84
target priority 81, **83**
visibility 82
shooting POAs 95, 99
shooting rolls to hit 95
sideways shifts **45**, 45
skill (quality levels) 14, 15, 17, 24
skirmishers 18, **25**, 26, 48, 55, 60, 64, 108
spearmen **18**, **77**, 129
starter armies 32–34
stepping forwards 54–55, **56**, **64**
straggling test 144
swordsmen 129

tabletop 12
tactical advice for beginners 154–157
target priority 81, **83**
terrain 12, 26, 36, 40–41, 131, 139–140
piece sizes **132**
placement and deployment area **146**, 146
placing dice rolls 140–141
time scale 126
training 14, 15–16, 129
troop function categories 18
troop types 12, 14–17, 127–130
see also individual entries
battle (non-skirmishers) 18
elite 15
foot 14, 30, 60, 98
mounted 14, 30, 147
shock 18, 48–49, **49**, 58–59, **59**
and terrain 40–41
troops who cannot charge 57
troops, bolstering and rallying 109–110, 112
troops, broken 100–101
troops based for other systems, using 127
troops leaving the table 50
turns 37–38, **44**, 44–45, **66**, 66–67, **167**, 168
see also wheeling

unusual situations **162**, 162, **163–167**

variable move distance (VMD) 47, 68
victory 118
visibility 82, 131, 132

wagons, battle 15, 41, 56, 57, 71, 73, 74, 75, 82, 91, 92, 96
wargaming, miniature, defined 8
weapons as capabilities 14, 16, 17
wheeling 23, 41, 43–44, **44**, 53, 74
see also turns

Zone of Interception (ZOI) **62**, 62

MOVEMENT AND COHESION

(A) BASIC MOVE SEQUENCE
1) IMPACT PHASE
Declare all charges, Intercept moves and Evade moves Resolve impact combat & post-combat cohesion tests
2) MANOEUVRE PHASE
Conform troop in close combat to enemy Make normal movement battle group by battle group Complex move tests as battle groups move
3) SHOOTING PHASE
Resolve shooting Post-shooting cohesion tests
4) MELEE PHASE
Resolve melee combat Post-combat cohesion tests
5) JOINT ACTION PHASE
Break-offs Complex move tests to stop pursuing or looting Move commanders Bolster or rally battle groups Move routers/pursuers

(B) MOVEMENT RATES	Open	Uneven	Rough	Diff.
Light foot	5	5	5	4
Medium foot	4	4	4	3
Heavy foot	3	2	2	1
Light Horse & Commanders	7	7	5	3
Cavalry	5	4	3	1
Knights/Cataphracts	4	3	2	1
Elephants	4	4	3	1
Light chariots	5	3	2	1
Heavy or scythed chariots	4	2	1	N/A
Battle wagons	3	2	1	N/A
Light artillery	2	1	1	N/A
Roads or slowing terrain:	+1 MU if in single base wide column			

KEY	
NO EFFECT	No effect
DISORDERED	-1 on CMTs. Lose 1 dice per 3 for shooting & close combat
	No Cohesion Test penalty
SEVERELY DISORDERED	-2 on CMTs. Lose 1 dice per 2 for shooting & close combat
	-1 on Cohesion Tests

(C) SIMPLE & COMPLEX MOVES		Troop type			
			Battle troops		
Type of move	Move to be made (*Advance* means a move from the Advances section below.)	Skirmishers	Drilled	Undrilled Cv/LCh	Other Undrilled
Charges	Any charge move that starts within reach of enemy	Simple	Simple	Simple	Simple
Advances	Any wheel or short move without a commander which starts, goes or ends <= 6 MUs from enemy:	Simple	Simple	Simple	Complex
	Any other forwards move which may include a single wheel	Simple	Simple	Simple	Simple
Double Wheels	Advance with 2 separate wheels in 1 move	Simple	Simple	Simple	Complex
Expansions	Expand 1 or 2 bases while stationary	Simple	Simple	Complex	Complex
	Expand 1 or 2 bases followed by a simple *advance*	Simple	Complex	Impossible	Impossible
Contractions	Contract 1 or 2 bases with simple *advance* >= 3 MUs before or after	Simple	Simple	Simple	Complex
	Contract 1 or 2 bases if stationary or advancing < 3 MUs before or after	Simple	Complex	Complex	Impossible
Turns	Turn 90 or 180 deg while stationary	Simple	Simple	Simple	Complex
	Turn 90 deg with simple *advance* before or after	Simple	Complex	Complex	Impossible
	Turn 180 deg with simple *advance* before or after	Simple	Impossible	Impossible	Impossible
	Turn 180 deg, move <=3 MUs with simple *advance* and turn back again	Complex	Impossible	Impossible	Impossible
2nd Moves	Simple *advance* if > 6 MU from enemy if commander +- BG or BL	Simple	Simple	Simple	Simple

COMPLEX MOVE TEST: ROLL 2D6						
	UNIT TYPE	PASS SCORE	Adjustments			
Quality re-rolls except for shock testing not to charge	Drilled or Skirmishers	7	Commander in LoC in range	+1	DISRUPTED or DISORDERED	-1
	Other Undrilled	8	Extra if he is with BG/BL Extra if he is IC	+1 +1	FRAGMENTED or SEVERELY DISORDERED	-2

QUALITY	AUTOBREAK ON
Elite	> 60% bases lost
Superior	> 50% bases lost
Average	> 40% bases lost
Poor	> 30% bases lost

(D) COHESION TEST Throw 2 dice. Quality Re-rolls apply.

	Immediately	At the end of the current phase	
Reasons to test	A battle group charged by other than light foot when FRG	A BG breaks within 3 MUs - Non-skirmishers ignore skirmishers	
	Losing a close combat	A commander in line of command is lost within 3 MUs	
	Suffering 1 HP3B from shooting - or taking 2 or more hits and shot at by artillery.	JAP	To bolster or rally a BG with a commander

Situation				
>= 1 HP2B from shooting	-1	Any one of….	Any troops shot at by artillery or firearms	-1
>= 1 HP3B from close combat	-1		Any troops testing for losing close combat vs El or SCh	
At least 2 more hits received than inflicted in close combat	-1		MF testing for losing close combat vs Mtd or HF in open	
>=25% losses overall	-1		Any troops testing for losing impact combat vs lancers	
Non-skirmishers with threatened flank	-1		Foot testing for losing impact combat vs impact foot	
More than 1 reason to test	-1	**Commanders and support**		
Current Cohesion State		Commander in LoC in range if BG is not in close combat, or with BG if it is in close combat.		+1
DISRUPTED or SEVERELY DISORDERED	-1			
FRAGMENTED	-2	Extra if he is IC		+1
BROKEN	-3	Battle Group has rear support		+1

RESULT	7 or more	Passed	Rise one cohesion level if testing to bolster or rally the battle group
	6, 5, 4, 3	Failed	Drop 1 cohesion level (unless testing to bolster or rally the battle group)
	2 or less	Failed	Drop 2 cohesion levels if testing for close combat in which BG received >= 2 more hits than inflicted, or if testing for seeing friends break or commander lost. Otherwise drop 1 cohesion level (unless testing to bolster or rally the battle group).

COMBAT

(A) SHOOTING RANGES	Effective	Maximum
Foot bows, longbows or crossbows	4	6
Sling, mounted bows or crossbows	4	–
Javelins or firearms	2	–
Heavy artillery	6	12
Light artillery	6	–

(B) COMBAT MECHANISM

SHOOTING	Dice	
Artillery (except when on battle wagons)	2 dice per base in effective range	
	1 dice per base outside effective range	
MF with Bw, XB or LB (Not Bw*)	1 dice per base of 1st shooting rank in effective range	
	1 dice per 2 bases of 2nd shooting rank or outside effective range	
Cav with Bw or XB (Not Bw*)	1 dice per base of 1st shooting rank	
	1 dice per 2 bases of 2nd shooting rank	
Chariots	1 dice per base	
Battle wagons	1 dice per base width from long edge only	
LF, LH or any javelins, sling, firearm or Bw*	1 dice per 2 bases in effective range	
	1 dice per 3 bases outside effective range	
IMPACT		
Scythed Chariots	3 dice per 1st rank base	
Others	2 dice per 1st rank base (BWg 2 dice per front rank base width)	
Supporting fire (Not LF vs foot)	1 rank of foot with Bw, LB, XB or Firearm in 2nd or (if bow) 3rd rank behind stationary MF/HF in combat: 1 dice per base. (0 dice vs flank/rear charge)	
MELEE		
El, Kn, all Ch, Artillery	2 dice per front rank base. No dice for rear rank bases of any type	
Battle wagons	2 dice per front rank base width. No dice for rear rank bases of any type	
Other troops	1 dice per base in 1st or 2nd ranks	
Overlaps	As above	
ALL		
LF or LH in impact or melee	Lose 1 dice per 2 unless LF vs LF or LH vs LH or LF, or any vs FRAGMENTED enemy	
THEN		
DISR or DISORDERED	Lose 1 dice per 3	Dice loss for Disruption, Fragmentation, Disorder or Severe Disorder is not cumulative, but whichever is worst applies.
FRAG or SEVERELY DISORDERED	Lose 1 dice per 2	
(d) QUALITY RE-ROLLS		
ELITE	Reroll 1's and 2's . Cannot go lower.	
SUPERIOR	Reroll 1's.	
POOR	Reroll 6's.	
SCORE TO HIT	**Shooting**	**Close Combat**
++	2	3
+	3	4
No POA	4	4
–	5	5
– –	6	5

(C) POINTS OF ADVANTAGE

SHOOTING

	Nearest rank of target is:		If shooting with:
Any one of...	Unprotected cavalry not in single rank	++	Longbow, bow, javelins, sling
	Protected cavalry not in single rank	+	Longbow, bow, javelins, sling
	Armoured cavalry not in single rank. Armoured knights	+	Longbow
	Cataphracts or heavily armoured knights	–	Bow, javelins, sling
	Elephants	+	Any except bow or sling
	Battle Wagons	–	Any except artillery
	Unprotected heavy or medium foot	+	Longbow, bow, javelins, sling
		–	Crossbow, firearm, artillery
	Armoured foot	–	Any except longbow
	Heavily armoured foot	–	Longbow, crossbow, firearm or artillery
		– –	Bows, javelins, sling
	Any other foot	–	Crossbow, firearm, artillery
Any		–	Any if shooting in impact phase, to rear or at/by BG in combat
In cover or behind field fortifications		–	Any except artillery

IMPACT

Any one of...	Impact Foot		++	against any foot
	Impact Foot		+	against any mounted, unless charging shock mounted
	Spearmen or pikemen if not charging			unless FRG or SEVERE DISORD or < 2 ranks of Sp or < 3 ranks of Pk
	Pk or Offensive Sp charging foot or non-shock mtd Defensive Sp charging Defensive Sp			unless SEVERE DISORDER or < 2 ranks of Sp or < 3 ranks of Pk
	Heavy weapon			against any foot
	Light spear (foot)			unless charging shock mounted
	Light spear (mounted)			against any if no other net POAs
	Elephants			against heavy or medium foot, BWg or any mounted
	Battle Wagons			against any mounted except elephants
	Knightly Lance	Only in open terrain		except against El, SCh, BWg or non-charging STEADY Pk/Sp
	Other Lance			except against lancers, El, SCh, BWg or non-charging STEADY Pk/Sp
	Heavy or Scythed Chariots			except vs skirmishers, lancers, El, BWg or non-charging STDY Pk/Sp
Mounted except El or SCh			+	against any medium or light foot
Extra for 4th rank of pikemen			+	unless FRAGMENTED
Charging flank or rear			++	**Net POA regardless of other factors**
Uphill or foot defending field fortifications or river bank			+	

MELEE

Any one of...	Skilled Swordsmen	+	against any except El, mounted Sw or STEADY Pk/Sp
	Swordsmen	+	against any except El, Sw, SSw or STEADY Pk/Sp
	Spearmen (>=2 ranks) or Pikemen (>=3 ranks)	+	unless FRAGMENTED or SEVERELY DISORDERED
	Heavy weapon	+	against any except SSw & skirmishers. Cancels enemy armour POA
	Elephants	+	against heavy or medium foot, BWg or any mounted
	Heavy or scythed chariots	+	against any except skirmishers, El, BWg or STEADY Pk/Sp
	Artillery	–	
Extra for 4th rank of Pikemen in open terrain		+	unless FRAGMENTED
Better Armour (front rank)		+	against any but Heavy Weapon, El, Ch, Art or BWg
Fighting enemy in 2 directions		–	
Uphill or foot defending field fortifications or river bank		+	

(D) DEATH THROW

Roll 1 Dice. (No re-rolls.) +1 on dice for elephants, artillery or battle wagons.	Score higher than number of hits received or lose a base
+2 on dice if shot at, or if won/drew close combat	If a base was lost, and there were more than 6 hits, deduct 6 from the hits and roll again for the remainder

GAME SET UP

TERRAIN	Maximum(Minimum)																
TERRITORY TYPE	Open	O.Field	Broken	Brush	E.Field	Plantn	Gully	Forest	Vinyds	Marsh	S.Sand	S.Hills	Village	Impass.	G.Hills	Road	River/Coast
DEVELOP ED	2	3			3(1)	2	1		3			1	(1)		2	1	1
AGRICULTURAL	2	4(2)			3	1	1		2			1	1		2	1	1
HILLY			3	3(1)		1	1	2		1		3(1)	1	1	3	1	1
WOODLANDS				2		2	1	4(2)		2		1	1		2	1	1
STEPPES	4(2)		4	2			1								1		
MOUNTAINS				2		1	1	1		1		4(2)	1	2		1	1
TROPICAL				2				4(2)		2		1	1	1	1	1	1
DESERT	2		2	2			1				4(2)	1		1	1	1	
COLOUR KEY	Open	Uneven		Rough				Difficult						Impass	Variable		

GAME SETUP PROCEDURE

1	Roll for Initiative – The player gaining the initiative chooses the territory type.
Selecting Terrain	
2	Player with initiative selects one of the 2 compulsory terrain pieces
3	The other player selects the other compulsory piece
4	The player with initiative selects 2–4 selections of available terrain He cannot choose both a coast and a river
5	The other player select 2–4 selections of remaining available terrain He cannot choose a river, a coast or a village
Placing Terrain	
6	Player with initiative places a river or coast if any Player with initiative places a village if any [including any integral hill] Player with initiative places his compulsory item
7	The other player places his compulsory item
8	Player with initiative places his open spaces if any The other player places his open spaces
9	Player with initiative places the rest of his terrain The other player places the rest of his terrain
10	Remove all open spaces
Army Deployment	For each number, each player in turn, starting with the player without initiative:
11	Places FFs <= 10 MUs from rear edge, <= 15 MUs if in central 1/3 of the table. Places his camp <= 10 MUs from his rear edge, or behind FF. Places any ambush markers in the 2 outer thirds of the table, <= 18 MUs from rear edge if without initiative, up to half-way across table if with initiative.
12	Records outflanking marches – commander, BGs and which flank.
13	Deploys BGs in alternate 25% batches. (See main rules). Skirmishers <= 15 MUs from rear edge, other troops <= 10 MUs from rear edge or behind FF.
14	Commits to dismounting if any.
15	Deploys commanders <= 15 MUs from rear edge.

PRE-BATTLE INITIATIVE MODIFIERS

+2	C-in-C is an inspired commander
+1	C-in-C is a field commander
+1	The army has 10–24 bases of cavalry, light horse, camelry or light chariots, excluding commanders
+2	The army has more than 24 bases of cavalry, light horse, camelry or light chariots, excluding commanders
Higher score has pre-battle initiative – re-roll if scores are equal.	

TERRAIN PLACEMENT

Dice Roll	Placement	Dice Roll	Placement
1	Touching opponent's long edge	2	Touching your own long edge
3	Touching side edge or coast in opponent's half	4	Touching side edge or coast in your own half
5	In opponent's half > 8 MUs from any edge	6	In your own half > 8 MUs from any edge
Terrain Adjustment Dice			
0–2	No change permitted	3–4	Slide up to 6 MUs
5	Slide up to 12 MUs or pivot	6+	Can remove piece entirely
–1 on adjustment dice score for compulsory terrain.		+1 on adj. dice score for impassable terrain, river or coast	

No piece can be placed (prior to adjustment) closer than 4 MUs to any other piece except:
- Any piece can be placed closer than 4 MUs to a coast, river or road.
- A road can be placed closer than 4 MUs to any piece, but not through it unless a village.
- A road must pass through or touch a village if there is one.

A river or a coast counts as 1 piece but 2 selections. A road counts as 1 piece and 1 selection.

Rivers and coasts can be removed, but not slid or pivoted.

AMBUSHES

The player with pre-battle initiative can place ambushes up to half way across the table from his side's rear table edge, in the two outer thirds of the table's width. The other player can place ambushes up to 18 MUs forward from his side's rear table edge, in the two outer thirds of the table's width.

Ambushes must not be visible from any part of the enemy deployment area for skirmishers (even if the enemy have no skirmishers). Battle groups can only ambush in terrain they could move in.

OUTFLANKING MARCH ARRIVAL TEST

Roll two dice for each outflanking march. (No re-rolls).		
Modifier	+1	If the flank march is led by a Field Commander
	–1	If the outflanking march includes medium or heavy foot
Score	Result	
9 or less	Roll again next turn	
10 or more	Successful arrival	

Straggling Test				
On the turn when the outflanking march should arrive, roll two dice for each battle group to see if it is straggling. Straggling battle groups will not arrive in time for the battle.				
Modifiers	+1	Drilled troops or skirmishers	–1	Medium or heavy foot
A battle group is straggling (and will not arrive) if it scores less than 5. Quality re-rolls apply.				

MARE GERMANICUM
Eboracum
OCEANUS ATLANTICUS
Londinium
MARE BRITANNICUS
Remi
Parisi
Alesia
GERMANIA
Regina
MARE CANTABRICUM
Avaricum
Bibracte
Burdigala
Asturia
Gergovia
Aquileia
Narbo
Genua
MARE ADRIATICUM
Massilia
Clusium
Asculum
Toletum
Ebora
MARE LIGUSTICUM
Arpi
Saguntum
Roma
Neapolis
Tarentum
FRETUM HURCLEUM
Gades
Carthago Nova
Thurii
MARE TYRRHENUM
Messana
Cathago
Syracuse